Hallucinogens and Culture

**Chandler & Sharp Series in
Cross-Cultural Themes**

GENERAL EDITOR

Douglass R. Price-Williams
  University of California, Los Angeles

CONSULTING EDITORS

L. L. Langness
Robert B. Edgerton
  both University of California, Los Angeles

Hallucinogens and Culture

Peter T. Furst

State University of New York at Albany
and Research Associate, Botanical Museum of Harvard
University

Chandler & Sharp Publishers, Inc.
11A COMMERCIAL BOULEVARD. NOVATO. CA 94947

Library of Congress Cataloging in Publication Data

Furst, Peter T   1922-
   Hallucinogens and culture.
   (Chandler & Sharp series in cross-cultural themes)
   Bibliography: p.
   Includes index.
   1. Hallucinogenic drugs.   2. Hallucinogenic drugs
and religious experience.   I. Title.
HV5822.H25F87   301.2'2   75-25442
ISBN 0-88316-517-1

EIGHTH PRINTING 1997

International Standard Book Number   0-88316-517-1
Library of Congress Catalog Card Number   75-25442
Printed in the United States of America

Book Design: Joseph M. Roter
Composition: Hansen & Associates Graphics

For Jill

CONTENTS

Preface   xi

Introduction   **1**

    An Ethnological Reply to a Statistical Question   2
    Ecstatic Shamanism as "*Ur*-Religion"   4
    Archaeological Evidence for the Earliest Hallucinogen   7
    Peyote: Sacred "Medicine" or "Dangerous Narcotic"?   9
    Other Pathways to "Alternate States"   10
    Hallucinogens and the Biochemistry of Consciousness   14
    The Social-Psychological Context as Crucial Variable   15
    Urgently Needed: An Integrated Perspective   17

**Chapter One.   "Idolatry," Hallucinogens, and
          Cultural Survival**   **19**

Chapter Two.   Tobacco: "Proper Food of the Gods"   **23**

    Gods and Men as Tobacco Addicts   24
    The Antiquity of Tobacco in America   27
    Psychedelic Enemas?   27
    The Sacred Pipe   29
    Tobacco Shamanism among the Warao   30

Chapter Three.   *Cannabis* (spp.) and Nutmeg Derivatives   **33**

    Cannabis spp.   34
    A New Finding: Three Species of *Cannabis*   34
    Nutmeg   36
    Nutmeg in European Medicine   36
    Nutmeg and Psychotherapy   37

Chapter Four. Ibogaine and the Vine of Souls: From Tropical Forest Ritual to Psychotherapy   **39**

Tabernanthe iboga   39
Iboga Cults in Tropical Africa   40
Male-Female Symbolism and Acculturation   42
Harmaline and Related Alkaloids   43
Amazonian Indians as Psychopharmacologists   45
Yajé and the Mythic Origins of Society   46
Hallucinogens and Jaguar Transformation   48

Chapter Five. Hallucinogens and "Archetypes"   **50**

The Transcultural Phenomenon   51
"Tiger, Tiger, Burning Bright . . ."   52
Journeys into Mythic Time   53
Yajé and the Origins of Art   54

Chapter Six. LSD and the Sacred Morning Glories of Indian Mexico   **57**

LSD and Parkinson's Disease   57
Historic Breakthrough: The Discovery of LSD   58
Ololiuhqui, Sacred Hallucinogen of the Aztecs   60
Ololiuhqui Identified   61
LSD-like Compounds in Morning-Glory Seeds   65
Ololiuhqui in Indian Religion   67
Morning-Glory Seeds as Divinity   67
Thwarting the Clergy   68
Morning Glory and Christian Acculturation   70
Morning Glory and Mother Goddess   70
God of Flowers and "Flowery Dream"   73

Chapter Seven. The Sacred Mushrooms: Rediscovery in Mexico   **75**

"Mushroom of the Underworld"   77
Mushroom Stones and the Cult of Sacred Mushrooms   79
Was the Fly-Agaric Sacred to the Maya?   81
Found at Last: A Living Mushroom Cult in Mexico   83
"Mycophiles" and "Mycophobes"   84
"A Soul-Shattering Happening"   85
The Mosaic Completed   86

Chapter Eight. The Fly-Agaric: "Mushroom of Immortality"   **89**
The Fly-Agaric and Intoxicating Urine   90
Chemistry and Effects   92

Chapter Nine. R. Gordon Wasson and the Identification
of the Divine *Soma*   96

The Elusive *Soma* Deity   97
Multidisciplinary Quest   98
Fly-Agaric Urine and the Identity of *Soma*   100
The Controversy Lives On   101
A New Road of Inquiry   103
Antiquity and Origins of the Mushroom Cult   103
Discovery of Hallucinogens: Deliberate or Accidental?   105
A Mexican Indian Mushroom Taxonomy   106
Hallucinogenic Mushrooms North of Mexico   107

Chapter Ten.   The "Diabolic Root"   109

A "Factory of Alkaloids"   111
"Mescaline": A Misnomer   112
The Sacred Quest for Peyote   113
Mythic Origins of Peyote   113
"We Are Newly Born"   116
The Dangerous Passage   117
"Where Our Mothers Dwell"   119

Chapter Eleven.   "To Find Our Life": Peyote Hunt of
the Huichols of Mexico   120

A Time to Walk   121
Food for Grandfather   121
The Ritual Kill   122
A Huichol Communion   124
"You Will See Your Life"   126
Uniqueness of the Shaman's Visions   131
The Children of Peyote   132

Chapter Twelve.   *Datura*: A Hallucinogen that Can Kill 134

Myth as History   137
Natural and Cultural History of *Datura*   138
Effects of *Datura* Intoxication   140
Datura among North American Indians   141
Initiation Rites in California   143
Transcending "Ordinary Reality"   144

Chapter Thirteen.   Hallucinogenic Snuffs and
Animal Symbolism   146

The *Virola* Tree as a Source of Snuff   147
Rapid Intoxication   152

Addiction: Snuff, No; Tobacco, Yes   152
Snuffing and Animal Art   153
Snuffing in Mexico   155

**Chapter Fourteen. The Toad as Earth Mother: A Problem
in Symbolism and Psychopharmacology**   **158**

Toad as Mediator and Dualistic Mother   159
Toad Mother and Culture Heroes   160
Psychotropic Properties of Toad Poison   161
Analogies in Asian Mythology   162
Toad and Toadstool   162
Magical Uses of Frog and Toad Poison   163

Chapter Fifteen. Hallucinogens and the Sacred Deer   **166**

American Indian Deer Symbolism: Asiatic Roots or
Independent Origins?   169
The Reindeer and the Sacred Mushroom   170
Deer-Mushroom Ecology in Mexico   172

Literature Cited   174
Index   183

ILLUSTRATIONS

Banisteriopsis caapi   43
Banisteriopsis rusbyana   44
Ololiuhqui (Rivea corymbosa). (From Hernández,
    Rerum medicarum, 1651.)   61
Rivea corymbosa   62
R. corymbosa, capsules and seeds   63
Ipomoea violacea   64
Ololiuhqui in art. Mural from Teotihuácan   71
Heimia salicifolia   73
Several Mushrooms   78
Amanita muscaria. The divine *Soma*; fly-agaric   99
Lophophora williamsii. Peyote in flower   110
Ramón, leader of the peyote quest   115
"There, there, the deer." A clone of peyote   123
Veradera. A peyote pilgrim   127
"Our game bags are full." Peyote plants and roots   128
Híkuri seekers. Peyote pilgrims in the desert   130
Datura. Two species, from an Aztec herbal   136
Sophora secundiflora   139
Anadenanthera peregrina   147
Virola theidora   148
V. callophylla   149
V. callophylloidea   150
Psychotria viridis   151
Bird-shaped snuffing pipes; Costa Rica   154
Deer, with peyote cactus; snuffing pipe; Monte Albán   155
Snuffing pipe in use; Colima   157

PREFACE

It is hoped that the following pages will demonstrate something of the essential interplay between nature and culture—between chemistry, mind set, and social and historical setting—in the use of hallucinogenic plants and other psychoactive substances by different peoples the world over. Obviously, many significant areas of research in psychopharmacology and ethnobotany, as well as some interesting and as yet little-understood nonchemical "techniques of ecstasy" have had to be slighted, in favor of in-depth treatment of some others of more general interest. Besides, this is an ongoing story: "new" botanical hallucinogens and other naturally occurring psychoactive substances—some perhaps never culturally exploited, others long forgotten by the people who formerly used them, and yet others successfully concealed for centuries from the prying eyes of outsiders—are even now being discovered and scientifically described and tested. Still more await botanical and pharmacological identification beyond the native terms under which they appear in the ethnohistorical literature or reports of travelers and ethnographers. Even for Indian Mexico or Amazonia, whose extensive psychoactive pharmacopoeia has been relatively well studied, we still do not know the identity of every species used in native ritual, prehistorically or at present, nor do we as yet fully understand the pharmacological or cultural role of additives to plants of known or suspected psychoactivity. Indeed, in the opinion of such authorities as Richard Evans Schultes, Director of Harvard's Botanical Museum, it is precisely the function of these additives to the botanical hallucinogens that presents one of the most exciting challenges to the modern investigator of the psychedelic phenomenon in indigenous societies. Clearly, then, there is a world yet to be discovered. The concerned reader is urged to keep up with the more specialized ethnobotanical publications and the rapidly growing literature on brain biochemistry and scientific and humanistic explorations into the uses and abuses of alternate states of consciousness.*

Many colleagues and publications were consulted in the writing of this book; while their contributions, personal or in print, are acknowledged in the text, they should know that without their generosity in sharing their expertise the task of writing it would have been impossible. In particular I would like to express my thanks to Dr. Johannes Wilbert, Professor of Anthropology and Director, Latin American Center, University of California at Los Angeles; to Dr. Weston La Barre, James B. Duke Professor of Anthropology, Duke University; and to R. Gordon Wasson, Honorary Research Associate, Botanical Museum, Harvard University. Special personal and professional thanks are owed to Richard Evans Schultes, who never failed to give generously of his time and knowledge, be it in helping to identify esoteric plant motifs in pre-Columbian art or in clarifying problems of botany and psychopharmacology encountered in the field. Professor Schultes also read the manuscript for botanical-pharmacological accuracy, but he is obviously not responsible for any shortcomings.

P.T.F.

Albany, N.Y.
March, 1976

---

*For example, the soon-to-be-published proceedings of a conference on alternate states of consciousness sponsored in 1975 by the Drug Abuse Council, Inc., and two earlier publications by the Council, *Altered States of Consciousness* (1975), and *"High" States: A Beginning Study*, by Norman E. Zinberg, M.D. (1974).

Hallucinogens and Culture

INTRODUCTION

If one were to look for landmarks in the study of hallucinogens in the nearly forty years since LSD-25 was first developed in a Swiss laboratory in 1938, a good many possibilities come to mind. One would be the discovery in that same year that a cult of divine psychedelic mushrooms had survived among Mexican Indians, and the rediscovery and systematic investigation of that cult in the mid-1950's. Another would be the identification of the seeds of morning glories as the sacred Aztec hallucinogen *ololiuhqui* in 1941, and the startling finding nearly twenty years later that its active principles are closely related to lysergic acid derivatives. Still another would be R. G. Wasson's definition of *Soma* as the psychotropic fly-agaric mushroom (1968). These discoveries have accompanied the realization over the past several years that the most important botanical hallucinogens are structurally related to biologically active compounds occurring naturally in the brain. For example, psilocybine and the psychoactive alkaloids in morning-glory seeds are indole-tryptamine derivatives and thus are similar in chemical structure to serotonine (5-hydroxy-tryptamine), while mescaline is related to noradrenaline. In addition, norepenephrine in the brain has been found to correspond structurally to caffeic acid, derived from chemicals found in several plants, including coffee beans and potatoes. Chemical systems active in the human brain, then, are now known to be close kin to growth-promoting substances in plants, including several that are powerfully psychoactive, a discovery of no mean evolutionary as well as pharmacological implications.

One of my own favorite landmarks is a "conversation across the disciplines" in 1970 between ethnobotanist Richard Evans Schultes and anthropologist Weston La Barre that has helped to place the whole psychedelic phenomenon in a culture-historical and ideological framework and has given it a theoretical time depth reaching back into the Paleolithic.

Schultes and La Barre were hardly strangers to the problem, or to each other. Schultes has long been the recognized authority on New World hallucinogens, and La Barre is a leading scholar in the anthropology and psychology of religion, author, among other works, of *The Peyote Cult* (1974, 1969, 1938), a classic study of the peyote religion of North American Indians. It was, in fact, peyote that originally brought them together, when, in 1936, Schultes, then a senior in biology at Harvard, accompanied La Barre, a doctoral candidate at Yale, to the Kiowa reservation in Oklahoma for field research on the nature and culture of peyote. La Barre incorporated the experience into his Ph.D. thesis and *The Peyote Cult*; for Schultes it led—via Mexico and his classic study of *ololiuhqui* (1941), and the first botanical identification of the sacred mushrooms of Oaxacan Indians—to a lifelong commitment to ethnobotany, especially the indigenous New World hallucinogens.

An Ethnological Reply to a Statistical Question

In 1970, La Barre published a significant paper in *Economic Botany*, "Old and New World Narcotics: A Statistical Question and an Ethnological Reply" (1970a), which sought for the first time to account in terms of culture history for the astonishing proliferation of sacred hallucinogens in Indian America. The "statistical question" was Schultes's: how was one to explain the striking anomaly between the great number of psychoactive plants known to the original Americans, who had discovered and utilized some eighty to a hundred different species, and the much smaller number—no more than eight or ten—known to have been employed in the Old World? From a strictly botanical point of view, one would have expected the reverse to be true: the Old World has a much greater land mass than the New; its flora is at least as rich and varied and contains as many potential hallucinogenic plants; humanity or protohumanity has lived there for millions of years (as against at most a few tens of thousands in the Americas) and has had immeasurably longer to explore the environment and experiment with different species. Given these circumstances, Schultes concluded, the answer could hardly be botanical but had to be cultural.

Quite so, replied La Barre. American Indian interest in hallucinogenic plants is directly tied to the survival in the New World of an essentially Paleo-Mesolithic Eurasiatic shamanism, which the early big-game hunters carried with them out of northeastern Asia as the base religion of American Indians. Shamanism is deeply rooted in the ecstatic, visionary experience, and the early Native Americans, as well as their descendants, were thus, so to speak, "culturally programmed" for a conscious exploration of the environment in search of means by which to attain that desired state.

It was La Barre's hypothesis, then, (1) that the magicoreligious use of hallucinogenic plants by American Indians represents a survival from a very ancient Paleolithic and Mesolithic shamanistic stratum, and that its linear ancestor is likely to be an archaic form of the shamanistic Eurasiatic fly-agaric cults that survived in Siberia into the present century, and (2) that while profound socioeconomic and religious transformations brought about the eradication of ecstatic shamanism and knowledge of intoxicating mushrooms and other plants over most of Eurasia, a very different set of historical and cultural circumstances favored their survival and elaboration in the New World.

These insights, to which Wasson's work on the sacred fly-agaric of Eurasia and the Mesoamerican mushrooms made no small contribution, have since been enlarged, in print and in the numerous public and private discussions which over the past several years have brought together some of us in related and complementary fields. The insights are, I believe, so fundamental to the understanding of traditional hallucinogens that it will be useful to spell them out in somewhat more detail by way of introduction to the topics covered in this book.

The American Indians are descendants of small Paleo-Asiatic hunting and food-gathering bands that migrated in the Late Paleolithic and Mesolithic into the New World across the 1300-mile-wide "land bridge" which then connected what are now Siberia and Alaska. The age of these early migrations is still a matter of dispute. Not counting some extravagant claims that range beyond a hundred thousand years, most scholarly estimates fluctuate from a high of 40-50,000 years ago for the oldest to 12-15,000 years for the terminal major movements before the melting of the glaciers raised the sea level by 200-300 feet and inundated the overland passage from Asia, while at the same time opening a new ice-free corridor for southward movement. There is an abundance of radiocarbon dates from Paleo-Indian occupation sites in North and South America that lie somewhere between these extremes. And we do know that some time before 10,000 years ago there were people virtually everywhere in the New World, from the Far North to the Tierra del Fuego. We also know that the original Americans sustained themselves with now extinct big game, especially mammoth and mastodon, giant sloth, Pleistocene camel and horse, as well as smaller animals and wild plants, and that their technology and general adaptations resembled by and large those of their contemporaries in comparable environments in Eurasia.

Adaptation, however, has to be understood holistically, comprising metaphysics or ideology as much as physical environment and technology. In other words, whatever their level of technological complexity, these first Americans moved in and interacted reciprocally with an ideational universe no less than the physical one, presumably with no more of a sharp dividing line between these two essential planes than one finds today in surviving hunting cultures and other traditional systems. It is probably not too much to say that mysticism, or religion, has always been a fundamental aspect of the human condition, with its beginnings reaching back perhaps to the primitive origins of self-consciousness.

But the first Americans were hardly "primitive." On the contrary, what little early skeletal material we have shows them to have been thoroughly modern *Homo sapiens*, ranging in physical type from Asiatic Caucasoid to nonspecialized Mongoloid, and generally resembling modern Indian populations. The direct ancestors of the American Indians, then, were not only biologically but also mentally the product of hundreds of thousands of years of human evolution in Asia to a modern type, and as such can be assumed to have shared with other Asiatic populations a well-developed symbolic and ritual system along with other aspects of religion originating in and adapted to their lifeway as hunters of game and collectors of wild vegetable foods.

Ecstatic Shamanism as *"Ur*-Religion"

Now, as we know from ethnology, the symbolic systems or religions of hunting peoples everywhere are essentially shamanistic, sharing so many basic features over time and space as to suggest common historical and psychological origins. At the center of shamanistic religion stands the personality of the shaman and the ecstatic experience that is uniquely his, in his crucial role as diviner, seer, magician, poet, singer, artist, prophet of game and weather, keeper of the traditions, and healer of bodily and spiritual ills. With his spirit helpers or familiars, the shaman is preeminently guardian of the physical and psychic equilibrium of his group, for whom he intercedes in personal confrontation with the supernatural forces of the Upperworld and Underworld, to whose mystical geography he has become privy through initiatory crisis, training, and ecstatic trance. Often, though not always or everywhere, the shaman's ecstatic dream has involved the use of some sacred hallucinogenic plant believed to contain a supernatural transforming power over and above the life force or "soul stuff" that in animistic-shamanistic religious systems inhabits all natural phenomena, including those we would classify as "inanimate." There is no question that shamanism has great antiquity: the archaeological evidence suggests, for example, that something very like the shamanistic religions of recent hunters was already present among the Neanderthals of Europe and Asia more than 50,000 years ago.* It

---

*There is now strong presumption that at least some Neanderthals were also accomplished herbal curers. At Shanidar cave in northern Iraq archaeologists discovered pollen clusters of eight kinds of flowering plants in association with an adult male skeleton. Originally thought to be the expression of the survivors' love and regard for their deceased relative and proof of the high spiritual development of these Neanderthals, the plant remains may actually have also been part of a curing shaman's medicine kit. No less than seven of the eight species represented by pollen grains in the burial have now been identified by the noted French palynologist A. Leroi-Gourhan as belonging to plants that still play a prominent role in herbal curing in the same area and elsewhere in the Old World (e.g. *Achillea*, whose Anglo-Saxon name, yarrow, means "healer"; *Althea*, or hollyhock, whose Greek name likewise means "healer"; *Senecio*, one of whose

is at least possible, though certainly not provable, that the practice of shamanism as an "archaic technique of ecstasy," to use the classic definition of Mircea Eliade (1964), may have involved from the first—that is, the very beginnings of religion itself—the psychedelic potential of the natural environment. This possibility is the more likely in that the reindeer—with which man, first as hunter and then as herder, has lived in an intimate relationship for tens of thousands of years—has itself a certain intriguing relationship with the hallucinogenic fly-agaric mushroom, even to the point of inebriation, a phenomenon that could hardly have failed to impress the Paleo-Eurasiatic peoples of long ago as much as it has impressed recent Siberian tribesmen (see Chapter 13).

Although they must have possessed ingenious means of protecting themselves against the rigors of the Arctic environment, comparable to those of the Eskimos and other Northern peoples, the early migrants from northeastern Asia could certainly be called "primitive" on the basis of their technological inventory alone. But we should not fall into the common error of equating technological complexity with intellectual capacity. On the contrary, when studied in depth as all too few have been, the intellectual cultures of some of the materially least complex peoples—African Bushmen, Australian Aborigines, Arctic or tropical-forest hunters, or the "primitive" preagricultural Indians of California, for example—have been found to rival in metaphysical complexity and poetic imagery some of the world's great institutionalized religions. Besides, as Schultes and others have often pointed out, the most "primitive" of food gatherers possess sophisticated and effective traditional systems of classification for the natural environment, and some of them long ago discovered how to prepare complex psychopharmacological and therapeutic compounds that became available to the industrialized world only with the rise of modern biochemistry. Mexican and Peruvian Indians, after all, experienced the otherworldly effects of mescaline thousands of years before Aldous Huxley.

No system, however conservative—and religion is extraordinarily so—is static, and much of what we find in the religions of Indian America was obviously elaborated *in situ* over a long time, in the context of adaptation to changing relationships with the environment. Nevertheless, there are demonstrably so many fundamental similarities between the core elements of the

---

common English names, groundsel, derives from an Anglo-Saxon word meaning "pus swallower," and *Ephedra*, horsetail, a genus containing the well-known nerve stimulant ephedrine). In the words of Columbia University archaeologist Ralph S. Solecki, who excavated the 60,000-year-old Shanidar cave burials, the presence of so many plants of proven medicinal value in one of the graves at least raises "speculation about the extent of the human spirit in Neanderthals" (Solecki, 1975:880-81). It is certainly tempting to speculate that if these Neanderthals, whom Solecki and other scholars now believe to be in modern humanity's direct line of evolution, possessed knowledge of so many effective medicinal plants, they may likewise have been familiar with some of the psychedelic flora of the region.

religions of the aboriginal New World and those of Asia that almost certainly at least in their basic foundations the symbolic systems of American Indians must have been present already in the ideational world of the original immigrants from northeastern Asia.

These foundations are shamanistic, and they include numerous concepts (recognizable even in the highly structured cosmology and ritual of the hierarchic civilizations, such as the Aztecs, with their institutionalized cyclical ritual and professional priesthood) such as: the skeletal soul of man and animal, and the restitution of life from the bones; all phenomena in the environment as animate; separability of the soul from the body during life (e.g., by soul loss, by straying during sleep, or by rape or abduction, or else the soul's deliberate projection, as by shamans in their ecstatic dreams); the initiatory ecstatic experience, especially of shamans, and "sickness vocation" for the latter; supernatural causes and cures of illness; different levels of the universe with their respective spirit rulers, and the need for feeding these on spirit food; qualitative equivalence of different life forms, and man-animal transformation—indeed, transformation rather than creation as the origin of all phenomena; animal spirit helpers, alter egos, and guardians; supernatural masters and mistresses of animals and plants; acquisition of supernatural or "medicine" power from an outside source. With the concept of transformation so prominent in these traditional systems, it is easy to see why plants capable of radically altering consciousness would have come to stand at the very center of ideology.

Now, as La Barre's original hypothesis was developed, while Asia and Europe formerly shared in this shamanistic world view, the Neolithic Revolution and subsequent fundamental socioeconomic and ideological developments, often cataclysmic in nature, long ago brought about profound changes in the old religions or even their total suppression (although ancient shamanistic roots are here and there still visible even in the institutionalized churches). In the New World, in contrast, the ancestral lifeway of hunting and food gathering, and the religious beliefs and rituals adapted to this lifeway, persisted in time and space to a far greater extent than in the Old; and moreover, the fundamental shamanistic base was much better preserved, even in the agricultural religions of the great civilizations that rose in Mesoamerica and the Andes, as well as of simpler farming societies.

Indeed, the two situations are really not even comparable. There are many historical reasons for this difference, but one that should be stressed is that prior to European colonization the New World as a whole never knew the intolerant fanaticism that is the hallmark of some of the major Old World religions, particularly Christianity and Islam, both of which massively transformed the areas in which they took hold—although, as we know, four centuries of Spanish Catholicism have failed to eradicate completely all traces of the pre-European past, and were spectacularly unsuccessful in the suppression of the sacred traditional hallucinogens. For it was generally characteristic even of the stratified, militaristic, and expansionist Indian civilizations that conquest by one group or another, if it affected religion at all, typically resulted in accretion or synthesis rather than in persecution, suppression, and forced conversion. These blessings of civilized life had to await the coming of the Europeans.

Without unduly idealizing the real situation, especially what eventually turned out to be nonadaptive aspects in such religions as that of the Aztecs, it is correct to say that most American Indians from north to south, and through all prehistory, seem to have valued above all individual freedom for each person to determine his own relationship to the unseen forces of the universe. In many cases this process of determination included personal confrontation of these forces in the ecstatic trance, often with the aid of plants to which supernatural powers were ascribed. Significantly, there is not a shred of evidence that this ancient situation was fundamentally affected even by the rise of political and religious bureaucracies, or that it ever occurred to these bureaucracies to exercise police power over the individual's right to transform his consciousness by whatever means he wished.

Archaeological Evidence for the Earliest Hallucinogen

This value given to freedom is especially noteworthy in that in *The Natural Mind* (1972), Dr. Andrew T. Weil has argued that "the desire to alter consciousness periodically is an innate, normal drive analogous to hunger or the sexual drive" (p. 17). While drugs are only one means of satisfying this drive, he maintained, it is nevertheless this inborn biological—as opposed to socioculturally conditioned—need of the psyche for periods of nonordinary consciousness that accounts for the near-universal use of intoxicants by peoples all over the world, on whatever level of cultural complexity, and apparently in all periods of human history.

Weil may well be correct; certainly he makes a persuasive cross-cultural case that the desire for temporary states of altered consciousness is embedded in the neurophysiological structure of the brain rather than in social conditioning. But while his hypothesis may be sound, for the present it must rest on circumstantial evidence. On the other hand, La Barre's proposition that the earliest Americans must have brought their fascination for the psychedelic flora with them from their Asian homeland, as a function of ecstatic visionary shamanism, now seems confirmed by prehistoric archaeology (La Barre's and Weil's are not, of course, mutually exclusive hypotheses).

What makes this proposition particularly interesting is that the evidence concerns one of the few physiologically hazardous (though not addictive) hallucinogens employed by American Indians. This is the so-called "mescal bean," which in reality has nothing to do with mescal (a distilled Mexican liquor produced from a species of agave) but is the red, beanlike seed of *Sophora secundiflora*, a leguminous flowering shrub native to Texas and northern Mexico. These seeds contain, like *Genista canariensis*, a nine-teenth-century import from the Canary Islands whose small yellow flowers are now ritually smoked by Yaqui shamans in northern Mexico, a highly toxic quinolizidine alkaloid called cytisine. In high doses cytisine is capable of causing nausea, convulsions, hallucinations, and even death from respiratory failure (Schultes, 1972a).

Notwithstanding such obvious disadvantages, *Sophora* seems to be the oldest and longest-lived New World hallucinogen; at least it is the earliest for which we have direct and sustained evidence. Historically, the potent seeds were the focus of a widespread complex of ecstatic visionary shamanistic medicine societies among the tribes of the Southern Plains, until in the final decades of the nineteenth century *Sophora* was finally replaced by the more benign peyote cactus, while the red-bean cults themselves were supplanted by the new syncretistic peyote religion that eventually was embraced as the Native American Church by 225,000 Indians from the Rio Grande in Texas to the Canadian Plains.

The first European mention of *Sophora secundiflora* dates back to 1539, when Cabeza de Vaca reported the seeds as an item of trade among the Indians of Texas. But its history can be extended to the very beginnings of the settlement of the Southwest by the early hunters coming down from the north. The radiocarbon laboratory of the Smithsonian Institution has now confirmed that the hallucinogenic mescal bean was well integrated not only into the preagricultural Western Archaic or Desert Culture, from its earliest levels to A.D. 1000, but that it was already known and employed by Paleo-Indians toward the end of the preceding Late Pleistocene big-game-hunting period, 10-11,000 years ago—not long after the cessation of the last overland migrations from Asia (Adovasio and Fry, 1975). At the very least this is strong circumstantial evidence for the La Barre hypothesis of Paleolithic roots for the hallucinogenic complex in the Americas.

Caches of *Sophora* seeds and associated artifacts and rock paintings reminiscent of the historic red-bean cults of the Southern Plains were found by archaeologists in a dozen or more rock shelters in Texas and northern Mexico, often together with another narcotic species, *Ungnadia speciosa*. At Frightful Cave, the earliest occurrence of *Sophora* was dated at 7265 B.C., with a margin of error of only 85 years in either direction. The seeds were also found in all the later cultural strata, up to the abandonment of the site. At Fate Bell Shelter in the Amistad Reservoir area of Trans-Pecos Texas, a region rich in ancient shamanistic rock paintings, the narcotic seeds of *S. secundiflora* and *U. speciosa* were found in every level, from 7,000 B.C. to A.D. 1000, when the Desert Culture finally gave way to a new way of life based on maize agriculture. Of the greatest interest, however, were the radiocarbon dates from Bonfire Shelter. This well-studied rock-shelter site yielded *Sophora* seeds from its lowest occupational stratum, known as Bone Bed II, dated at 8440 to 8120 B.C., or well into the Late Pleistocene big-game-hunting era. Indeed, the hallucinogenic seeds were found with Folsom and Plainview-type projectile points and the bones of a large extinct species of Pleistocene bison, *Bison antiquus.*

It is certainly noteworthy that apparently a single hallucinogen, the *Sophora* bean, should have enjoyed an uninterrupted reign of over 10,000 years— from the ninth millenium B.C. well into the nineteenth century and the disintegration of traditional Indian culture—as the focus of ecstatic-visionary shamanism, and for all but a few centuries of that enormous span of time in the context of the well-documented, conservative, and evidently highly successful homogeneous ecological adaptation we know as the Desert Culture of southwestern North America. This is all the more extraordinary in that of all the many native hallucinogens only the genus *Datura* ("Jimsonweed") poses so great a physiological risk as does *Sophora secundiflora.* Clearly, the individual, social, and supernatural benefits ascribed to the drug must have outweighed its disadvantages.

Peyote: Sacred "Medicine" or "Dangerous Narcotic"?

Without necessarily advocating unrestricted availability of every hallucinogen less demonstrably risky to health than *S. secundiflora* or *Datura*, one would hope that lessons would soon be drawn from the abundant cultural and psychopharmacological data available to us for most of the botanical hallucinogens that have played a major role in the context of magicoreligious rites and curing practices, particularly among American Indians. Peyote, to mention only one, has a proven cultural history of more than 2000 years in Mesoamerica, and is likely to be far older still than its first botanically recognizable representation in archaeological tomb art dating to the period from 100 B.C. to A.D. 100. More than 10,000 Huichols and many other Mexican Indians continue to deem peyote sacred and charged with great therapeutic powers for body and mind. For nearly a quarter-million North American Indians, their own efforts and those of their allies among anthropologists and civil libertarians over the past decades have finally made peyote use legal within the framework of the Native American Church. But for those outside that church, the bitter-tasting spineless little cactus plant is supposed to be so dangerous to the individual and to society that its possession for "unlawful" purposes or sale to others can (at least under New York State's retrogressive drug law) result in punishment as harsh as that for dealing heroin—with the measurable *direct* social costs running well into the hundreds of thousands of dollars for a successful conviction resulting in long incarceration. This in the face of a vast body of scientific evidence, as freely available in print to legislators and the law-enforcement establishment as it is to the academic community! Despite the work of generations of scholars, from anthropologists and ethnobotanists to pharmacologists and psychiatrists, then, it seems as though in our social policies we have not advanced very far beyond the superstitious fulminations of sixteenth-century Spanish Inquisitors in Mexico and their particular means for dealing with a core element of traditional Indian religion, one they feared and abhorred as the Devil's own handiwork but also one that, if Weil and other students of consciousness are right, is inseparable from the human condition itself.

The chapters that follow are not intended as an exhaustive treatment of hallucinogens, but mainly as a selective introduction to the botany and pharmacology of psychoactive substances *in their cultural context*. For, quite apart from purely biochemical effects, as several field workers have noted, it is primarily the mind set and the culture of the user and his social group that determine the nature and intensity of the ecstatic experience and how that experience is interpreted and assimilated.

Other Pathways to "Alternate States"

Nor do I mean to imply that psychoactive plants or animal secretions have always and everywhere been the only, or even the principal, means of achieving altered states of consciousness. On the contrary, over vast areas of North America many aboriginal peoples achieved the same ends by nonchemical means: fasting, thirsting, self-mutilation, torture, exposure to the elements, sleeplessness, incessant dancing and other means of total exhaustion, bleeding, plunging into ice-cold pools, near-drowning, laceration with thorns and animal teeth, and other painful ordeals, as well as a variety of nonhurtful "triggers," such as different kinds of rhythmic activity, self-hypnosis, meditation, chanting, drumming, and music. Some shamans may also have used mirrors of pyrite, obsidian, and other materials to place themselves into trances, as some Indian shamans in Mexico still do. Most dramatic of known techniques were surely the spirit-quest ordeals of certain Plains Indian tribes, such as the Oglala Sioux and the Mandan.

George Catlin, a Pennsylvania lawyer born in 1796 who in the mid-1800's became the dean of documentary painters of the American Indian and his aboriginal culture, and who was one of the few white men privileged to witness the entire ceremony, has left us a vivid account as well as paintings and drawings of the vision-seeking ordeal practiced by the Mandan (Donaldson, 1886). Already greatly weakened from hunger and thirst and four consecutive sleepless days and nights, the candidates had holes pierced with knives through the flesh of their shoulders or breasts. Through these holes they were suspended by skewers and thongs from the center pole of the great Medicine Lodge. The vision seeker's shield, bow, quiver, and other belongings were suspended from still more skewers passed through other parts of his body, and in many instances even a heavy bison skull was attached to each arm and leg. Attendants with long poles caused his body to twirl ever faster until the candidate, streaming with blood, passed out from the pain, his medicine bag dropping from his hands and his body hanging apparently lifeless.* He was then lowered to the ground and allowed to recover, but the ordeal was not over. There was still the sacrifice of the little finger of his left hand (which was chopped off and offered to the Great Spirit), to be followed by a furious race around an altar, with the bison skulls and other weights dragging behind the candidate, until he could endure no more and fell in a dead faint. With that collapse, the purpose of the ordeal—which took place in connection with the great Sun Dance festival at the end of the summer bison hunt—was accomplished. Whites generally interpreted the ritual as a test of courage and fortitude, or preferred to see it as an example of Indian "cruelty," but in fact it belongs well within the general tradition of the ecstatic spirit quest, however extreme it may be as an example of the drugless vision-inducing ordeal.

Interestingly enough, ordeals of this type if not necessarily of the same intensity were not uncommon even in ancient Mexico, notwithstanding the widespread use of plant hallucinogens to achieve altered states of consciousness. Self-mutilation is depicted in the ritual art of different pre-Hispanic cultures and periods, from about 1300 B.C. to the Conquest, and bloodletting rites that must have inflicted severe pain (including perforation of the penis, tongue, and other organs with cactus thorns, stingray barbs, and other sharp instruments) are described in the early ethnohistoric literature on Maya and central Mexican customs. The Maya may even have practiced a vision-quest ritual resembling that described by Catlin for the Great Plains. I am familiar with at least one naturalistic Maya figurine from the island of Jaina, in the Gulf of Campeche, depicting what seems to be a priest with four perforated folds of flesh on his bare back, one pair on each side. The body and the arms and legs are so positioned by the sculptor as to suggest that the figure was meant to be suspended from the holes pierced in the skin—much like the vision seekers in one of Catlin's Mandan paintings.

A famous carved Maya monument, dated ca. A.D. 780, Lintel 25 from the ceremonial center of Yaxchilán in the Usumacinta region of Chiapas, depicts a richly attired kneeling woman in the act of drawing through her tongue a twisted cord, set with large sharp thorns. In the literature, such extremely painful rites are often discussed in terms of blood sacrifice—blood being the most precious gift to the supernaturals in ancient Mesoamerican thought—but in point of fact they must have constituted a violent shock to the system, sufficient to bring about alterations in consciousness to the point of visions. At the very least they would have created the proper mind-set to

---

*Twirling, as Weil (1972) has noted, is also a technique by which children in many cultures the world over seek to alter the normal or everyday state of consciousness.

receive and interpret such visions. Indeed, a magnificent relief carved on another monument, Lintel 24, in the same Yaxchilán temple seems to depict just that kind of ecstatic phenomenon, with a woman gazing transfixed at the figure of a warrior emerging above her from the wide-open jaws of a writhing serpent or dragon. Whether or not such visions might have been facilitated by a combination of physical ordeal and hallucinogenic mushrooms of the kind that abound in the Usumacinta basin cannot be stated with certainty in the present state of our knowledge of ancient Maya religion. At the same time, we should not assume that all apparently painful bloodletting rites were so in fact. Even where the shock to the system was sufficient to trigger an alternate state of consciousness, the perception of pain could have been blocked by a properly trained individual;* indeed, there are sixteenth-century accounts by Spanish observers of self-sacrificial rites involving severe laceration of the penis where no pain was said to have been felt and no blood flowed. In this connection it might be noted that in depictions in Maya art of bloodletting rituals of the most severe kind the expressions of the individuals involved are calm and serene, lacking any indication of physical suffering.

Actually, some kind of ordeal, usually in the form of deprivation of normal food, drink, sleep, and sex, for varying lengths of time, is almost always the essential precondition for the ritual use of hallucinogens, and clearly plays an important role in the intensification of the ecstatic experience. As an example, when the Huichol peyote pilgrim finally arrives in Wirikúta, the sacred country in the north-central Mexican desert where he (or she) is to harvest the hallucinogenic cactus, he has already traveled some 300 miles from his homeland (traditionally on foot), and he is physically close to exhaustion. He has had little or no sleep since setting out. He has kept himself at a fever pitch of emotion by the realization of the gravity and sacredness of the enterprise on which he is embarked and its importance to the well-being of his people, by incessant dancing and singing, and by the observance of innumerable rituals along the way. He has eaten virtually nothing and little or no water has quenched his thirst. Salt is strictly forbidden for the duration of the pilgrimage, and for many days before and after. Finally, he has smoked

---

*Research by scientists of several countries, including the United States, Great Britain, and Sweden, has recently uncovered evidence that the body spontaneously manufactures pain-killing chemicals whose structure and effects appear to be very like those of morphine and that within the mammalian brain, including that of humans, there are molecules that are highly specific opiate receptors which chemically join such opium derivatives as heroin and morphine. The United States scientists involved in this important research include Drs. Gavril Pasternak and Solomon H. Snyder of Johns Hopkins University and Dr. Avram Goldstein of Stanford. Drs. John Hughes and H. W. Kosterlitz in Aberdeen, Scotland, and Dr. Lars Terenius in Uppsala, Sweden, have been making breakthroughs in the same field. Apart from helping to account for spontaneous mitigation of pain in severe trauma situations, one hope is that the new discoveries will be useful in the treatment of opiate addiction.

many ritual cigarettes of the extremely potent native *Nicotiana rustica* tobacco wrapped in cornhusk, and he may also have purified himself symbolically and literally by eating impressive quantities of the same tobacco, whose content of nicotine and other alkaloids is far greater than that of commercial cigarettes. He is thus already at a very different level of consciousness, so much so that it is not necessary for him to be under the influence of the peyote alkaloids to perceive the plant in its animal form when the leader of the pilgrimage exclaims, at the sight of the very first cactus: "Ah, there he is at last, Our Elder Brother, the divine Deer, who gives us our life!" In the course of the rites that follow, in the peyote country and back home in the Sierra, Huichols will literally saturate themselves with peyote, chewing it incessantly for days and nights on end, getting little sleep and eating little normal food, until the entire social and natural environment and the individual's relationship to it take on a wholly mystical dimension. The metabolic system has been altered, and it is in that mystical state that the shamans interpret the visions—their own and those of others—in accordance with the traditional cultural norms and the magical-animistic world view that permeates Huichol ideology.

If sleep or food deprivation or extreme fatigue and physical pain could be employed, with or without chemical aids, to affect mental balance—or, putting it another way, to facilitate a different kind of psychic equilibrium— how much more drastic must be the effects of the powerful, even deadly, poisons that also played a role of some importance in the traditional systems of altering consciousness and, in the case of the frog-poison ordeals of South American Indians, still do so even now?

The great sixteenth-century chronicler Fray Diego Durán has left us a vivid description of the sort of toxic substance which the Aztec priests of Tezcatlipoca took both internally and externally to place themselves in the proper mental state to serve the deity and interpret his words. Known as *teotlacualli*, food of god or divine food, it included "poisonous beasts, such as spiders, scorpions, centipedes, lizards, vipers, and others," which were caught for the priests by young boys and kept by them in large numbers in the priestly school:

This was the divine food with which the priests, ministers of the temples, and especially those with whom we are dealing, smeared themselves in ancient times. They took all these poisonous animals and burned them in the divine brazier which stood in the temple. After these had been burned, the ashes were placed within certain mortars, together with a great deal of tobacco; this herb is used by the Indians to relieve the body so as to calm the pains of toil. In this it is similar to Spanish henbane, which, when mixed with lime, loses its poisonous qualities, though it still causes faintness and is harmful to the stomach. This herb, then, was placed in the mortars together with scorpions, live spiders, and centipedes, and there they were ground producing a diabolical, stinking, deadly ointment. After these had been crushed, a ground seed called *ololiuhqui* was added, which the natives apply to their bodies and drink to see visions. It is a drink which has inebriating effects. To all this were added hairy black worms, their hair filled with venom, injuring those who touch them. Everything was mixed with soot and was poured into bowls and gourds. Then it was placed before the god as divine food. How can one doubt that the men smeared with this pitch became wizards or demons, capable of seeing and speaking to the devil himself, since the ointment had been prepared for that purpose? (Durán, 1971:115-16).

According to Durán, the priests painted themselves with this fearsome mixture and, rendered unafraid of wild animals and other dangers by their magic potion, set forth at night to visit dark caves and "somber, fearful cliffs." The same ointment or pitch was also used in curing rites, when it was applied to the affected parts of the patient's body to deaden the pain.

Who, indeed, could doubt the power of such a mixture on the mind as well as the body? Covering large surface areas of the body for prolonged periods, containing not only venoms that would be deadly if they entered the blood-stream directly but also the potent alkaloids of tobacco and morning-glory seeds (*ololiuhqui*), *teotlacualli* at the very least would have had to cause serious skin reactions, if it was not actually absorbed to some degree into the system. In either event, it could well have had more or less drastic effect on the body's metabolism, with some alteration in the user's state of consciousness, even if he did not actually intoxicate himself with infusions of the sacred hallucinogenic *ololiuhqui*, as Aztec priests are known to have done, and some native Mexican curers still do, for the purpose of divination.

Hallucinogens and the Biochemistry of Consciousness

The entire subject of chemical substances in nature and their relationship, actual or potential, to alternate* states of consciousness is vast and complex. It extends toward the origin of what Jung called "archetypes," mythmaking and common world-wide themes in oral tradition (especially the strikingly similar content the world over of funerary, heroic, and shamanistic mythology), art and iconography, traditional cultural systems of perceiving and ordering reality that differ drastically from the so-called "scientific" western model, conceptions of Otherworlds, death and afterlife, mysticism, and, indeed, what we call religion itself. And, much as we think we already know, in truth we have made barely a beginning in these cultural areas, just as we are only just coming to grips with the fact that even in our waking hours our minds are constantly flipping back and forth between discrete, or alternate

---

*The substitution of "alternate" for the customary "altered" was suggested by Dr. Norman Zinberg (1974) "in order," he writes, "to avoid the idea that the change alters consciousness from the way it *should* be." Nevertheless, most authorities on "high states" agree with C. T. Tart (1972) that these constitute "a qualitative alteration in the overall pattern of mental functioning, such that the experiencer feels his consciousness is radically different from the way it functions normally."

(but nonetheless complementary), inward- and outward-directed states, and that this phenomenon bears directly on the use and effects of psychedelics. There are, of course, degrees of intensity in the experience of the inward-directed state of consciousness: obviously a peyote "high" is not of the same order as daydreaming, even if similar neurochemical processes are at work in the brain. If one were to reduce to its essentials the complex chemical process that occurs when an external psychoactive drug such as psilocybine reaches the brain, it would then be said that the drug, being structurally closely related to the naturally occurring indoles in the brain, appears to interact with the latter in such a way as to lock a nonordinary or inward-directed state of consciousness temporarily into place, presumably by blocking out certain areas or chemicals involved in "ordinary" modes of awareness.* In any event, whatever the biochemical processes involved—while we should beware of overestimating as of undervaluing the impact that the discovery of psychoactive plants and other life forms by early human populations may have had on the evolution of world views or ideology—there are obviously wide implications, biological-evolutionary as well as philosophical, in the discovery that precisely in the chemistry of our consciousness we are kin to the plant kingdom.

The Social-Psychological Context as Crucial Variable

Finally, a word about the need for an anthropological and culture-historical perspective. The ways in which and the purposes for which so-called "primitive" or traditional societies and those of industrialized nations employ chemicals capable of triggering alternate states of consciousness are obviously very different, as are the attitudes with which such drugs and their effects are viewed. As the following pages make clear, in the preindustrial or tribal world, psychotropic plants are sacred and magical; they are perceived as living beings with supernatural attributes, providing for certain chosen individuals such as shamans, and under certain special circumstances for ordinary people as well, a kind of bridge across the gulf that separates this world from Otherworlds. By common agreement, in the "primitive" societies the breakthrough in plane which the extraordinary chemicals in these plants facilitate is considered to be essential for the wellbeing of the individual and the community. The ecstatic trance experience or truly altered state of consciousness triggered by the natural alkaloids, and its culturally conditioned content and

---

*This is an area of research in which Dr. Joel Elkes, formerly Psychiatrist-in-Chief, The Johns Hopkins Hospital, Baltimore, Maryland, has done considerable pioneering work. It might be noted that even in drug "highs" of great intensity, such as with *Psilocybe* mushrooms or peyote, it is nevertheless sometimes possible to alternate between inward- and outward-directed states by the simple device of opening and closing one's eyes. At least I have found this to be so, and I have seen Indians make the same transitions during rituals.

subsequent interpretation, are fully consistent with traditional religious-philosophical systems that value and even encourage individual pathways to the supernatural powers and personal confrontation with them, however these be conceived or named. The evidence, archaeological and otherwise, is such that we can say with certainty that most societies, if not all, that still employ hallucinogenic plants in their rituals have done so for centuries, not to say millennia. The plants have a cultural history: they are accounted for by traditions in which all members of the society share.

Indeed, we can go so far as to say that the psychotropic plants have helped determine the history of the culture, inasmuch as it is typically in the ecstatic initiatory trance experience that the individual confirms for himself the validity of tribal traditions he has heard his elders recite from earliest childhood:

When one considers that datura results in mental images of tremendous intensity, it is no wonder that a Cahuilla boy after his first vision under its influence became a firm believer in mythic traditions. Datura enabled him to glimpse the ultimate reality of the creation stories in the Cahuilla cosmology. The supernatural beings and aspects of the other world that he had been told about since childhood were now brought before his eyes for the ultimate test—his own empirical examination. He has seen them. They are real. . . . Once the Cahuilla neophyte was convinced by his own perceptions, he was thenceforth locked into the entire Cahuilla cosmology, dramatically, with community guidance and support. (Bean and Saubel, 1972:62-63)

The magic plants, then, act to validate and reify the culture, not to afford some temporary means of escape from it. The Huichol of Mexico, like the Cahuilla of Southern California or the Tukano of Colombia, returns from his initiatory "trip" to exclaim, "It is as my fathers explained it to me!" One takes peyote, he says, "to learn how one goes being Huichol." It is hardly to learn "how one goes being American" (or German, or English, or Mexican) in the conventional sense that LSD or DMT are employed in the West. And yet, objectively, the chemistry of these drugs differs little from that of the sacred plants of the tribal world, LSD being similar to the natural alkaloids in morning-glory seeds, while dimethyltryptamines are prominent in the hallucinogenic snuffs of South American Indians. And *Cannabis* (spp.), which thirty million contemporary Americans are said to have smoked recreationally at least once, and probably more often, has replaced the potent *Psilocybe* mushroom in the divinatory curing rituals of some Mexican Indian shamans, who easily place themselves in ecstatic trances with a plant that, from the strictly pharmacological point of view, is not in fact comparable to *Psilocybe*.*

---

*With other states following Oregon's example in reducing penalties for personal use of marihuana to the level of a traffic fine, similar federal legislation presently being considered in Congress, and the Alaska State Supreme Court ruling that personal use in the home is not a crime, the situation is clearly changing, however belatedly and slowly, and however irrelevantly for the hundreds of thousands of Americans branded for life as felons by antiquated federal and local statutes. The movement toward decriminalization of *Cannabis* use received a major boost

Urgently Needed: An Integrated Perspective

It is clearly society, not chemistry, that is the variable, since the same or chemically similar drugs can function so differently in different cultural situations, or be venerated over centuries as sacred, benign, and culturally integrative in some contexts but regarded in others as inherently so evil and dangerous that their very possession constitutes a serious crime. Likewise, it is obviously culture and the attitudes and stereotypes it fosters—not any inherent characteristics or even their measurable medical and social consequences—that make one "social" drug, alcohol, legally and morally acceptable to us, and another, marihuana, not. Addictive narcotics such as heroin are a different matter, of course, from nonaddictive hallucinogens, but to say that here too we urgently need to apply the essential cultural (that is to say, anthropological) perspective is not to underrate the seriousness of the problem —quite the contrary. However, I suspect that until a holistic perspective, integrating anthropology, biology, and psychology, has become so fully accepted (by the general public no less than the drug-research, lawmaking, and law-enforcement establishment) as to be second nature, resort to any but officially approved or commercially touted drugs to alter consciousness will always be perceived as objectionable. Thus I suspect that use of drugs not "approved" will remain at the level of an "epidemic," yielding neither to the most repressive laws nor to the most massive spending for "education" and rehabilitation.

If that suspicion were unfounded, would we not be more worried about the effects of nicotine than about those of THC? And, while by no means underrating the seriousness of the heroin threat, would we not be less agitated over an estimated quarter million heroin addicts, and adopt more intelligent social policies to deal with the problem (including even such "unthinkable" alternatives to the black-market drug empire as legalized heroin maintenance)

---

in 1975 with the publication of *Ganja in Jamaica*, by Vera Rubin and Lambros Comitas (1975), a medical anthropological study of chronic marihuana use sponsored by the Center for Studies of Narcotic and Drug Abuse, National Institute of Mental Health. The study found no indications of organic brain damage or chromosome damage from long-term chronic use of *ganja* (the folk name for marihuana in Jamaica); no significant psychiatric, psychological or medical differences between chronic smokers and nonsmokers of *ganja*; and no loss of motivation. The only correlation that could be found between *ganja* and crime was a technical one: *ganja* cultivation and possession are technically crimes. The "single medical finding of interest," writes former Pennsylvania Governor Raymond P. Shafer in his foreword to the book, "is the indication of functional hypoxia among heavy, long-term chronic smokers." However, he notes, *ganja* in Jamaica is customarily mixed with tobacco and *ganja* smokers are also generally heavy cigarette smokers; hence it was impossible to distinguish between clinical effects of *ganja* and tobacco smoking and cigarette smoking, the conclusion being that smoking *per se* may be responsible for impairment of respiratory efficiency. Again pointing up culture as the crucial variable in the use and effects of a drug was the finding that, as Governor Shafer notes, in contrast to the alleged "amotivational" effects generally attributed to marihuana in the United States, in Jamaica *ganja* "serves to fulfill values of the work ethic."

than by the truly epidemic proportions of alcoholism? Against three to four hundred thousand opiate addicts in the United States (certainly a shocking figure) there are nevertheless ten to twelve million confirmed alcoholics and millions more "problem drinkers" with enormous potential for harm to themselves and society. Whatever the personal and social damage of heroin addiction and its functional relationship to street crime and corruption, there is a demonstrable correlation between drinking and many thousands of annual highway deaths, as well as homicide, child abuse, and other violence, with a total social cost immeasurably higher than that attributable to heroin. Moreover, as Brecher (1972) and others have shown, excessive use of alcohol carries far greater potential than heroin for organic deterioration. This is not to advocate heroin over alcohol, certainly, nor to minimize the tragedy which heroin addiction represents for so many individuals and their families, but only to underscore that in disregard of everything we know of alcohol as a dangerous drug, "getting high" with it carries but a fraction of the social and legal stigma we as a society attach to other mind-altering substances. Facts, then, are seemingly irrelevant—at least they are less relevant or decisive than cultural conditioning.

CHAPTER ONE

"IDOLATRY," HALLUCINOGENS,
AND CULTURAL SURVIVAL

Almost as soon as Europeans set foot on American soil at the end of the fifteenth century, first in the Antilles and soon afterwards on the continent itself, they took note with varying degrees of fascination and revulsion of a strange indigenous custom they were later to recognize as an indispensable aspect of aboriginal religion and ritual in many parts of the New World: ecstatic intoxication with different plants to which the native peoples ascribed supernatural power, and which the Spaniards, not surprisingly, associated with the Devil's untiring effort to impede the victory of Christianity over traditional Indian religion.

In a sense they were right: the missionary clergy correctly perceived the sacred mushrooms, morning-glory seeds, peyote, snuffs, tobacco, and other "magical" (that is, consciousness-transforming) plants as obstacles to total conversion, since their continued use, in secret and under the constant threat of the most cruel punishment, from public flogging to burning alive at the stake, served to confirm and validate the traditional symbolic and religious world views of some of the aboriginal peoples and to consolidate resistance against their total destruction. And in fact, as ecclesiastical writers of later centuries were forced to admit, the great expenditure of missionary zeal, the preaching, and the punishment seemed in the end to have accomplished little more than to drive these practices underground, where they were even harder to combat. Or else the Indians had managed to work peyote, morning-glory seeds, and other sacred plants so subtly into Christian doctrine and ritual that they could lay claim to practicing proper respect for the Virgin Mary and the saints even while continuing to seek spiritual guidance with the aid of the divine inebriants of the pre-European past. The Spaniards, of course, saw this combination as clever deceit; which in a way it was—in defense of the integrity of the traditional culture; on the other hand, such synthesis of Christian with pre-Conquest belief and ritual was an expectable consequence of culture contact and acculturation.

It is important to note that the early missionary fathers more often than not were content to accept as true the reports they heard from the Indians of the wondrous effects of the magical plants, especially in connection with divination and curing, the two areas in which the native hallucinogens played their most important role. What they seem to have objected to primarily—apart from their aversion to any kind of intoxication among their Indian charges— was that Christ was missing from the system; for that reason the supernatural effects could only be explained in terms of the Devil, who unceasingly tried to maintain and enlarge his ancient hold on the native souls whose salvation the Spaniards were convinced was their divine mission. Hernando Ruiz de Alarcón, a seventeenth-century divine who was commissioned by his bishop to investigate and uproot whatever indigenous belief and ritual had survived the first century of Spanish rule in Morelos and adjacent parts of central Mexico, devoted much of his *Tratado* of 1629 to Indian worship and use of the sacred morning glories, peyote, mushrooms, and tobacco, expressing the fear that these ancient "idolatrous" practices of the Indians might prove attractive enough to spread to the lower strata of Spanish colonial society.

The earliest European accounts of ritual intoxication date from the initial voyages of discovery toward the end of the fifteenth century. One Fray Ramón Pané was commissioned by Christopher Columbus, on his second voyage in 1496, to observe and set down the ceremonies and "antiquities" of the Arawakan-speaking Taino Indians on the island of Hispaniola, whom even the Spaniards recognized as a notably gentle people with an advanced culture (which, however, was soon to decline disastrously in response to European cruelties and previously unknown diseases). Pané described rites in which the natives inhaled an intoxicating herb they called *kohobba*,* "so strong that those who take it lose consciousness" and believe themselves to be in communication with the supernatural world. The Indians snuffed the potent powder through foot-long tubes, he reported, and "sorcerers" (i.e. shamans or curers) customarily took the drug along with their patients so as to learn the cause of the affliction and its proper treatment. The same sort of direct

---

Kohobba, whose use died out in the Antilles after the Conquest, along with hundreds of thousands of the native population, was made from the seeds of an acacia-like tree, *Anadenanthera peregrina*, which are rich in tryptamines and from which a number of Indian tribes in northeastern South America still prepare their intoxicating snuffs. Initially, however—indeed, until the early twentieth century—*kohobba* was generally identified with tobacco, an understandable error since tobacco was, and continues to be, used in similar ways elsewhere in South America. It is even possible that *kohobba* or a closely related word was also applied to intoxicating snuffs based mainly on tobacco.

psychic bond between healer and patient is still common in drug-assisted folk therapy in Mexico as well as Peru.

In the first decades of the sixteenth century, the Spanish conquerors of Mexico found the Indians there in possession of a considerable psychoactive pharmacopoeia that included several kinds of sacred mushrooms, peyote, *Datura* (a genus that may not have been unfamiliar to the invaders since it also played a role in medieval European medicine and witchcraft), an especially potent species of tobacco called *piciétl*, and a variety of other native plants with strangely "otherworldly" effects whose chemistry has only recently been clarified. Prominent among the latter are certain species of morning glories whose psychedelic seeds were held especially sacred—to the point of divinity—by the Aztecs and by peoples of central Mesoamerica, and whose active principles the scientific world was surprised to learn only a few years ago are closely allied to the synthetic hallucinogen LSD-25.

Nor was it different in South America. All across the continent, from the small-scale societies of tropical-forest manioc planters and hunters and collectors of wild foods to the complex civilization of the Incas in the Andes, the early explorers and missionaries found the drug-induced ecstatic trance—what we now call transformation of consciousness—to be an integral aspect of shamanistic religion. As we now know, the Indians of South America even more than those in Mesoamerica not only discovered and experimented with the psychoactive properties of many plants in their different environments, but also successfully tried combinations of unrelated species for the purpose of activating their psychedelic principles or heightening their effects.

For the native inhabitants in its path, the military, economic, and spiritual conquest of South America was—as it has continued to be in such areas as Amazonia—an almost unrelieved tragedy. Nor did it have the benefit of a Las Casas crying out for justice for the Indians, or even the painstaking kind of ethnography that is the Mexican legacy of Fray Bernardino de Sahagún, a remarkable sixteenth-century Franciscan who, like a few other churchmen of his time, was blessed with an insatiable and even largely sympathetic curiosity that caused him to compile for posterity all he could learn from Aztec informants of the native civilization that the Spaniards, himself included, had come to destroy. Sahagún's *Florentine Codex* and other writings include an impressive array of herbal lore which, together with the botanical and medicinal compilations of his learned contemporary, the royal physician Francisco Hernández, is the indispensable starting point for any botanical, taxonomical, or ethnographic investigation of the sacred hallucinogens. The beautifully illustrated mid-sixteenth-century Aztec herbal known as the *Codex Badianus* may also have been composed under the auspices or inspiration of Sahagún. For the century following the Conquest, the treatises of Jacinto de la Serna and of Ruiz de Alarcón are essential for an understanding of the continued functions of traditional hallucinogens, especially tobacco, morning glories, peyote, and mushrooms, during the early Colonial period, and the ways in which these were affected by, or managed to evade, the processes of culture change and Christian acculturation.

Although there are references in the Colonial literature to ritual intoxication by means of plants, for South America the pre-nineteenth-century sources are not very satisfactory, and apart from Alexander von Humboldt's identification and discussion of one of the two major sources of hallucinogenic snuff on the Orinoco, there is little that could be called scientific. It is in fact no exaggeration to state that practically everything we know today of the botany, taxonomy, chemistry, and even anthropology of the ritual hallucinogens of South America ultimately had its genesis in the work of the modern ethnobotanists—from the Yorkshireman plant explorer Richard Spruce to Harvard's Richard Evans Schultes. Spruce in 1851 collected and named the first specimens of *Banisteriopsis caapi*, which he identified as the source of the intoxicating drink of Upper Amazonian Indians. Schultes's field research in the American tropics and in Mexico since the late 1930's has directly or indirectly led to the botanical, chemical and cultural identification of most of the vegetal hallucinogens of the New World, a task that is nonetheless not yet complete and will undoubtedly continue for years to come.

CHAPTER TWO

TOBACCO: "PROPER FOOD OF THE GODS"

The Spanish clergy from the first classified tobacco alongside peyote, morning glories, and mushrooms as a ritual intoxicant of traditional Indian culture. This fact may come as a surprise, but the ministers of the Colonial church knew whereof they spoke.

The natural and cultural history of tobacco (*Nicotiana* spp.) as an aboriginal American cultigen—as much unknown to the rest of the world less than 500 years ago as were chocolate, maize, and rubber—is too complex and too extensive to fit into these pages. But we can hardly ignore it in the present context, not so much because as used by us today it is potentially one of the most physiologically damaging substances known, but rather because in much of the traditional Indian world tobacco was and still is considered to be the special gift of the gods to humanity, given to assist mankind in bridging the gulf between "this" world and "the other"—the world of the gods themselves. In many cases this view involves employing tobacco to attain precisely the kinds of mystical states, or the characteristically shamanistic ecstatic trance, that we commonly associate only with the better recognized vegetal hallucinogens. To mention only one example from Mexico: not only before the Conquest but centuries later the curing shamans of Aztec-speaking communities used *piciétl* (*Nicotiana rustica*), in conjunction with chants of certain origin myths, to place themselves in what we might call "mythic time"—a time when everything was possible—and to enlist the supernatural power of the creator gods and their primordial handiwork in the restoration of the patient's health and equilibrium. This use is about as far removed from hedonistic smoking as one can get. We will have occasion to refer to this particular Aztec phenomenon again in another chapter.

Such things did not escape the attention of the Spanish chroniclers, and should have led to many detailed investigations since, but in the modern ethnographic literature a recent study of tobacco intoxication and shamanism, with its underlying mythological and cosmological complex, among the Warao Indians of Venezuela (Wilbert, 1972) is literally the only competent in-depth treatment of this important topic.

Gods and Men as Tobacco Addicts

I do not wish to imply that tobacco was universally employed to trigger alternate states of consciousness. On the contrary, it probably served a greater variety of sacred purposes than any other plant in the New World, among its most important and virtually universal functions being that of divine sustenance for the gods, mainly in the form of smoke; it also served as an indispensable adjunct of shamanic curing, primarily as a supernaturally charged fumigant but sometimes also as a panacea. Yet there seems to have been at least an element of incipient intoxication in shamanistic smoking in many Indian societies of North and South America, and real tobacco intoxication, to the point of a radical altering of consciousness or psychedelic trance, was certainly of considerable importance in the ecstatic complex of the New World as a whole. This element, together with what we know today of the chemical activity of *Nicotiana*, justifies assigning tobacco—as the Indians themselves did—to the psychedelic flora, but with this important difference: in contrast to the plants that we usually call hallucinogens, of which not a single species has been known to be addictive, tobacco may be so. There seems to be no scientific reason to doubt, and more than enough evidence to suggest (including observations among and testimony by South American Indians) that tobacco is not just psychologically habituating, as some have maintained, but that it does in fact result in physical dependency—i.e., is addictive in the true sense of the word, a fact that many Indian populations recognized and codified in their mythologies, even to the point of assigning to their gods the same physical and psychological craving for tobacco they observed in their shamans, themselves archetypically the mythmakers. Anthropologist Johannes Wilbert (personal communication) notes that various North and South American Indian societies share a tradition that in giving tobacco to the people the supernaturals failed to hold any back for themselves ("not even one pipe," the Fox quote the Gentle Manitou). Inasmuch as the gods crave tobacco as their essential spirit food (usually though not always or everywhere in the form of smoke), by this act of generosity they could be said to have placed themselves in a position of dependency, subject to manipulation by religious practitioners. However, since the people likewise depend on the good will of the supernaturals, the relationship was one of reciprocity and interdependency, differing fundamentally from Judeo-Christian concepts. Because of the similarity of tobacco rituals and beliefs in widely separated areas of aboriginal North and South America, Wilbert thinks they diffused long ago from a common point of origin along with the first plants themselves.

Edward Brecher *et al.* (1972) having adequately dealt with the problem of tobacco addiction in the context of contemporary American society (pp. 209-244), there is no need to dwell on it here. What concerns us, rather, is the traditional use of *Nicotiana* as a ritual and very sacred inebriant, concerning which some Indians were, and are, well aware of its tendency to addict, even if they did not phrase it in quite those terms.

The genus *Nicotiana* belongs, with *Datura* ("Jimsonweed") and such important food plants as the tomato and potato, to the nightshade or potato family (Solanaceae), which also includes a number of important narcotic genera, such as *Atropa* (*A. belladonna*). There may be as many as 45 different species of tobacco, most of them the result of cultivation, but only a few achieved wide pre-European dissemination. The most prominent of these are *N. tabacum*, which may have originated as a cultivated hybrid of two other species in the eastern valleys of the Bolivian Andes, spreading from there across northern South America into the West Indies and to lowland Mexico, and *N. rustica*, another cultivated hybrid that is found from the Andes to Canada, rivalling maize in its pre-European distribution. In the Great Basin of western North America, particularly in California and the adjacent Nevada and Arizona desert, three other species, *N. bigelovi* Watson, *N. attenuata*, and *N. trigonophylla*, were the important tobaccos in native ritual. *N. glauca* Graham, the so-called "tree tobacco" that is found growing all over the foothills on the Pacific coast of California, is a comparatively recent import from South America that was apparently never employed by California Indians in aboriginal times (Zigmond, 1941).

Although other alkaloids may contribute to the psychedelic aspects of *Nicotiana* intoxication, the most important active principle is nicotine, a pyridine alkaloid that occurs in the aboriginal species in much higher concentrations (up to four times) than in modern cigarette tobacco. It is nicotine that produces the craving for tobacco in confirmed smokers, as it does among Indians who use it in great amounts for ritual rather than pleasure. The nicotine content of *N. rustica* is significantly greater than that of *N. tabacum*, which, along with the fact that *N. rustica* is also the hardier of the two species and requires less attention in cultivation, probably accounts for its far more extensive geographical and cultural distribution. In any event, being more powerful, *N. rustica* was much more widely employed in metaphysical and therapeutic contexts. It was the sacred *piciétl* of Aztec ritual and medicine, also the divine tobacco of the Indians of the eastern Woodlands and also, probably, the *petúm* of aboriginal Brazil. Today, secular smoking of commercial tobacco for pleasure, wholly unknown in the Americas in pre-European times, is probably general among most Indian populations, excepting those in the remote interior of South America. Nevertheless, the aboriginal

Indian tobaccos have nowhere passed into secular use. Even many relatively acculturated Indians who participate to one or another degree in the national economy still make a distinction between white man's tobacco and their own. Commercial cigarettes or cigars may be freely smoked at any time (and are sometimes even used ceremonially), but the powerful *N. rustica* continues to be everywhere reserved for traditional metaphysical and therapeutic purposes. This differentiation is also emphasized in the terms applied to the traditional species. For example, the Huichols of Mexico refer to *N. rustica* as "the proper tobacco of the shaman," while the Seneca of New York call it *oyengwe onwe*, "real tobacco." At the same time, it seems that some Indians, the Huichols included, are aware that *N. rustica* is not without danger; among the Huichols there are even reports of imbibers of tobacco infusion falling ill with what is apparently nicotine poisoning. There are also stories of peyote pilgrims dying after a tobacco purification ordeal in the course of the quest for peyote. Considering the very high nicotine content of *N. rustica*, occasional accidents of this sort are certainly possible.

The importance of tobacco in Huichol shamanism is especially interesting because it is yet another example of the functional and symbolic coexistence of tobacco with a sacred hallucinogen, in this case peyote. The shaman to whom tobacco is said to belong is not only the actual shaman of a particular group but also the principal deity, the "First Shaman," Our Grandfather, the deified fire, who established tobacco as well as the peyote ritual, and to whom *N. rustica* is ceremonially sacrificed, not only in the peyote rites but in all other ceremonies. Furthermore, tobacco smoke is as essential to shamanic curing among the Huichols as it is everywhere else in American Indian shamanism. Huichol shamans "with a bad heart"—i.e. in their malevolent role, as sorcerers—also use tobacco to speed "arrows of sickness" to their victims, a phenomenon of which we will hear again shortly. My Huichol informants say that evil shamans have their own special tobacco, which may or may not be true in the literal sense, but which in any case reminds one of a Carib Indian tradition of a mythological contest between a good and a bad shaman. At one point the good shaman challenges his rival to reveal all the kinds of tobacco he has, and when the other fails to enumerate more than ten, shows him up by magically producing many more varieties of his own (Koch-Grünberg, 1923:213-214).

Tobacco also enters into the contest between the Young Lords or Hero Twins in the Popol Vuh, the sacred book of the Quiche Maya of highland Guatemala, and the rulers of the Underworld. The latter challenge their visitors from the Upperworld to keep two cigars lit through the night. The Hero Twins pass the test by placing fireflies at the tips of their cold cigars, only pretending to smoke incessantly, and relighting their still fresh cigars in the morning, a feat that mystifies the rulers of the dead. As a matter of fact, the Tzotzil Maya of Chiapas, Mexico, still believe that tobacco shields one from the evil beings of the Underworld and from death, and the Lacandón Maya of the Usumacinta region even now offer the first tobacco harvested to their gods in the form of cigars (Thompson, 1970). Similar practices and traditions abound all over the Americas.

The Antiquity of Tobacco in America

How ancient is tobacco in the New World? Its spectacular aboriginal distribution and the striking similarity of tobacco ideology suggest that it is very old indeed. It is entirely possible that the progenitors of *N. rustica* and *N. tabacum* are the most ancient cultivated plants in the Americas, older even than the earliest varieties of maize and other native American food plants, whose initial domestication in southeastern Mexico dates to ca. 4000-5000 B.C. There is of course no reason why the first cultigens should not have been intended to feed the spirit rather than the stomach. In any event, tubular stone pipes, probably (though not certainly) for tobacco smoking, rivaling in age the earliest primitive Mexican maize, have been found in California—and smoking is not even believed to be among the oldest methods of tobacco use! By the time of Columbus there was virtually no Indian population, from Canada to southern South America, to whom one or another of the major species of tobacco was not sacred and that did not either cultivate it or obtain it by trade from their neighbors. This was true as much for societies that also used other psychoactive species as for those that did not. Not only did *Nicotiana* enjoy a far wider geographical and cultural distribution than any other vegetal hallucinogen, but it was also consumed in many more ways and for many different purposes, from shamanic intoxication to feeding the gods, to curing. Best-known and probably most common is smoking, but it was also drunk, snuffed, licked, sucked, eaten, and even injected rectally as enemas, a technique that permits especially rapid absorption of the active principles into the blood stream, while bypassing the digestive system and thereby avoiding unpleasant side effects.

Psychedelic Enemas?

The rubber enema syringe is actually a South American Indian invention, but other suitable materials were also employed for the bulb. Intoxicating as well as medicinal enemas have been described both in the earliest European accounts of native customs, dating to the sixteenth century, and in the more recent ethnographic literature. Tobacco juice, *ayahuasca* (*Banisteriopsis caapi*), and even a species of *Anadenanthera* (*A. colubrina*) whose seeds (*huilca* or *wilka*) were used for hallucinogenic snuff and in intoxicating beverages, all seem to have been employed for enemas in western South America. Very early Quechua dictionaries mention *huilca* syringes, and the sixteenth-century chronicler Poma de Ayala (1936) likewise reports enemas made from these potent hallucinogenic seeds among the Inca. Enema syringes also appear in the pictorial art of the Moche civilization, which predates the Incas by more than a thousand years. Sahagún mentions enemas in Aztec medicine, but does not tell us the purpose for which they were employed. Not so the Anonymous Conqueror (1917), another sixteenth-century Mexican source, who writes of the Huastec Indians of Veracruz that, not content with intoxicating themselves by drinking their "wine" (actually *pulque*, the fermented juice of the agave cactus), they also injected it rectally.

It has only recently come to light that the ancient Maya, too, employed enemas. Enema syringes or narcotic clysters, and even enema rituals, were discovered to be represented in Maya art, an outstanding example being a large painted vase dating A.D. 600-800, on which a man is depicted carrying an enema syringe, applying an enema to himself, and having a woman applying it to him. As a result of this newly discovered scene, archaeologist M. D. Coe was able to identify a curious object held by a jaguar deity on another painted Maya vessel as an enema syringe. If the enemas of the ancient Maya were, like those of Peruvian Indians, intoxicating or hallucinogenic, they might have been compounds of fermented *balché* (honey mead), itself a very sacred beverage, fortified with tobacco or with morning-glory-seed infusions. Of course they could also have been a tobacco infusion alone.

The suggestion that the ritual enemas of pre-Hispanic Mesoamerica were in fact not just medicinal or therapeutic in our sense but, like those of the Incas, were meant to affect the user's state of consciousness and place him in touch with the supernaturals, is supported not just by the sixteenth-century and later evidence from South America but also by the recent discovery of peyote enemas among the Huichols of the western Sierra Madre in Mexico (Timothy Knab, personal communication). The Huichol syringe is made of the femur of a small deer, with a bulb of deer bladder instead of rubber, closely resembling Plains Indian deer-bone enema syringes in the collections of the Museum of the American Indian in New York. Huichols say shamans who take a peyote infusion rectally instead of by mouth (whole or ground in a specially consecrated mortar) do so because their stomachs are weak and cannot tolerate the very bitter and astringent plant, which often causes nausea and even severe vomiting; however, I suspect that inasmuch as the sacred cactus is itself equated with, and identified as, deer (see Chapters 10 and 11), the practice probably has deeper symbolic meaning.

The tobacco enema is presumably a relatively recent refinement in the history of nicotine ecstasis, while the drinking of tobacco in the form of a syrupy infusion may be among the earliest. The juice, produced by steeping or boiling of the leaves, can either be taken by mouth or imbibed through the nostrils, in which case the active principles are absorbed more quickly into the system. Tobacco drinking to induce the desired trance state, often in great amounts and after prolonged periods of fasting, was and is especially common in shamanic initiation among Amazonian Indians, where it is often followed by the neophyte's first introduction to the ritual *Banisteriopsis caapi* beverage, whose most important active principles are harmala alkaloids. Tobacco infusions, imbibed through the nostrils, are also well-integrated in the symbolic system and psychopharmacology of drug-assisted folk therapy in urban Peru, where, for example the healer administers it both to his patients and to himself in conjunction with the mescaline-containing *San Pedro* cactus (Sharon, 1972).

More or less rapid intoxication by eating raw or prepared tobacco, or by snuffing, or more gradual intoxication by sucking, are probably also very old. Snuffing is common, especially in South America, where pulverized tobacco, mixed with wood ashes or some other alkaline preparation to facilitate release of the active principles, is inhaled either alone or in combination with some other psychoactive species. What is often called chewing in the literature should more properly be described as sucking, since the quids prepared of powdered or crumbled tobacco and lime (or ashes) are not actually chewed but held in the mouth, between the gums and the teeth, and sucked for hours, allowing the juice to trickle down the throat. This technique of gradual nicotine intoxication was aboriginally so widespread, from the Northwest Coast of North America through California deep into Amazonia, that it must surely rank among the earliest methods. It is still the common practice among the Yanomamö (Shiriana, Waika) of the Upper Orinoco as well as other aboriginal populations of tropical South America. Significantly, the Yanomamö, who also employ powerful intoxicating tryptamine snuffs in their shamanistic rituals, apparently can and do go for long periods without snuffing but say they suffer physical discomfort if they are deprived of their tobacco quids for even short periods of time (Chagnon *et al.*, 1971). Powdered tobacco mixed with lime in the form of a quid or cud is also one of several ways in which *Nicotiana* was and is used among both the highland and lowland Maya, as it was throughout Middle America (Thompson, 1970). The early literature lists alleviation of fatigue, hunger, and thirst, and also ritual intoxication among the principal reasons for the practice.

The Sacred Pipe

Considering its enormous geographic spread in the Americas at the time of European discovery, as well as the probable age of stone tobacco pipes in California, the inhaling (often called "drinking" or "eating") of tobacco smoke by the shaman, as a corollary to therapeutic fumigation and the feeding of the gods with smoke, must also be of considerable antiquity. Tobacco was and still is smoked by shamans and other participants in shamanic ritual in many different ways—as cigarettes and cigars with wrappings of corn husk or other plant materials, of which some may well have been themselves psychoactive; in cane tubes up to three feet in length; or in tubular or elbow pipes of varying design and of different materials. Such pipes were often of simple construction, but others, especially in North America, were frequently real works of art on which much care and ritual was lavished, representing humans, animals, or supernatural beings and activities associated with the "medicine" or spirit power of their owners. Simple or complex, however, the manufacture of the pipe never was solely a matter of technology. It was a sacred art, often an elaborate ceremonial lasting over many days, fully commensurate with the divine nature of tobacco and the metaphysical purposes for which the pipe was intended. Perhaps the following, summarized from a description of pipe manufacture among the Navaho (Tschopik, 1941) will help us appreciate this better:

While a pipe is made, no one may talk or laugh and great care is taken that nothing be broken. Pipes may be made by either men or women, who are usually specialists in this art. Both must observe strict rules about handling of their tools and other objects; for example, tools may be passed only between thumb and index finger and in no other manner. A pipe maker usually makes two pipes at a time, and if a man and a woman are both making pipes, two pairs are produced (this relates to Navaho insistence on male-female balance and balance in general). The pipe maker generally makes a black, crooked, conical male pipe that is used in hunting rituals, and a white, straight, conical female pipe which is employed in the Blessing Way ceremony. Pipes are made from clay which deer, antelope, elk, jackrabbits, or prairie dogs have chewed in order to extract salt. The water used for mixing the clay likewise has a mystical bond with deer, for plants that have been knocked down by deer while feeding are soaked in it before it is added to the clay. The paste is rolled out between the palms of the hands and modeling is done with the fingers. The pipe is smoothed with a wooden scraping tool and saliva produced as the maker chews "deer medicine." The pipe is bent into the desired shape and perforated longitudinally while the clay is still soft.

When it is finished the maker—whether man or woman—must sing four songs (four being the sacred number), after which the pipes are decorated with bits of stone or shell, in recognition of the materials with which the gods made the first tobacco pipes. Then, after more songs have been sung, the pipes receive names. Navaho pipes are dried for four days, either inside the hogan or in the crotch of a tree. If a dog should urinate on the drying pipes they cannot be used in any ceremony. During the drying period the makers must take sweat baths and wash their clothing.

The finished and dried pipe is fired in a small pit that is specially dug. A flat rock is placed at the bottom and the pipe laid on it with the bowl end facing east. Only one pipe at a time is fired. It is covered with tinder and the fire is allowed to burn down to ashes before the pipe is removed. The ashes are cooled with water, a ritual act believed to bring rain. Four more days of ceremonies must pass before the pipe can be painted. If four pipes have been made, each is painted with a different color, representing one of the four sacred directions and one of the sexes—i.e. a black male pipe stands for east, a white female pipe for north, a yellow male pipe for west and a blue female pipe for south. (Tschopik, 1941:56-62)

Tobacco Shamanism among the Warao

As a fitting conclusion to our consideration of tobacco as a divine—but addictive—inebriant, and by way of introduction to the psychedelic flora as a whole, let us look briefly at the tobacco ideology of the Warao, a Venezuelan Indian society that at least until the most recent times managed to escape the destructive effects of acculturation and maintain its highly successful traditional lifeway as riverine fishermen in the delta of the Orinoco. As Wilbert (1972:55-83) tells us, the Warao, of whom there are more than 10,000, use no other hallucinogen but tobacco. More than that, their astonishingly complex metaphysical universe is quite literally held together and sustained by tobacco smoke, through the agency of their shamans, who smoke incessantly to fulfill the primordial promise to the gods that there be abundant tobacco smoke as their proper and only food and as the shaman's means of communication with the Otherworld. The shaman's cigar is a long and slender cane tube, up to two feet in length, filled with powerful charges of tightly rolled leaves of black tobacco that is perfumed with a fragrant resin to make it attractive to the gods. In the course of shamanizing, shamans may smoke ten, twenty, thirty, and even more of these giant cigars, never exhaling but "eating" the smoke until it suffuses their entire system. So "lightened" by tobacco, the shamans ascend in their ecstatic trances to the zenith and travel to their respective master spirits on celestial bridges constructed of tobacco smoke, as are the houses to which they retire after death. A curing shaman's tobacco smoke is therapeutic, but in their negative role these shamans can also speed projectiles of sickness and death to their victims with the aid of powerful blasts from their reversed cigars.

For the novice shaman the most crucial undertaking of his life is his initiatory tobacco trance, when, after a long fast and instruction by the master shaman, speeded upward by the smoke of his sacred cigar, he at last embarks upon a journey that takes him to the ends of the Warao universe. Along the way he must travel on slippery paths across a yawning defile, evade the knives of demons, the snapping beaks and talons of raptorial birds, and the jaws of alligators and other terrifying creatures, until at the moment of greatest rapture, having successfully negotiated the final obstacle of clashing gates, he is wafted, "buoyant as a puff of cotton," toward his celestial encounter with the supreme spirit in the House of Tobacco Smoke.

Awakening from his tobacco trance, the novice shaman feels newborn, confident of the truth of the ancient traditions because they have been validated by his own ecstatic experience. The new shaman and the tobacco medicine powder that has lodged in his chest are still feeble and tender, but after a month of eating little, avoiding certain odors, and smoking incessantly, he grows strong, ready to take his place as one of the guardians of his community's physical and metaphysical integrity.

But like all shamans, he will always need tobacco and will experience great physical and psychological distress when tobacco is in short supply. Then his people will say, "Our shaman is sick, he craves tobacco."

In his book, *Maya History and Religion* (1970), the great English Maya scholar J. Eric S. Thompson devotes an entire chapter to the meaning and uses of the divine tobacco among the Maya and their neighbors, from which I wish only to quote the summation (pp. 122-123) as peculiarly pertinent to all that was said above:

This review makes clear the extent to which the taking of tobacco in every form permeated Indian life in ancient Middle America. The attitude of noble, priest, and commoner was imbued at times with something approaching mysticism, as when tobacco was personified or even deified or when it was accepted as an ally fighting beside man to overcome fatigue or pain or to ward off so many ills of the human flesh. There is deep beauty there which we, in our materialistic world, bombarded with advertising on television and in print of some young man lighting a girl's cigarette as a prelude to conquest, are unable to share or even to perceive. The relationship is that of compline to a blast of the Beatles and their sad imitators.

Aside from the fact that in the meantime cigarette advertising has been banned from television and that one can think of lots worse than the Beatles to set against the Night Song, no one could have said it better.

CHAPTER THREE

CANNABIS (SPP.) AND NUTMEG DERIVATIVES

With upward of a hundred species thus far botanically and chemically identified in the psychoactive pharmacopoeia of different peoples of the world, the great majority of them in the Americas, it is nonetheless a fact that there are many more potential hallucinogens in the plant kingdom than have ever been discovered or utilized. The plant world is so enormous that not even all its members have been classified, with estimates ranging up to 800,000 for the total number of species in the floras of the two hemispheres. The hallucinogens among them are concentrated mainly in two families: (1) The *fungi*—from the primitive *Claviceps*, the ergot parasite of rye and other Old World grasses, to the sacred mushrooms of Mesoamerican Indians and the spectacularly beautiful *Amanita muscaria*, or fly-agaric, of Eurasian shamanism. (2) The *angiosperms*, that vast family of plants whose seeds are enclosed in an ovary. In contrast, the gymnosperms, comprising seed plants with naked seeds not enclosed in an ovary (such as the conifers); ferns; lichens; algae; bacteria; and bryophytes (nonflowering plants with rhizoids instead of true roots, comprising the mosses and liverworts), all seem to be lacking in psychedelically active members (Schultes, 1972a).

The hallucinogenic properties themselves can be ascribed to two broad groups—nitrogenous and non-nitrogenous (i.e. lacking a nitrogen atom). Of these two groups, the former, comprising mainly alkaloids closely related to the amino acids (the building blocks of proteins) and derived in their majority from the indolic amino acid tryptophane, plays by far the greater role. Among these alkaloids, the tryptamines are the most important hallucinogens (Schultes, 1970, 1972a). Interestingly enough, the nitrogenous compounds are cosmopolitan while the non-nitrogenous compounds, classified into two

33

main divisions, the dypenzopyrans, which include the cannabinols in marihuana and hashish (*Cannabis* spp.), and the phenylpropenes, found in nutmeg
(*Myristica fragrans*), are strictly Old World. There is still a third group,
comprising the alcohols, but these are beyond the scope of this book, even
though alcohol is of course a drug and is in fact widely employed for ritual
intoxication, rather like the vegetal hallucinogens.*

Cannabis spp.

The literature on the hemp plant, *Cannabis*, scientific and popular, is such
that we need hardly add to it here. Also, strictly speaking, its best-known
modern product, marihuana, the "new social drug," is not a psychedelic but
an euphoriant. But there is some significant new information on the genus
Cannabis that has not been widely disseminated. Moreover, the active principles of *Cannabis* are perfectly capable of psychedelic effect, and have been
so used through history, especially in Asia, probably long before hemp fiber
began to assume economic importance.

A New Finding: Three Species of *Cannabis*

"Spp." is the conventional abbreviation for species in the plural. It may
come as something of a surprise that contrary to conventional wisdom *Cannabis* should be treated as a multispecies genus rather than as a single species,
Cannabis sativa L., with several geographical or ecological varieties (e.g. *C.
mexicana*, *C. americana* [*gigantea*], and *C. indica*) but not separate species.
In this I follow a new determination by Schultes and his colleagues (1974:
337-360), who have now accepted as correct the findings of Russian plant
geneticists in the 1920's and 1930's that *Cannabis sativa* is not alone but is
only one of three separate species, the others being *C. indica* and *C. ruderalis*.
This differentiation is by no means an idle taxonomical exercise, of significance only to a handful of botanists and plant taxonomists. As Schultes and
his coworkers point out, considering the great economic and therapeutic
importance of this multipurpose plant to man since he first cultivated it
perhaps as much as 10,000 years ago, and the fact that the drug it yields
continues to be the focus of considerable controversy as well as medical
experimentation, the time "is long overdue when a full study of *Cannabis*
taxonomy must be initiated" (p. 357). Moreover, there is an intriguing legal
aspect: much marihuana legislation, not only in the United States but, largely
because of American pressure, in other countries as well, is based precisely

---

*Schultes (1970) mentions an alcohol-containing plant, *Lagochilus inebrians*, whose leaves
and other parts have long been used to brew an intoxicating tea by such peoples of central Asia as
the Tajik, Tartar, Turkoman, and Uzbek. A crystalline material called lagochiline, isolated from
the plant in 1945, was at first thought to be an alkaloid, but recent studies have shown it to be a
polyhydric alcohol.

on the single-species theory which Schultes and his colleagues now reject as scientifically untenable.

That there is considerable variability in the strength of marihuana and other preparations of *Cannabis* has long been generally known, to scientists as well as social users. A variety of factors, particularly environmental ones, are usually cited to account for the phenomenon. But Schultes *et al.* have become convinced that there are, in fact, significant chemical differences between different species,

... not only in the cannabinolic content but in other constituents, such as the essential oils, flavonoids and possibly several other classes of secondary compounds. Lamarck suggested as early as 1783 that the content of the intoxicating principle was higher in *Cannabis indica* than in *C. sativa*. In the intervening 200 years, during which the epithet *indica* has been used, there has usually been the inference that it is a more strongly intoxicating form of *Cannabis*. Unfortunately, however, almost no chemical studies have been made in association with taxonomic studies nor on the basis of voucher specimens. Throughout the modern Russian literature there exists the inference, if not outright claim, that the cannabinolic content of *Cannabis indica* is higher than that of *C. sativa* and *C. ruderalis*. Pertinent to species differentiation on a chemical basis may be the unexpected, recent discovery, made independently by several workers, that chemical differences in *Cannabis* appear to be based more on a genetic basis than on environmental or edaphic factors. If this be so, then it may add still another argument for specific differentiation in the genus. (Schultes *et al.*, 1974:354-355)

Whatever the final taxonomic and phytochemical determinations, *Cannabis*, whose original home is somewhere in central Asia, where its only truly wild representatives can now be found and from where it diffused in early times to other parts of the Old World—and after the Conquest, to the New World as well—is today adapted to almost all inhabited parts of the globe, and virtually all climates, either as cultivated plants or as weeds that escaped from cultivation. The literary, folkloric, historical, and archaeological evidence for its use in ancient medicine and as a ritual intoxicant is extensive, beginning with what is generally believed to be the earliest reference to the therapeutic value of *Cannabis* in a Chinese treatise on pharmacology attributed to the legendary emperor Shen Nung and said to date from 2737 B.C. (cf. Brecher *et al.*, 1972; Emboden, 1972a). *Cannabis* actually had a wide variety of medical uses in the United States between 1850 and 1937; it was listed as a recognized medicinal drug in the United States Pharmacopoeia until 1942 and is still so included in its British counterpart. Largely because of public or official hysteria over recreational marihuana use, medical demand for *Cannabis* extracts was until recently very low, but beginning in 1971 there has been a sharp upturn in experimental use of *Cannabis* as medication for a variety of disorders, including alcoholism, heroin and amphetamine dependence, emotional disturbance, and even glaucoma. (See Brecher *et al.*, 1972.)

Nutmeg

Nutmeg, like mace a product of the fruit of the nutmeg tree, *Myristica fragrans*, has long been a popular spice—and historically, an important medicament in Asia, the Near East, and Europe—of which the United States alone consumes between five and six million pounds a year, mainly as a food flavoring in baking and cooking. It is used especially in doughnuts, and around Christmas time there is always a marked upsurge in its popularity as a savory ingredient in eggnog and hot toddy.

Less well-known perhaps is the fact that in large doses nutmeg acts on the central nervous system as an hallucinogenic intoxicant, though, let it be said at once, with bizarre physical and mental symptoms and with such distinctly unpleasant after-effects as extreme nausea, headache, dizziness, and dryness of the nose and throat. The psychoactive properties of nutmeg, which have been noted by physicians since early times, present a whole series of interesting cultural and psychopharmacological problems, especially since two of its essential oils, safrol and myristicin, are the basis of two synthetic drugs, MDA and MMDA, amphetamine derivatives that have become important in psychotherapy.

The ancient world is full of tales of nutmeg as a narcotic medicament with wondrous healing properties for a great variety of ailments, from kidney disease to chronic irritability to impotence. Unfortunately, as Weil (1967), who made a study of experimentation with nutmeg intoxication among students and United States prison populations* has noted, reliable historical data on nutmeg's being deliberately used as a psychoactive agent are hard to come by, although there are a number of early accounts of the effects of nutmeg intoxication, and the nutmeg is specifically referred to as a "narcotic fruit" in the Ashur Veda, an early Hindu work dealing with medicine and the prolongation of human life.

Nutmeg in European Medicine

Nutmeg achieved great importance in European medicine in the Middle Ages, but it was apparently unknown to the Greeks and Romans. In fact, it does not seem to have reached Europe until the first centuries of the Christian era, presumably through the agency of Arabian spice traders. Arab physicians set down its numerous therapeutic applications as early as the seventh century, but in Europe it is nowhere mentioned in literature until the twelfth century, and its source, the Banda (Nutmeg) Islands in the East Indies, was to remain unknown until the Portuguese reached them in 1512. It is not generally realized that early exploration by the Portuguese and their European rivals

---

*Malcolm X, for example, describes his prison experience with nutmeg intoxication in his *Autobiography* (1964).

was largely spurred by the search for nutmeg and other precious spices of the Orient, which in those days were much sought after not as condiments but as medicines, among them narcotics and aphrodisiacs as well as panaceas. Nutmeg was, in fact, widely regarded as an effective aphrodisiac and still enjoys that reputation in the Near East, where Yemenite men take it to enhance potency. It is also still very much a part of the popular pharmacopoeias of Malaysia and India, where it is prescribed for such ills as heart trouble, intestinal disorders, kidney disease, and even irritability in children.

In European medicine nutmeg achieved its greatest fame in the 1700's, but with the advent of modern medicine its popularity gradually diminished—until in the late nineteenth century it made a sudden and dramatic comeback with a veritable epidemic of nutmeg intoxication among American and British women who mistakenly thought large doses of the spice could induce overdue menstruation and even abortion. According to Weil, this completely erroneous idea, whose origins are a mystery, occasionally still surfaces in the United States.

Nutmeg and Psychotherapy

The two drugs mentioned above, MDA and MMDA, do not occur in nature. They are the result of amination of the essential oils of nutmeg. If similar processes occur naturally in the human body it would help to explain the subjective effects of nutmeg. MDA (methylene dioxyamphetamine) is an amination product of safrol, and the closely related MMDA (3-methoxy-4,5-methylene dioxyphenyl isopropylamine) is a synthetic compound derived from the addition of ammonia to myristicin, the most important primary constituent of nutmeg. Safrol is also present in other spices, most prominently in oil of sassafras, which consists about 80 percent of safrol. In modest quantities sassafras oil serves as a flavoring, in larger doses it has been used as a medicament, and of course sassafras tea has long been widely enjoyed. Neither sassafras oil nor sassafras tea, however, have the reputation of nutmeg as a psychoactive agent (Shulgin *et al.*, 1967).

In a new book, *The Healing Journey* (1973), the Chilean-born psychiatrist Claudio Naranjo has outlined some of his experiences with MDA- and MMDA-assisted psychotherapy.* Naranjo calls these agents "feeling enhancers," and he differentiates them as psychedelic ("mind-manifesting") agents as distinguished from *hallucinogens* or *psychotomimetics* because they

---

*Notwithstanding his enthusiasm for the psychotherapeutic potential of MDA, Naranjo (p. 77) properly sounds this word of caution: MDA has recently proved to be toxic to certain individuals and at varying dose levels; as is true of chloroform, among other drugs, what may be a regular dose to most patients may prove fatal to some. Typical warning signals of MDA are confusion, skin reactions, and profuse sweating. Hence, he writes, compatibility of individual patients must be ascertained with progressively increasing test doses before commencing any therapeutic MDA session.

do not result in extraordinary perceptual phenomena or depersonalization and do not mimic psychotic states. In psychotherapy, he writes, MDA is valuable because it characteristically induces what is called "age regression," a state in which the patient, while retaining awareness of the present self, vividly reexperiences particular childhood events and is able to verbalize these past experiences far more expressively than is the case with other drugs that have been so used. While he calls MDA the "drug of analysis," capable of returning the patient deep into his troubling past far more quickly than is usual with traditional psychoanalysis and less traumatically than with LSD, MMDA induces ecstatic or peak experiences of the here and now, again without the temporary disintegration of personality and other drastic psychic effects that often accompany the use of LSD in psychotherapy, creating instead

. . . an *intensification* of feelings, symptoms, and visual imagination rather than a qualitative change thereof. The value of such an intensification in the psychotherapeutic process lies mainly, perhaps, in that clues to the significant issues take more frequently the therapist's and patient's attention than they otherwise would, whereas, in the normal situation, much of the time and effort in a therapeutic process may go into cutting through a veil of verbiage and automatisms that form part of the habitual social role. With MMDA, there is a more prompt access to the patient's underlying *experience*, or symptoms resulting from its denial and distortion. (p. 122)

CHAPTER FOUR

IBOGAINE AND THE VINE OF SOULS: FROM TROPICAL FOREST RITUAL TO PSYCHOTHERAPY

Naranjo's application of psychedelics to mental therapy at this point provides a convenient pharmacological bridge for us, from the numerically small though significant non-nitrogenous substances to the infinitely more numerous and culture-historically more dramatic nitrogenous hallucinogens. Also, in contrast to the nutmeg derivatives MDA and MMDA, which do not occur naturally but are the result of *in vitro* amination, ibogaine and harmaline, the other two psychedelics which Naranjo found most useful, are very much in evidence in the natural world itself—as are the tryptamines, ergolines, isoquinolines, phenylethylamines, and tropanes in the major hallucinogens of the New World, or the isoxazoles of the fly-agaric mushroom, *Amanita muscaria*.

Ibogaine is derived from an equatorial African bush, *Tabernanthe iboga*, whose hallucinogenic roots are employed in the Bwiti ancestor cult, the MBieri curing cult, and other nativistic religious movements in tropical sub-Saharan West Africa. Harmaline is one of the principal harmala alkaloids in *Banisteriopsis caapi*, the sacred vine of ecstatic Amazonian shamanism, in related species of the Malphighiaceae, and in *Peganum harmala*, an Old World plant known also as Syrian rue.

Tabernanthe iboga

Twelve closely related indole alkaloids have been isolated in *T. iboga*, a member of the Apocynaceae, or dogbanes, a family consisting of tropical herbs, shrubs, and trees characterized by a milky juice, often showy flowers,

39

and simple entire leaves. *T. iboga*, which occurs wild in the equatorial underforest but is also cultivated widely around villages adhering to the cults, has yellowish or pinkish-white flowers and a small, sweetish-tasting, non-narcotic fruit that is sometimes used as a medicine against barrenness. Although the family as a whole is rich in alkaloids, *T. iboga* is the only member definitely known to be used as an hallucinogen, with ibogaine apparently the principal psychoactive constituent (Schultes, 1970).

Iboga or *eboka* has interested the Europeans since the 1800's, when its ritual use was first reported by explorers of Gabon and the Congo. In the last decades of the nineteenth century the German colonial administration of northern Gabon, then German Kamerun, encouraged its use as a central stimulant on tiring marches and colonial labor projects. French medical scientists studied ibogaine—now known to function as a monoamine oxidase inhibitor in the brain—intensively around the turn of the century and adopted it into official medicine as the first antidepressant of its kind, long before the advent of Tofranil, iproniazide, and similar drugs. The first modern psychiatrist to adopt it on a sustained basis as an adjunct to psychotherapy seems to have been Naranjo, who reported his initial results with the drug in 1966. Since then, ibogaine has passed into wider psychiatric use, especially in South America.

Because I want to devote more space in this chapter to the harmala alkaloids, whose subjective effects in psychotherapy sometimes strikingly resemble those reported from the aboriginal cultural context, the discussion of ibogaine will be limited to a summary of its role in African cults (for a wider discussion of its application to psychiatry see Naranjo's *The Healing Journey*, pp. 174-228).

Iboga Cults in Tropical Africa

The first significant modern anthropological examination of *Tabernanthe iboga* is that of James W. Fernandez, who studied its role in the Bwiti and MBieri cults of the Fang of Gabon in the larger context of reformist and nativistic African religious movements. What follows is based on a paper published by him in 1972.*

In the Fang tongue *T. iboga* is called *eboka*. The principal active alkaloid is mainly concentrated in the root bark, and it is this that the Fang employ for ecstatic inebriation, in the form of raspings, ground up as powder or soaked in water and drunk as an infusion. How much of the drug is consumed depends on the context. The regular way is to ingest small doses of *eboka* (two to three teaspoonfuls for women and three to five for men) in powdered form before and in the early hours of the ceremonies. The second way is to take truly massive doses once or twice in the career of the cult member for the purpose

---

*A recent article by H. Pope in *Economic Botany* (1969) also contains much valuable ethnobotanical and historic data.

of initiation and to "break open the head" in order to effect contact with the ancestors. The regular doses amount to about 20 grams in all, containing 75-125 mg. of ibogaine. This is sufficient to bring about the desired ecstatic dream state in which one travels outside one's body to Otherworlds, where the ancestors dwell and where one learns to do their work (as distinct from the burdensome and psychologically disorienting demands of the rapidly modernizing world outside the tropical rain forest). The massive initiatory dose is very much greater, from forty to sixty times the threshold dose, when the effects make themselves felt. However, in very high amounts *eboka* is toxic; not surprisingly, as in the *toloache* (*Datura inoxia* or *meteloides*) initiation cults of Southern California Indians, and the red-bean rites of the Southern Plains, overdose deaths from *eboka* have occasionally been reported.*

How old is the use of *T. iboga* in equatorial Africa? That is difficult to estimate, but the Fang themselves credit its origin to the Pygmy people of the Congolese rain forest, who were there long before the Fang arrived from the north and who are, in fact regarded by them as their saviors, having shown them how to survive in the unfamiliar and frightening forest environment. *Eboka*, goes a Fang story recorded by Fernandez (pp. 245-246), was given to the people by the last of the creator gods, Zame ye Mebege:

> He saw the misery in which blackman was living. He thought how to help him. One day he looked down and saw a blackman, the Pygmy Bitumu, high in an Atanga tree, gathering its fruit. He made him fall. He died and Zame brought his spirit to him. Zame cut off the little fingers and the little toes of the cadaver of the Pygmy and planted them in various parts of the forest. They grew into the *eboka* bush.

Eventually the dead man's wife came searching for him. She was told by a disembodied voice to eat of the root of an *eboka* plant that grew at the left of the mouth of a cave, and of a mushroom (!) that grew on the right. She did so and suddenly the bones of the dead with which the cave was filled came to life, revealing themselves as her husband and other deceased relatives. They told her that she had found the plant that from then on would enable members of the Bwiti cult to see the dead.

---

*The Fang employ several other plants with hallucinogenic properties, but none plays the pervasive ritual role of *eboka*. One is *Alchornea floribunda*, called *alan*. In large amounts *alan* produces a state that is interpreted as passing over to the land of the ancestors. Some branches of the Bwiti cult mix *alan* and *eboka*. The latex of *Elaeophorbia drupifera* is mixed with oil to form eyedrops that seem to affect the optic nerves, producing bizarre visual effects. Yet another is hemp (*Cannabis* sp.), which in some branches of Bwiti is smoked after the ingestion of two or three teaspoonfuls of *eboka*. The smoke symbolizes the travel of the soul to the roof of the Bwiti chapel, where it mingles with the ancestors. Although hemp has long been smoked in Gabon, most branches of Bwiti reject it as a foreign plant that distracts the members from proper ritual matters. Like South American Indians, Fang women also make quids of tobacco and ashes which they hold in their cheeks or under the tongue and which are said to produce a state of pleasant lassitude. (Fernandez, 1972:242-243)

Male-Female Symbolism and Acculturation

The mushroom of the origin myth is a white fungus with a large cap that is sometimes consumed in the Bwiti cult and that also plays a role in herbal concoctions. No psychoactive properties have been reported, but the mushroom has not been studied ethnobotanically or chemically.

Fernandez points out several important elements in the myth. First, it clearly identifies the *eboka* plant with the deep forest and the Pygmies as an agent of transition that enables the people to pass from the familiar village deep into the dark and mysterious forest that holds the secrets of death (recalling that the Fang themselves once made the traumatic transition from the open savannah lands to the north into the equatorial rain forest). Second, there is the universal image of the cave as the place of death and rebirth. Third, the story of the discovery of *eboka* by the wife emphasizes the crucial role of women in the cult. While in the MBieri curing cult women are dominant, in Bwiti men and women have an equal place. However, the cult directs itself to the female principle of the universe: Nyingwan Mebege, author of procreation and guarantor of a prosperous life. Fernandez also notes that Bwiti *eboka* is the left-hand plant—the left side of the chapel is female— while the phallic mushroom stands at the right, or male, side, repeating the directional juxtaposition of *eboka* and mushroom at the entrance to the mythic cave of death and rebirth.

Finally, Fernandez draws attention to a certain eucharistic implication of the planting of parts of the Pygmy who upon his death became *eboka*:

This makes the consumption of the roots an act of communion with the Pygmy—originator of the cult who had been chosen by Zame and brought to heavenly abode. Hence we have in the eating of *eboka* a eucharistic experience with similarities to Christian communion. How much of this is a syncretism with Christianity and how much is original with the Fang is difficult to say. One can suspect more of the former. For not only do members of Bwiti practice communion, employing *eboka* instead of bread, but they also boast of the efficacy of *eboka* over bread in its power to give visions of the dead. Some of the more Christian branches of Bwiti, not fully cognizant with the origins legend, even speak of *eboka* as a more perfect and God-given representation of the body of Christ! (p. 247).

This syncretistic view of the meaning of *eboka* is strikingly similar to what we find today in Mexican mushroom rituals (see Chapter Seven) which likewise blend Christian with traditional Indian elements and identify the mushroom with Christ. But I rather suspect that there is more to the eucharistic implication than just Christian acculturation. In the first place, the origin myth in which a dismembered Pygmy transforms into the sacred hallucinogenic plant is essentially similar to the Colombian Indian tradition of the *Yajé* Woman and her baby, whose dismembered body becomes *Banisteriopsis caapi* (see below). This myth is certainly not influenced by Christian beliefs, any more than is the Huichol story of peyote as the transformed flesh of the

BANISTERIOPSIS *Caapi*

(Spruce ex Griseb.) Morton

ritually slain deer deity (see Chapter Ten). Again—the manner in which on the peyote hunt the first peyote—the flesh of the slain deer god—is divided and distributed to his companions by the officiating shaman cannot but recall the Eucharistic "Take, eat, this is my body." Yet there is little question that the Huichol ceremony is pre-European and that its eucharistic element is no more "Christian" than was the communal eating of the dismembered body of the transsubstantiated "god-impersonator" in the sacrificial rite of the Aztecs. Indeed, this act of ritual cannibalism reminded some of the early Spaniards so uncomfortably of the rite of the Eucharist that they tried to explain it away as vile distortion of Christian communion by the Devil himself!

Harmaline and Related Alkaloids

Hallucinogenic harmala alkaloids (harmine, harmaline, harmalol, and harman), which belong to the *beta*-carbolines, were originally isolated from an Old World perennial *Peganum harmala*, or Syrian rue. Syrian rue, the traditional source of the characteristic red dye of Turkish carpets, is at home

**BANISTERIOPSIS
Rusbyana** (Ndz.) Mort.

in the Mediterranean and central Asia, but it has several close relatives in the southwestern United States and Mexico, of which none, so far as is known, has ever been employed hallucinogenically. Nor do we know of any deliberate psychedelic use of *Peganum harmala*, even though the plant is a very old folk remedy of whose intoxicating potential Arab physicians and folk healers of the Orient must surely have been aware since antiquity (Schultes, 1970:576).

Syrian rue is actually only one of at least eight plant families of the Old and New Worlds in which harmala alkaloids are now known to be present. Botanically the most numerous and culturally the most interesting of these is *Banisteriopsis*, a malpighiaceous tropical American genus that comprises no less than a hundred different species, of which at least two, *B. caapi*, discovered and named by Spruce in the mid-nineteenth century, and *B. inebrians*, and quite possibly others, such as *B. muricata*, are the basis of the potent hallucinogenic ritual beverages the Indians of Amazonia call, depending on the local language, by such terms as *caapi* (more correctly, *kahpi* or *gahpi*), *mihi*, *dapa*, *pinde*, *natéma*, *yajé*, etc. In Quechua, the language of the Incas of pre-Hispanic Peru and of millions of Andean Indians today, the drink is eloquently called *ayahuasca*, meaning "vine of the souls," a term that has been adopted also by some non-Quechua Indians east of the Andes. *Yajé* (or *yagé*) is a Tukanoan word widely employed in the northwest Amazon, and for the reason that by far the best anthropological analysis ever written on the complex mythological, symbolic, and social meanings of the *Banisteriopsis* drink in the aboriginal world comes from the Tukanoan Desana of Colombia (Reichel-Dolmatoff, 1971, 1972), that is what we will call it here.

According to Schultes (1972a:38), the earliest chemical studies were probably carried on *B. caapi*, and it is this plant also of which Louis Lewin wrote in the 1920's, when the first psychotherapeutic experiments with an extract of harmala alkaloids were carried out in Germany. Originally a number of *Banisteriopsis* alkaloids were described under such names as telepathine, yageine, and banisterine, but all these were eventually identified as harmine, which is contained, along with harmaline and *d*-tetrahydroharmine, in the bark, stems, and leaves of *B. caapi* and *B. inebrians*. These psychedelic alkaloids have been found to be amazingly long-lived—much more so than those, for example, in the sacred mushrooms of Mexico. Pieces of the stems of the type material of *B. caapi* which Spruce collected in Brazil in 1851, and which were eventually deposited in England after first being lost in the Brazilian wilderness for nearly a year under conditions that hardly favored preservation, were recently submitted to laboratory tests at Schultes's suggestion, to see how much, if any, of the active principles had been retained. To everyone's astonishment, they were found to contain—after 115 years!—practically the same concentration of active harmine as did material that had been freshly collected. Harmala alkaloids have also been isolated from *Cabi paraensis*, another malpighiaceous genus that has many uses in Brazilian folk medicine, but here again no deliberate intoxicating use is known.

In addition to the two principal species of *Banisteriopsis* from which *yajé* is known to be made, there is still another that figures in this complex, *B. rusbyana*, whose stems and leaves, oddly enough, do not contain the *beta*-carboline alkaloids characteristic of *B. caapi* and *B. inebrians* but instead yield tryptamines, a pharmacological phenomenon to which we will refer again when we get to the problem of hallucinogenic snuffs. For the moment let it be said only that the way the Indians use *B. rusbyana* suggests that long before the advent of modern chemistry, they discovered for themselves that the alkaloids of certain plants require the addition of others to become psychedelically effective.

Amazonian Indians as Psychopharmacologists

No one can tell when the Indians of the upper Amazon discovered the "otherworldly" effects of the vine of the souls. But we are probably not far wrong in suggesting that it is at least as old as the characteristic Tropical Forest Culture, which was based on intensive root-crop agriculture and which seems to have been well-established as early as 3000 B.C. or even before (Lathrap, 1970). Tukanoan mythology places the origin of *yajé* at the very beginning of the social order, when it is said to have appeared in human form soon after the male Sun had fertilized the female Earth with its phallic ray and the first drops of semen had become the original people. Among them appeared *Yajé* Woman, who bore a child that was human in shape but also had the quality of light, for it was *yajé* and caused the men to have visions. *Yajé* Child was dismembered, every man appropriating for himself a part of its body. In turn, each of these became a *yajé* vine, which the Tukano equate with lines of descent of their different phratries. As a result of this original act, each phratry has its own particular kind of *yajé* (based not on species differentiation but on different external appearances of the plant and the ways its effects are perceived). Descent also forms the basis for the criteria by which different parts of the plant are chosen for the preparation of the hallucinogenic drink (Reichel-Dolmatoff, 1972).

When properly performed according to the sacred traditions, the entire *yajé* ritual, from the initial cutting of the vine and the preparation of the drink to the interpretation of the hallucinogenic effects, is highly formalized and circumscribed from beginning to end by a series of ceremonial requirements and taboos. The pottery vessel that will hold the liquid is a ceremonial object symbolizing the maternal womb and the creative process of gestation. The different symbols with which it is decorated represent fertilization and fecundity, including, on its base, a painted vagina and clitoris. Before the vessel can be used it must be ritually purified with tobacco smoke.

Yajé and the Mythic Origins of Society

As described by Reichel-Dolmatoff (1972:97-102), the *yajé*-drinking ceremony commences in the communal house after nightfall with ritualized dialogues that recount the Creation Myth and the genealogies of the exogamous phratries, the origins of humanity, of *yajé*, and of the social order being commemorated with song and dance to the accompaniment of instrumental sounds: a phallic rattle staff that symbolizes the primordial fertilizing ray of the Sun, the rhythmic pounding of wooden tubes, and the rubbing of a turtle shell with wax to imitate the croaking of a frog. Each distribution of *yajé* is formally introduced by the blowing of a decorated clay trumpet. The *yajé* is distributed at prescribed intervals and with ritual gestures and speechmaking by the headman, who fills the cups from the sacred maternal *yajé* vessel, while the men sit or continue their dancing. As the *yajé* effects increase so does the precision with which the dancers coordinate their movements, until at last they seem to be dancing as one body. The hallucinations are called "*yajé* images," and the Indians say that the order in which they appear is fixed: some are seen after the third cupful, others after the fourth, and so on. To have bright and pleasant visions one must have abstained from sexual intercourse and have eaten only lightly on the preceding days (exactly as in the peyote rituals of the Huichols of Mexico). At intervals an old man or someone who lays claim to esoteric knowledge describes his visions and interprets them publicly: "This trembling which is felt is the winds of the Milky Way," or "That red color is the Master of the Animals." The women meanwhile keep to themselves at one end of the house. As a rule they do not drink but participate with shouts of encouragement or derisive laughter when someone vomits or refuses a proffered bowl or cup.

What Reichel-Dolmatoff* writes of the subjective reasons why the Indians take *yajé* is of the greatest interest, not just because of what it reveals specifically about the psychocultural mechanisms of the social group involved, the Tukanoan Desana of the Vaupés of Colombia, but also because of its sometimes striking similarity to other such aboriginal "psychedelic" rituals; a comparison with the meaning of peyote among the Huichols, as described later in these pages, will immediately demonstrate this similarity.

In the first place, the Tukano say that one who has had the *yajé* experience awakens as a new person, a true Tukano, fully integrated and at one with his traditional culture, for what he has seen and heard in his ecstatic *yajé* trance has confirmed and validated the ancient truths of which the shamans and elders have told him since childhood. This is exactly what my Huichol friends told me many times of the meaning of their initiation into the magic of the peyote quest: "We went to find our life; we went to see what it is to be Huichol." Let me quote some salient passages from Reichel-Dolmatoff's account:

> According to our informants of the Vaupés, the purpose of taking *yajé* is to return to the uterus, to the *fons et origo* of all things, where the individual "sees" the tribal divinities, the creation of the universe and humanity, the first human couple, the creation of the animals, and the establishment of the social order, with particular reference to the laws of exogamy. During the ritual the individual enters through the "door" of the vagina painted on the base of the vessel.† Once inside the receptacle he becomes one with the mythic world of the Creation. . . . This return to the uterus also constitutes an acceleration of time and corresponds to death. According to the Indians, the individual "dies" but is later reborn in a state of wisdom, because on waking from

---

*For other significant recent anthropological literature on *Banisteriopsis* in its aboriginal context see Michael J. Harner's *The Jivaro: People of the Sacred Waterfalls* (1972) and *Hallucinogens and Shamanism*, M. J. Harner, ed. (1973). For those who read German, Koch-Grünberg's *Vom Roraima zum Orinoco* (1917-1928) contains much information on *Banisteriopsis* and other hallucinogenic plants in the mythology and practice of shamanism in Venezuela, the Guianas, and Brazil, and of course R. E. Schultes's many publications are an essential source not only of botanical and pharmacological but also ethnographic data.

†Among the sacred places on the ritual itinerary of the Huichol peyote pilgrimage to Wirikúta. the divine, paradisiacal land of the peyote and place of ultimate origins and primordial truths, there is one called "The Vagina."

the *yajé* trance he is convinced of the truth of his religious system, since he has seen with his own eyes the personifications of the supernaturals and the mythic scenes. . . .

According to the Tukano, after a stage of undefined luminosity of moving forms and colors, the vision begins to clear up and significant details present themselves. The Milky Way appears and the distant fertilizing reflection of the Sun. The first woman surges forth from the waters of the river, and the first pair of ancestors is formed. The supernatural Master of the Animals of the jungle and waters is perceived, as are the gigantic prototypes of the game animals, and the origins of plants—indeed, the origins of life itself. The origins of Evil also manifest themselves, jaguars and serpents, the representatives of illness, and the spirits of the jungle that lie in ambush for the solitary hunter. At the same time their voices are heard, the music of the mythic epoch is perceived, and the ancestors are seen, dancing at the dawn of Creation. The origin of the ornaments used in dances, the feather crowns, necklaces, armlets, and musical instruments, all are seen. The division into phratries is witnessed, and the *yuruparí* flutes promulgate the laws of exogamy. Beyond these visions new "doors" are opening, and through the apertures glimmer yet other dimensions, which are even more profound. . . . For the Indian the hallucinatory experience is essentially a sexual one. To make it sublime, to pass from the erotic, the sensual, to a mystical union with the mythic era, the intra-uterine stage, is the ultimate goal, attained by a mere handful, but coveted by all. We find the most cogent expression of this objective in the words of an Indian educated by missionaries, who said, "To take *yajé* is a spiritual coitus; it is the spiritual communion which the priests speak of."

Hallucinogens and Jaguar Transformation

Reichel-Dolmatoff's essay concerns *yajé* in the social setting; elsewhere he has written of shamanism and jaguar transformation and the role of *yajé* and other intoxicants in this context. It is in fact a common phenomenon of South American shamanism (reflected also in Mesoamerica) that shamans are closely identified with the jaguar, to the point where the jaguar is almost nowhere regarded as simply an animal, albeit an especially powerful one, but as supernatural, frequently as the avatar of living or deceased shamans, containing their souls and doing good or evil in accordance with the disposition of their human form (Furst, 1968). This qualitative identity of shaman and jaguar is reflected in the fact that in a number of Indian languages the terms for shaman and jaguar are identical or closely related (e.g. *yai* or *dyai* = shaman, jaguar, in several Tukanoan languages). Shaman-jaguar transformation is closely linked to the ecstatic trance, by means of tobacco or *Anadenanthera* or *Virola* snuff among some peoples, the *Banisteriopsis caapi* among others, or, as is often the case, tobacco followed by *yajé*. For some peoples *B. caapi* is the shaman's vine *par excellence*, his ladder to the Upperworld, his means of achieving transcendence. "This vine," an Indian informant told the German ethnographer Theodor Koch-Grünberg (1923:388), who traveled widely among the Indians of the Guianas, Venezuela, and northern Brazil in the early decades of this century, "contains the shaman, the jaguar."

Since there are good shamans and bad—i.e. witches or sorcerers—and since both are able to transform themselves into jaguars, it is to be expected that the great jungle cat can appear as a malevolent and frightening demon in unpleasant *yajé* experiences, not uncommonly in association with giant snakes such as the anaconda. That even a Tukano can have an occasional "bad trip" with *yajé* is confirmed by Reichel-Dolmatoff (1972). There are instances, he reports (p. 103), when he is nearly overcome by the nightmare of the jaguar's jaws or the menace of snakes that draw near while he, paralyzed with fright, feels their cold bodies winding themselves around his extremities.*

---

*My Huichol informants explained "bad trips" as the consequence of imperfect purification prior to a peyote pilgrimage, especially on the sexual plane. An incestuous relationship (the most serious infraction of the ethical code) is almost certain to result in a terrifying rather than pleasant drug experience. However, such negative experiences are not attributed to peyote; rather, say the Huichols, someone who has transgressed and not purified himself before going out to collect peyote will be supernaturally misled into mistaking another hallucinogenic cactus, *Ariocarpus retusus*, for the true peyote, *Lophophora williamsii*, and will suffer terrible psychic agonies instead of seeing "what it is to be Huichol" in vividly colored peyote dreams.

CHAPTER FIVE

HALLUCINOGENS AND "ARCHETYPES"

In the preceding chapter it was suggested that visions of jaguars, anaconda snakes, and the like are expectable images in a tropical forest setting. After all, one would hardly expect psychedelic visitations from Asian tigers or African lions among the Tukano; they would be even less likely here than in the urban slums of Amazonian Peru, where healers called *ayahuasqueros* employ the "vine of the souls" in the psychotherapeutic curing of supernaturally caused illnesses, especially those associated with witchcraft. Such emotional or psychosomatic maladies are a common complaint among the culturally and economically uprooted and psychologically disoriented Indians who have left, or been displaced from, their traditional lifeway in the forest (cf. Marlene Dobkin de Rios, *The Visionary Vine: Psychedelic Healing in the Peruvian Amazon* [1972]).

There is nevertheless a distinct possibility that harmaline and other alkaloids are biochemically involved in the formation of what Jung called archetypes, and that to this category belong big cats of whatever species happen to be familiar to the individual. Claudio Naranjo makes precisely that case in *The Healing Journey* and some of his previous writings. As it happens, such a thesis, which has a psychological as well as biochemical basis, is not inconsistent with what has been written by Harner, Reichel-Dolmatoff, Koch-Grünberg, and others about the effects of harmala alkaloids on the Indians, by Harner (1973) about his own experiences and *yajé* as a transcultural phenomenon, and by Naranjo himself about non-Indian subjects in experimental settings. All this is obviously important enough, not alone in the specific context of *Banisteriopsis*, to warrant some consideration here.

Harner (1973:154-194), lists the following common themes in the *yajé*

50

experiences that have been collected over the years from Indian informants in different parts of Amazonia:

(1)   The soul is felt to separate from the physical body and to make a trip, often with the sensation of flight.

(2)   Visions of jaguars and snakes, and to a much lesser extent, other predatory animals.

(3)   A sense of contact with the supernatural, whether with demons, or in the case of missionized Indians, also with God, and Heaven and Hell.

(4)   Visions of distant persons, "cities" and landscapes, typically interpreted by the Indians as visions of distant reality, i.e. as clairvoyance.

(5)   The sensation of seeing the detailed enactment of recent unsolved crimes, particularly homicide and theft, i.e., the experience of believing one is capable of divination.*

The Transcultural Phenomenon

Among the transcultural *yajé* experiences of South American Indians Harner lists auditory hallucination and visions of certain geometric forms, auras, one's own death, combats with demons and animals, bright colors, constant changing of certain shapes that seem to dissolve into one another, and the like. However, he cautions (p. 173), it must be remembered that all of the peoples who traditionally use *Banisteriopsis* occupy a similar tropical forest environment and, however far apart, the total content of their cultures is rather similar; these similarities could account for the striking similarity in their *yajé* experiences.

What Reichel-Dolmatoff has written about the meaning of the *yajé* experience in relation to certain universal or at least widespread themes and symbols in prehistoric art and in present-day Tukanoan imagery is very much to the point here and I will return to it below. But even more immediately pertinent to the question raised by Harner are the harmaline experiments of Naranjo with a group of non-Indian subjects, as well as a biochemical peculiarity of harmala alkaloids that places the whole problem in the context of the chemistry of the brain. Harmaline is of special interest, writes Naranjo

. . . because of its close resemblance to substances derived from the pineal gland of mammals. In particular, 10-methoxy-harmaline, which may be obtained in vitro from the incubation of serotonin in pineal tissue, resembles harmaline in its subjective effects and is of greater activity than the latter. This suggests that harmaline (differing from 10-methoxy-harmaline only in the position of the methoxy group) may derive its

---

*This sensation explains why one of the harmala alkaloids of *Banisteriopsis caapi* was originally called "telepathine."

activity from the mimicry of a metabolite normally involved in the control of states of consciousness.*

Among the typical harmaline trance symbols or experiences that many of Naranjo's subjects reported were felines, snakes, dragons, birds, flight, sun, passage through perilous regions, descent and ascent, death and rebirth. This experience is all very familiar from the shamanistic world, but one particular harmaline dream among those cited by Naranjo is especially pertinent not only because it mirrors in many of its details the characteristic experience of initiatory ecstasy but also because it even echoes some familiar themes from the cosmologies of ancient China and pre-Hispanic Mesoamerica. The subject in this case is a woman.

"Tiger, Tiger, Burning Bright . . ."

Her dream begins with tiger eyes as the initiatory image, soon followed by many faces and sleek bodies of big cats of different colors. From these images there emerges a large and powerful Siberian tiger, an animal of grace and beauty whom she feels compelled by a great longing to follow to the ends of the world. The tiger takes her to the edge of a high plateau, from where she glimpses a deep abyss filled with liquid fire or molten gold in which many people are swimming:

> The tiger wants me to go there. I don't know how to descend. I grasp the tiger's tail, and he jumps. Because of his musculature, the jump is graceful and slow. The tiger swims in the liquid fire as I sit on his back. . . . (Naranjo, 1973:154)

They swim on together and she sees a monstrous crocodile-headed serpent-like animal swallowing a woman. Frogs and toads suddenly appear around her as the fiery pond turns into a stagnant, greenish swamp full of primitive life forms. But she rides her protective tiger safely through the terrifying images to the far shore, followed by the great serpent. A cosmic battle ensues between her protective tiger and the snake, in which she intervenes on the tiger's side. The snake is vanquished, it disintegrates like a mechanical toy, and she and her feline guardian travel onward together, side by side, her arm draped around the animal's neck. They come to a high mountain and ascend it along a zigzag path that leads upward through a forest. At the top there is a crater. Tiger and woman wait there for a time, until there is an enormous eruption:

---

*In man the pineal gland, which rises conelike from the third ventricle of the brain, is a vestigial organ, representing more evolved forms in lower vertebrates and their long-extinct reptilian ancestors. The pineal body has sometimes been thought to be the seat of the soul. Serotonin is a neuro-transmitter agent that occurs naturally in the mammalian brain, including that of man, and, interestingly enough, also in the venom of toads (*Bufo* spp.). The highest concentrations of serotonin have been found in the brains of schizophrenics. See also the first footnote in Chapter Six, below.

The tiger tells me I must throw myself into the crater. I am sad to leave my companion, but I know that this last journey I must travel. I throw myself into the fire that comes out of the crater. I ascend with the flames toward the sky and fly onward. (Naranjo, 1973:155)

Experiences such as this during a single exposure to the effects of harmaline, Naranjo writes,

. . . constitute a plunging of the mind into an area of myth, transpersonal symbols, and archetypes, and thus constitute an analogue to what is the essence of initiation in many cultures. Typically, for instance, the puberty ordeals are occasions when the young are brought into contact (with or without drugs) with the symbols, myths, or art works which summarize the spiritual legacy of their culture's collective experience. The attitude toward the world that is expressed by such symbols is regarded as important to maturity and to the order of life in the community, and for this reason its transmission is reverently perpetuated, made the object of initiations and of other rituals or feasts in which the people renew their contact with, or awareness of, this domain of existence, irrelevant to practical life but central to the question of life's meaning. The harmala-alkaloid-containing drinks of South American Indians are not only employed in puberty rituals but also in the initiation of the shamans, primitive psychiatrists whose expertise in psychological phenomena is revealed, for instance, in the fact that they are frequently expected to understand the meaning of dreams. (1973:152-153)

Journeys into Mythic Time

All of this is very true, and obviously is of great significance not only to psychology and psychotherapy but also to the ethnology of religion and the ecstatic experience. But it is important to note that the phenomenon of "plunging the mind into myth" or mythic time, that is, into a time when everything is possible, is larger than the choice of a particular alkaloid or group of related alkaloids, because, as we know, other plants with active principles that belong to different groups than the harmala alkaloids are also used in this manner. And similar experiences can also be obtained without any drug. So the cultural context has to be stressed again as being at least as important as the subjective effects of a certain drug.

Transposition from the "here and now" to the "there and then" is common in the initiatory experience, whether in the *yajé* ritual of the Tukano or in the peyote quest of the Huichols, which Weston La Barre (1970b) has characterized as "probably the closest to the pre-Columbian Mexican rite." It is especially important in shamanic curing, precisely because in the mythic "there and then," experiences of transformation, or being and becoming, are the normal order, and all manner of ordinarily difficult or impossible things respond with ease to the efforts of the gods, who are themselves the original and most powerful of shamans. To illustrate what I mean, let me digress for a moment from the contemporary *yajé* complex and modern psychotherapy and return to sixteenth- and seventeenth-century central Mexico and the world of the Nahuatl-speaking curer.

In the course of analyzing the extraordinary corpus of shamanic incantations collected in Ruiz de Alarcón's *Tratado* of 1629, historian Alfredo
López Austin (1973) has found that the synthesis of mythic chants and
mind-manifesting drugs (e.g. *picíetl* [*Nicotiana rustica*], and also peyote,
mushrooms, and *ololiuhqui* [morning-glory seeds]) assists the process of
curing in two ways: one, it gives the shaman or "magician" the gift of
clairvoyance—the perceptive capability of discovering the occult reality of
things, the "supernatural in the natural," in actual time and space, and of
achieving contact and communication with supernatural beings that have
become visible to him. Second, myth and magic plant

. . . permit him to break free from the actual time and space and travel to a world in
which the action that is being attempted (the cure) is both feasible and more effective.
In short, chant and drug enable him to act in the here and now or there and then.

For example, to set a fractured limb (which he does pragmatically by
splinting) the shaman invokes the magic powers of the drug and chants the
myth of the journey of the God Quetzalcóatl to the land of the dead, Mictlán,
to obtain the bones of the dead of a previous creation and with them to
recreate a new race of humanity. In the myth a quail caused Quetzalcóatl to
fall and break the bones. The shaman identifies the evil spirit that has taken
possession of the fracture with this mythic quail, and he identifies himself
with a divinity that has the power of counteracting the evil and reconstituting
the broken bones of the dead. He even calls the fractured limb of his patient
"bone of the world of the dead." "Aha," we say, "this is obviously what
anthropologists call analogous magic." But that is too simplistic, and it fails
to appreciate the philosophical subtleties of the Aztec perception of mythic
times in relation to the here and now. It is not, writes López Austin, that the
expulsion of the evil that has taken possession of the fracture is identified with
the myth of the taking and breaking of the bones of the dead and their re-
constitution into living beings. Rather,

the mythical element "fractured bone" is the fissure through which the magician slips
in order to avail himself of a favorable point in time. He does not attempt to relate
analogically a divine event with a result that he wishes to obtain in the real world. It is
not simply analogic magic. The magician does not want analogies; he wants a moment
of time that by virtue of being of the Creation, and hence critical, abnormal, is also
malleable, pliable, subject to easier manipulation than any other.

None of the above invalidates Naranjo's thesis, especially with respect to
archetypes; but it does extend the mythic experience as such beyond the
boundaries of a specific psychedelic. This will be especially evident in the
peyote quest (Chapters Ten and Eleven).

Yajé and the Origins of Art

According to Reichel-Dolmatoff (1972), the Tukano attribute everything
we would call "art" to the images that occur in the *yajé* dream. The striking

polychrome designs that adorn the fronts of communal houses, the abstract motifs on their pottery, bark cloths, calabashes, and musical instruments—all these, they say, first appeared and consistently recur under the influence of the psychedelic drink. Not only is there consensus about the forms of these motifs, but in addition their meaning is codified, each having a fixed value as an ideographic sign.

According to the Tukano, the geometric or nonrepresentational motifs, which are interpreted in terms of exogamy, incest, fertility, and the like, appear with the onset of *yajé* intoxication, and are followed by scenes from the mythic world, with well-defined images of animals—especially felines and reptiles, birds and other beings, and themes whose models are familiar from the natural and social environment of the tropical forest. It would seem, then,

. . . that in a state of hallucination the individual projects his cultural memory on the wavering screen of colors and shapes and thus "sees" certain motifs and personages. (Reichel-Dolmatoff, 1972:110)

Furthermore, there is nothing secret about the content of the dreams. The ecstatic trance experiences are shared, and their interpretation is often done publicly by the shamans and others respected for esoteric knowledge and wisdom. Thus a consensual fixing of images, and their meaning, in accordance with the common cultural pattern, could easily develop and be transmitted through time.

But that does not account completely for the striking parallels among the nonrepresentational images described and drawn by Tukano informants. The problem becomes even more complex,

. . . if we consider it from the perspective of artistic inspiration. It is amazing to note how frequently the [geometric] design motifs . . . appear in the petroglyphs and pictographs of the region and far beyond. It would not be difficult to find parallels to these motifs in other prehistoric artifacts, such as the decorations of ceramics or the rock carvings of ancient indigenous cultures. It could be argued that we are dealing with such elementary motifs that they could have evolved independently in any place and era, for they are simply circles, diamonds, dots, and spirals, and nothing more. But are they really that elementary? (Reichel-Dolmatoff, 1972:111)

The Colombian anthropologist suggests that both the corpus of nonrepresentational images and their ethnographic and archaeological parallels might have arisen from the organic effects of *yajé* and perhaps other hallucinogens. Considering the known antiquity of the psychedelic complex among American Indians, he writes, we might conceive of "great cultural zones" wherein, since very ancient times, a certain hallucinogen was ritually employed, giving rise to a body of symbols and motifs that gradually came to be culturally fixed or institutionalized, along with their interpretations. This is all the more plausible, he argues, in that it is typically the shamans, the bearers of the magicoreligious traditions, who are also the artists of their societies and who are ultimately responsible for the symbolic images that appear on the artifacts of the culture and on the living rock in their environment.

That different hallucinogens tend to produce similar geometric or abstract images has been recognized by some investigators of the psychedelic phenomenon since the 1920's. Recent long-term experiments at the University of California at Los Angeles also indicate an organic basis for specific sensations in fixed sequences reported by many subjects under the influence of hallucinogenic drugs. What is new is the suggestion that the commonality of abstract or geometric symbolic art through time and space might likewise have a biochemical origin.

Might this be extended to include motifs we would call representational—specifically the great cats, the snakes, and the birds that recur in so many *yajé* dreams? Certainly feedback and projective mechanisms are at work here: feline, reptilian, and avian motifs predominate in the cosmologies, the myths, and the art of prehistoric as well as contemporary Indian societies from Mexico south. But these have to have started somewhere: might they in fact be archetypes, embedded deeply in the unconscious since very ancient times, to be released, perhaps, by biochemical stimuli? Are there, then, biopsychological explanations rather than culture-historical ones for the parallels in ancient Chinese ritual art to the feline-reptilian-avian symbol complex of the New World?* Or are both only two sides of the same coin, interdependent rather than mutually exclusive? And how is one to understand the similarities in the *yajé* experiences of Indians, anthropologists, and volunteers in psychotherapeutic experiments?

That something ties all these transcultural and transpersonal phenomena together seems obvious. How much is due to the chemistry of consciousness and how much to culture, however, remains a large unanswered question.

---

*The "dragon" is the synthesis of these three cosmic elements, as is the "Feathered Serpent" of Mesoamerica.

CHAPTER SIX

LSD AND THE SACRED MORNING
GLORIES OF INDIAN MEXICO

For Dr. Albert Hofmann of Sandoz Ltd., a well-known Swiss pharmaceutical house headquartered in Basel, his finding in 1960 that the psychedelically effective principles of morning-glory seeds were nothing else than lysergic acid derivatives, closely related to synthetic LSD-25, was, as he wrote later, like "closing a magic circle" on a research series that began more than twenty years earlier with the discovery of LSD and that finally embraced some of the most interesting of the divine hallucinogens of Indian America.

LSD and Parkinson's Disease

In a very real sense the circle is also closing with respect to Hofmann's hope, expressed at the time of his epoch-making discovery of LSD, that because of its ability to mimic certain mental illnesses the drug might prove useful in their treatment. In fact, LSD has been employed to that end over the years by some psychiatrists, often with beneficial results. However, the potency of LSD and the severe legal limitations imposed in recent years on its use even under controlled scientific conditions have caused psychotherapists to turn to other chemical agents, such as those discussed in a previous chapter.

Recently, however, scientists at the School of Medicine of the University of California at Los Angeles have made some significant discoveries about the interaction of LSD with dopamine, one of the neurotransmitter agents in the brain, that may lead not only to a better understanding and eventual treatment of schizophrenia, the mental disorder to which the LSD "high" is a kind of temporary analogue, but even of such physically, rather than mentally, crippling disorders as Parkinson's disease (*UCLA Weekly*, 1975:4). The investigators, Drs. Sidney Roberts and Kern von Hungen and Diane F. Hill, determined that adenyl cyclase, an enzyme in nervous tissue that is stimulated by naturally occurring neurotransmitter agents, is also stimulated by the action of LSD on receptors for one of these neurotransmitters, dopamine. In addition, LSD blocked the stimulatory actions of dopamine and other neurotransmitters (agents that aid in conducting impulses along nerve cells, specifically bridging the gap, or synapse, between them), such as serotonin and norepeninephrine. These, as noted in the Introduction to this book, are themselves structurally closely related to powerful plant growth hormones; dopamine, moreover, has also been identified with the giant saguaro cactus (*Carnegiea gigantea*) of Arizona and northern Mexico (Bruhn, 1971:323).

Schizophrenia is thought to be a disease of dopamine hyperactivity; victims of Parkinson's disease, on the other hand, suffer from dopamine insufficiency, which is partially offset nowadays by the administration of a new drug, L-dopa, often in combination with Tofranil or some other amphetamine. The adenyl cyclase experiments enabled the UCLA team to show that dopamine receptors are present in the higher regions of the brain, which are concerned with the more complex experiences and thus are more likely to be the seat of alternate states of consciousness, or "hallucinations." Their work, report the UCLA investigators, makes it appear that the psychotic mimicking effects of LSD, first noted by Hofmann more than thirty years ago, may also be related to hyperactivity of brain dopamine systems. These insights have obvious implications for work on new drugs for schizophrenia on the one hand and Parkinson's disease on the other; recognition of their biochemical kinship was, of course, still far off in the distant future when Hofmann correctly predicted the ultimate benefits of LSD for brain research. Nor did he suspect at the time that "primitive" psychotherapy had been making effective use of a natural compound very like LSD for hundreds, perhaps thousands, of years.

Lysergic acid, Hofmann (1967) has explained,

. . . is the foundation stone of the ergot alkaloids, the active principle of the fungus product ergot. Botanically speaking ergot is the sclerotia of the filamentous fungus *Claviceps purpurea* which grows on grasses, especially rye. The ears of rye that have been attacked by the fungus develop into long, dark pegs to form ergot. The chemical and pharmacological investigation of the ergot alkaloids has been a main field of research of the natural products division of the Sandoz laboratories since the discovery of ergotamine by A. Stoll in 1918. A variety of useful pharmaceuticals have resulted from these investigations, which have been conducted over a number of decades. They find wide application in obstetrics, in internal medicine, in neurology and psychiatry. (p. 349)

Historic Breakthrough: The Discovery of LSD

The significant part of our story begins in 1938, when Hofmann and an associate, Dr. W. A. Kroll, discovered *d*-lysergic acid diethylamide, a derivative of ergot. Because it was the twenty-fifth compound in the lysergic acid series to be synthethized at Sandoz, it was named LSD-25, the designation under which it was to become famous; but at the time, since tests on animals showed nothing of pharmaceutical interest, it was laid aside without being tested on humans, Five years later, on April 16, 1943, in the course of working with two other ergot derivatives, Hofmann suddenly experienced feelings of restlessness and dizziness, so much so that he was compelled to go home. Later that afternoon, as he subsequently wrote in his notebook, while lying down in a semiconscious and slightly delirious state he suddenly experienced "fantastic visions of extraordinary realness, and with an intense kaleidoscopic play of colors," a condition that endured about two hours, and in the course of which self-perception and the sense of time itself were changed.

At that time LSD was not actually suspected as the cause, but as it happened, he had that same morning recrystallized d-lysergic diethylamide tartrate while working with two other ergot derivatives. Their effects were well known, however, and because he suspected that he might have accidentally ingested some of the LSD compound, he decided to test the chemical under more controlled conditions. The following week he administered to himself what he then took to be a very small dose of one-quarter of one milligram (actually, as he discovered and as we now know, a very substantial amount) and soon found himself in for a six-hour-long and often highly dramatic "trip." Thus began the saga of LSD-25, the most potent psychoactive or "psychedelic" compound known up to that time, whose discovery ushered in a whole new era of exploration into the nature of the unconscious and the historical role of hallucinogens in the evolution and maintenance of metaphysical and even social systems. And inasmuch as it opened new vistas for the cross-cultural and multidisciplinary investigation of what has been called "inner space," one cannot but agree with psychologist Duncan B. Blewett (1969) that the discovery of LSD marked, together the splitting of the atom and the discovery of the biochemical role of DNA, the basic genetic material of inheritance, one of the three major scientific breakthroughs of the twentieth century.*

---

*As this book was nearing completion, the nation's newspapers were filled with disclosures of large-scale secret experimentation with LSD by the Pentagon and the Central Intelligence Agency on many hundreds (more than 1500 in the Army's tests alone) of human subjects, of whom at least some were not informed beforehand what drug they were being given—a method that has been characterized as unethical by, among others, such medical authorities as Dr. Judd Marmor, President of the American Psychiatric Association. The secret tests, whose results were not accessible to the general scientific community, continued for at least a dozen years into the late nineteen sixties—in other words, long after LSD was made illegal, extensive campaigns were mounted on the national and local level to convince the public of its dangers, and its unauthorized manufacture, possession, sale, use or even free distribution made subject to lengthy prison terms. The *New York Times* of August 1, 1975, quoted Dr. Albert

Ololiuhqui, Sacred Hallucinogen of the Aztecs

Among the several sacred hallucinogens that were apparently too vital to the individual and social equilibrium of Indian Mexico to be suppressed after the Conquest, and that took on the trappings of Christian iconography without losing their essential pre-Christian meanings, was *ololiuhqui*. *Ololiuhqui* (*ololuc*), an Aztec word meaning "round thing," contains no clue to its botanical identity, any more than does *teonanácatl*, food or flesh of the gods, the name by which the Aztecs called certain hallucinogenic mushrooms. Although Ruiz de Alarcón (1629) declined to identify the source of *ololiuhqui*, there should have been no doubt from the first that the term referred to the lentil-shaped light-brown seeds of the morning glory, for Hernández had accurately pictured the plant in his sixteenth-century study and Mexican botanists had long identified it as *Rivea corymbosa*.

Nevertheless, prior to 1941, when Schultes published a definitive review of the sacred morning glories and once and for all identified *ololuc* or *ololiuhqui* as *R. corymbosa*, its identity was subject to controversy, primarily because a noted American botanist, William A. Safford, had no faith in the botanical knowledge of the Aztecs, of the early Spanish scholars, or even of his Mexican colleagues. In 1919, Dr. Blas Pablo Reko, an Austrian-born Mexican scholar who was later to collaborate with Schultes in Mexico, had collected *ololuc* seeds and identified them as *R. corymbosa*. Safford (1915, 1920) confirmed the botanical determination, but because no intoxication followed ingestion of the seeds, and because no psychoactive alkaloids had ever been found in any Convolvulaceae, the order to which the morning glories belong, he insisted that the real *ololiuhqui* had to be the seeds of

---

Hofmann to the effect that he was repeatedly approached during the late nineteen-fifties by United States Army researchers looking for a way to mass-produce large quantities of the drug; he had never been told the reason for the Army's interest, he said, but from the extremely large quantities being discussed assumed that it was for weapons research. Whereas a standard experimental dose was in the range of 250 to 300 micrograms, he said, the Army was interested in finding a process that could produce "many kilos" (a microgram is one millionth of a gram, a kilo one thousand grams). "The Army people came back many times," Dr. Hofmann told reporters, "every two years or so, to see if any technological progress had been made," adding that the visits stopped after other researchers succeeded in developing such a process in the early nineteen-sixties. He also said he personally did not like what the Army was after, "because I had perfected LSD for medical use, not as a weapon. . . . In any case, the research should be done by medical people and not by soldiers or intelligence agencies," especially in light of the serious risks posed by the potent psychochemical.

It must seem to many the height of irony and of official cynicism that even as civilian medical research with LSD was being severely hampered by legal restrictions, and thousands of Americans, mostly young people, were being jailed and marked for life with felony records on LSD-related charges, the drug was being covertly administered to other thousands to see if it might prove useful for chemical warfare, while the Army was seeking ways to have it manufactured in quantities equivalent to literally tens of millions of individual experimental doses!

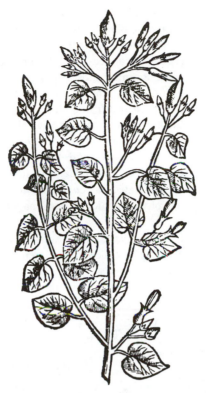

Ololiuhqui (Rivea corymbosa). As illustrated by Francisco Hernández in his
Rerum medicarum Novae Hispania thesaurus . . ., published in Rome in 1651.

Datura inoxia (*meteloides*) (*toloatzin*), whose intoxicating effects were said
to resemble those reported for *ololiuhqui* (they do not, in fact). Safford was
wrong, of course, as he was also in his claim that *teonanácatl* was not a
mushroom, as reported by Sahagún and other early chroniclers, but probably
was nothing else than peyote, whose dried and shriveled "buttons" Sahagún
and other early observers, and the Aztecs themselves, had supposedly mis-
taken for mushroom caps! So much for ethnocentricity in science.

Ololiuhqui Identified

In 1934 Reko published the first historical review of *ololiuhqui* use, and
again identified it—correctly—with *Rivea corymbosa*. Three years later, C. G.
Santesson (1937) finally dispelled the notion that the Convolvulaceae, specifically *R. corymbosa*, lacked hallucinogenic principles, although the precise
nature of the psychoactive alkaloids could not be determined. Then, in 1939,
Schultes and Reko, while on a field trip through Mexico, for the first time
encountered a cultivated species of *R. corymbosa* in the courtyard of a

Zapotec Indian *curandero* in Oaxaca, who was using the seeds in divinatory curing rites. Schultes subsequently reported *ololuc* being used among such Oaxacan Indians as the Mazatecs, Chinantecs, Mixtecs, and others; since then, the list has been greatly expanded, not only for *R. corymbosa* but for the other major hallucinogenic morning glory, *Ipomoea violacea*, whose seeds are called *badoh negro* in Oaxaca, and which in pre-Hispanic times was the sacred divinatory hallucinogen *tlitliltzin* (Wasson, 1967a). This species is known in the United States under such names as Heavenly Blue, Wedding Bells, Blue Stars, Summer Skies, and others. In 1941, Schultes published his now classic monograph on *R. corymbosa* and the divine hallucinogen *ololiuhqui*. Thus at least the botanical identification of *ololiuhqui* and its mother plant, known to the Aztecs as *coatl-xoxouhqui*, green snake plant, was settled, although its phytochemical determination had to wait another twenty years.

Meanwhile—in fact, just the year before Schultes and Reko collected the first unquestionably identifiable voucher specimen of *Rivea corymbosa* in

RIVEA
corymbosa (L.) Hall. f.

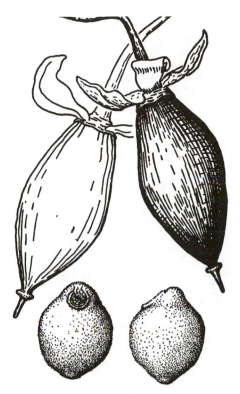

Rivea corymbosa. Capsules and seeds.

Oaxaca—LSD had been discovered and synthethized in Switzerland. It was this event and subsequent research at Sandoz into psychotomimetic alkaloids that caused the French mycologist Roger Heim to send samples of *teonanácatl* mushrooms to Hofmann, "on the assumption that the necessary conditions for a successful chemical investigation would be present in the laboratory in which LSD was discovered" (Hofmann, 1967:350). They were; Hofmann discovered psilocybine and psilocine as the active principles of the most important hallucinogenic fungi. Close collaboration followed with Heim and with the American ethnomycologist R. Gordon Wasson, and this in turn led directly to the startling discovery of the active principles of *R. corymbosa* and *I. violacea*.

In the interim, there were to be two more research reports on the effects of morning-glory seeds. Santesson had been certain that alkaloids were present but was not able to identify them. In 1955, the Canadian psychiatrist Humphrey Osmond, who had long been interested in the use and effects of peyote, especially in the context of the Native American Church among Canadian Indians, experimented on himself with *ololiuhqui* seeds. His experience did

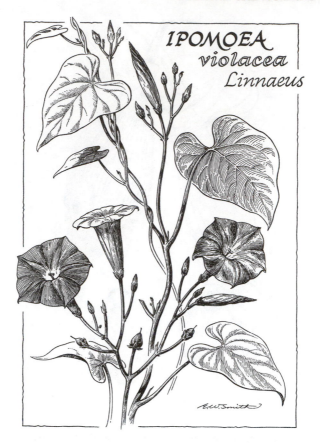

IPOMOEA
violacea
Linnaeus

not duplicate that reported historically from Mexico, but after taking 60 to 100 seeds he passed into what he described as a state of listlessness, accompanied by increased visual sensitivity and followed by a prolonged period of relaxed well-being. In 1958, V. J. Kinross-Wright published the entirely negative results of *ololiuhqui* experiments with eight male volunteers, of whom not a single one reported any effect whatever, even though individual doses ranged up to 125 morning-glory seeds!

But this hardly squared with the accounts of the early chroniclers, nor with the modern observations of Schultes and others. Quite apart from set and setting, which, as we know, are crucial variables in the use of any hallucinogen, the problem evidently lay in the manner of preparation of the seeds. To quote Wasson (1967a):

In recent years a number of experimenters have taken the seeds with no effects and this has led one of them to suggest that the reputation of *ololiuhqui* is wholly due to autosuggestion. These negative results may be explained by inadequate preparation.

The Indians grind the seed on the *metate* (grinding stone) until it is reduced to flour. Then the flour is soaked in cold water, and after a short time the liquor is passed through a cloth strainer and drunk. If taken whole, the seeds give no result, or even if they are cracked. They must be ground to flour and then the flour is soaked briefly in water. Perhaps those who took the seeds without results did not grind them, or did not grind them fine enough, and did not soak the resulting flour. The chemistry of the seeds seems not to vary from region to region, and seeds grown in the Antilles and Europe are as potent as those grown in Oaxaca. I have taken the black seeds (*Ipomoea violacea*) twice in my home in New York, and their potency is undeniable. (p. 343)

In 1959, Wasson sent Hofmann a sample of seeds in two small bottles. With it came a letter, identifying one as having been collected in Huautla de Jiménez, the Mazatec village that has become famous as a center of the living mushroom cult, and the other in the Zapotec town of San Bártolo Yautepec. The first batch, wrote Wasson (quoted in Hofmann, 1967), he took to be *ololiuhqui*, i.e. the seeds of *Rivea corymbosa*. Upon botanical investigation, this proved correct. The Zapotec seeds, which were black and angular rather than light-brown and roundish, were identified as *Ipomoea violacea*, the *badoh negro* of Zapotec *curanderos* and the *tlitliltzin* of the Aztecs.

LSD-like Compounds in Morning-Glory Seeds

Initial chemical-analytical studies with Wasson's small samples proved exciting enough—they indicated the presence of indole compounds structurally related to LSD and the ergot alkaloids. These preliminary results caused Hofmann to ask Wasson for larger quantities of these interesting seeds. Wasson enlisted the aid of the veteran Mexican ethnologist Roberto Weitlaner, like B. P. Reko of Austrian birth, an untiring field ethnologist even when he was well into his seventies, and his daughter Irmgard Weitlaner Johnson, herself a noted specialist in pre-Columbian and contemporary Indian textiles. With the assistance of the Weitlaners, father and daughter, Wasson was able to send Hofmann 12 kilograms of *Rivea corymbosa* seeds and 14 kilograms of the seeds of the blue-flowered *Ipomoea violacea*.

With these considerable quantities, which reached Hofmann in the early part of 1960, he was able to isolate their main active principles and identify them as ergot alkaloids—*d*-lysergic acid amide (ergine) and *d*-isolysergic acid amide (isoergine). These are closely related to *d*-lysergic acid diethylamide (LSD):

From the phytochemical point of view this finding was unexpected and of particular interest because lysergic acid alkaloids, which had hitherto only been found in the lower fungi of the genus *Claviceps*, were now for the first time found to be present in higher plants, in the plant family Convolvulaceae.

The isolation of lysergic acid amides from *ololiuhqui* thus caused a research series to close like a magical ring.

It was the discovery of lysergic acid diethylamide (LSD) as a highly active psychotomimetic agent, during investigations on simple acid amides, that our research in the field of hallucinogenic compounds commenced. It was within the framework of this activity that the Mexican magic fungi came to our laboratories. It was during the course of these investigations that the personal contact was made between the writer and R. G. Wasson and it was as a result of this contact that the investigations of *ololiuhqui* were conducted. In this magic drug, lysergic acid amides, which made their appearance in the initial stages of our psychotomimetic research, were again found as active principles. (Hofmann, 1967:351-352)

Schultes (1970) notes that the nomenclature and taxonomy of the Convolvulaceae are still in a state of confusion. *Rivea*, mainly an Asiatic genus of woody vines, has five Old World but only one New World species, *R. corymbosa*, which occurs, in addition to Mexico and Central America, in the southernmost United States, parts of the Caribbean, and on the north coast of South America. *R. corymbosa* is known in the literature by at least nine synonyms, the two most common being *Ipomoea sidaefolia* and *Turbina corymbosa*. *Ipomoea*, a genus of climbing herbs and shrubs, comprises at least 500 species in warm and tropical parts of the hemisphere. *I. violacea* ("Heavenly Blue," etc.), is also often called *I. tricolor* or *I. rubro-caerulea*. The psychotropic principles of *R. corymbosa* and *I. violacea* are shared by other morning-glory species, but the degree to which any of these were or still are used by Indians is not known. However, the fact that some are called by popular names that allude to intoxicating properties (e.g. *arbol loco*, crazy tree, or *borrachera*, drunkenness, a term that is also applied to *Datura*), suggests that these are at least known, if not actually utilized.

Presumably to head off their popularization as an inexpensive natural psychedelic in the United States commercial seeds of Heavenly Blue and other varieties were ordered coated with a noxious substance. Since the artificial coating is not inheritable, nothing, of course, would prevent hallucinogenic use of subsequent generations of seeds.

Nonetheless, for whatever reason, and despite the fact that the natural chemistry of morning-glory seeds is far more reliable than that of synthetic hallucinogens available on the black market, except on the West Coast* they seem not to have become integrated to any notable extent into the drug subculture. Nor do we have any indication that morning glories ever entered ritual contexts in the Old World or even in South America. Thus the discovery and utilization of their psychic effects apparently belongs exclusively to the Indians of Mexico.

---

*The seeds of the so-called "Hawaiian wood roses" *(Argyreia* spp.)—actually not roses at all but with the morning glories members of the Convolvulaceae—achieved some popularity for easily accessible "highs," which, however, turned out to have extremely unpleasant after-effects, such as nausea, constipation, vertigo, blurred vision, and physical inertia (Emboden, 1972b:26). Their complex chemistry includes amides of lysergic acids.

Ololiuhqui in Indian Religion

According to Dr. Francisco Hernández, that learned and observant physician to the Spanish crown who studied the medicinal lore of Indian Mexico in the sixteenth century and whose great work on the plants, animals, and minerals of New Spain was published in Rome in 1651,

. . . when the priests wanted to communicate with their gods, and to receive messages from them, they ate this plant (*ololiuhqui*) to induce a delirium. A thousand visions and satanic hallucinations appeared to them.

Morning-Glory Seeds as Divinity

Actually, as the Spaniards quickly saw, *ololiuhqui*, like the mushrooms and other magical plants, was more than just a means of communication with the supernatural. It was itself a divinity and the object of worship, reverently preserved within the secret household shrines of village shamans, curers, and even ordinary people in the early Colonial era. Carefully hidden in consecrated baskets and other dedicatory receptacles, the seeds were personally addressed with prayers, petitions, and incantations, and honored with sacrificial offerings, incense, and flowers. *Ololiuhqui* was apparently considered to be male. It could even manifest itself in human form to those that drank the sacred infusion. Accounts of the worship of the seeds and other sacred plant hallucinogens as divinities are too specific and they occur too often in the Colonial literature to be dismissed out of hand as mere ethnocentric misconstructions of indigenous belief. In fact, if one looks at peyote among the Huichols, or the mushrooms in central Mexico and Oaxaca, one finds the same sort of identification with the divinities: peyote is the divine deer or supernatural master of the deer species, addressed as Elder Brother and merging with some of the leading deities, and the sacred mushrooms are personified and addressed as "ancestors," "ancient ones," "little princes of the waters," "little saints," and the like.

As mentioned, the best early source on *ololiuhqui*, as on seventeenth-century indigenous beliefs and practices in general, is Ruiz de Alarcón's *Tratado* on the "idolatries and superstitions" of the Indians of Morelos and Guerrero. Several chapters of this important work are devoted to what their author calls "the superstition of the *ololiuhqui*," to which, he complains repeatedly, the Indians continued to attribute divinity in the face of the severest denunciations and punishment. Worse, he writes, the same "superstition" threatened to spread to the lower strata of Colonial society, for which reasons he said he felt compelled to refrain from identifying the plant botanically, except to say that it was a vine growing profusely along the banks of rivers and streams in his native Guerrero and neighboring Morelos (as it still does).

The Indians had special incantations that they addressed to the divine *ololiuhqui* to cause him to appear and assist in divination and the curing of illnesses:

"Come hither, cold spirit, for you must remove this heat (fever), and you must console your servant, who will serve you perhaps one, perhaps two days, and who will sweep clean the place where you are worshiped." This conjuration in its entirety is so accepted by the Indians that almost all of them hold that the *ololiuhqui* is a divine thing, in consequence of which . . . this conjuration accounts for the custom of veneration of it by the Indians, which is to have it on their altars and in the best containers or baskets that they have, and there to offer it incense and bouquets of flowers, to sweep and water the house very carefully, and for this reason the conjuration says: ". . . who will sweep (for) you or serve you one or two days more." And with the same veneration they drink the said seed, shutting themselves in those places like one who was in the *sanctasanctórum*, with many other superstitions. And the veneration with which these barbarous people revere the seed is so excessive that part of their devotions include washing and sweeping (even) those places where the bushes are found which produce them, which are some heavy vines, even though they are in the wildernesses and thickets. (Ruiz de Alarcón, 1629)

Thwarting the Clergy

The Indians, he complains, seemed always to find new ways to thwart even the best efforts of the clergy, including himself as the investigating emissary of the Holy Office, hiding their supplies of *ololiuhqui* in secret places, not only because they were afraid of discovery and punishment by the Inquisition, but for fear that *ololiuhqui* itself might punish them for having suffered it to be desecrated by the touch of alien hands. Always, he reports, the Indians seemed to be more concerned with the good will of *ololiuhqui* than the displeasure and penalties of the clergy. Moreover, they often pretended to cooperate in the denunciation of "idolatry" only so as to better conceal its practice. The following story of such a denunciation, involving a woman who had some *ololiuhqui* in her possession and several of her relatives, will serve as an illustration.

It seems that the woman had been involved in a domestic quarrel and one of her male relatives had admitted to Ruiz de Alarcón that she owned a basket filled with the sacred seeds. Ruiz de Alarcón wanted to check the house immediately, but his informant asked if he might be allowed to do it alone, for he knew her hiding places and would be able to determine quickly if the *ololiuhqui* and all the other things he had denounced were still in the house. Ruiz de Alarcón agreed and let the relative do the searching alone; the man soon returned to report that the basket was nowhere to be found. Ruiz de Alarcón had the woman and her sister placed under arrest and after questioning them "with all diligence" for an entire day, they finally admitted that at the first sign of danger they had quickly removed all the *ololiuhqui* from the oratory and divided it into many small segments, each to be carefully secreted in a different place:

When she was asked why she had denied it so perversely she answered, as they always do, "Oninomauhtiaya," which means, out of fear I did not dare. It is important to indicate that this is not the same fear which they have for the ministers of justice for the punishment they deserve, rather (it is) the fear that they have for this same *ololiuhqui*, or the deity they believe resides in it, and in this respect they have their reverence so confused that it is necessary to have the help of God to remove it; so that the fear and terror that impedes their confession is not one which will annoy that false deity that they think they have in the *ololiuhqui*, so as not to fall under his ire and indignation. And thus they say (to it), "Aconechtlahuelis," "may I not arouse your ire or anger against me."

This particular round of investigations completed, the good friar returned to Atenango, seat of his benefice in what is now the state of Guerrero. Here,

. . . knowing the blindness of these unfortunate souls, to remove from them such a heavy burden and such a strong impediment to their salvation,

he began to preach at once against *ololiuhqui*, ordering the vines that grew along the river to be cleared away, and casting quantities of the confiscated seed into the fire in the presence of its owners. With this, he writes, "Our Lord was served." The Indians, predictably, didn't see it that way at all, and when he soon fell seriously ill, they promptly credited the ailment to the displeasure of *ololiuhqui*,

. . . for not having revered it, it being earlier angered by what I had done to it: this is how blind these people are.

He recovered and to prove the Indians wrong, he chose a solemn feast day to assemble the entire *beneficio* for another, more impressive burning of *ololiuhqui*. He ordered an enormous bonfire built, and into it,

. . . with all of them watching, I had almost the totality of the said seed which I had collected burned, and I ordered burned and cleared again the kind of bushes where they are found.

Alas, the old ways persisted:

Such is the diligence of the devil that it works against us, for by his cunning we find each day new damage in this work, and thus it is good if the ministers of each jurisdiction are diligent in investigating, extirpating and punishing these consequences of the old idolatry and cult of the devil. . . .

As Wasson (1967a) notes, throughout these references of early Colonial times

. . . there runs a note of sombre poignancy as we see two cultures in a duel to the death—on the one hand, the fanaticism of sincere Churchmen, hotly pursuing with the support of the harsh secular arm what they considered a superstition and an idolatry, and, on the other, the tenacity and wiles of the Indians defending their cherished *ololiuhqui*. The Indians seem to have won out. Today in almost all the villages of Oaxaca one finds the seeds still serving the natives as ever present help in time of trouble. (pp. 339-340)

Morning Glory and Christian Acculturation

The subtle manner in which the sacred morning-glory seeds have become interwoven with Christian elements is evident in a step-by-step description, paraphrased by Wasson (1967a) from an account dictated by a Zapotec Indian *curandera*, Paula Jiménez of San Bártolo Yautepec:

> First, a person who is to take the seeds must solemnly commit himself to take them, and to go out and cut the branches with the seed. There must also be a vow to the *Virgen* in favor of the sick person, so that the seed will take effect with him. If there is no such vow, there will be no effect. The sick person must seek out a child of 7 or 8 years, a little girl if the patient is a man, a little boy if the patient is a woman. The child should be freshly bathed and in clean clothes, all fresh and clean. The seed is then measured out, the amount that fills the cup of the hand, or about a thimble full. The time should be Friday, but at night, about 8 or 9 o'clock, and there must be no noise, no noise at all. As for grinding the seed, in the beginning you say, "In the name of God and of the *Virgencita* ("dear little virgin"), be gracious and grant the remedy, and tell us, *Virgencita*, what is wrong with the patient. Our hopes are in thee." To strain the ground seed, you should use a clean cloth—a new cloth, if possible. When giving the drink to the patient, you must say three Pater Nosters and three Ave Marias. A child must carry the bowl in his hands, along with a censer. After having drunk the liquor, the patient lies down. The bowl with the censer is placed underneath, at the head of the bed. The child must remain with the other person, waiting, to take care of the patient and to hear what he will say. If there is improvement, then the patient does not get up; he remains in bed. If there is no improvement, the patient gets up and lies down again in front of the altar. He stays there a while, and then rises and goes to bed again, and he should not talk until the next day. And so everything is revealed. You are told whether the trouble is an act of malice of whether it is an illness. (pp. 345-346)

Morning Glory and Mother Goddess

In Spanish the seeds of the morning glory are commonly known as *semilla de la Virgen*, seed of the Virgin. The extraordinary importance of the *doncella*, *niña* or young maiden, in the preparation of the morning-glory infusion as well as the sacred mushrooms and other divinatory agents has been noted by Wasson (1967a), who thought the Indians might have seized on Christian iconography in this connection because it was already familiar to them in their own supernatural system. I think he was quite right: these associations may well have deep roots in the psychedelic complex of pre-Hispanic Mexico.

In 1940, long before the identification of plants in pre-Columbian art assumed its present significance in relation to hallucinogenic research, ar-

Ololiuhqui in art. Once thought to represent the male rain god Tlaloc, this spectacular mural from Teotihuácan, Mexico, dated ca. A.D. 500, actually depicts a great Mother Goddess and her priestly attendants with a highly stylized and elaborated morning glory, *Rivea corymbosa*, the sacred hallucinogenic *ololiuhqui* of the Aztecs.

chaeologists uncovered a complex of mural paintings at Tepantitla, a compound of sacred buildings within the great pre-Hispanic city of Teotihuácan, which flourished from the first to the eighth century A.D. north of the present Mexico City. These paintings have been dated to the fifth or sixth century A.D., when Teotihuácan was not only the greatest urban center in the New World but one of the largest cities anywhere, with perhaps as many as 100,000-200,000 inhabitants.

The most prominent elements in the mural are a deity from which flows a stream of water that covers the earth and feeds its vegetation, and above the central figure a great vine-like plant with white funnel-shaped flowers at the ends of its many convoluted branches. Seeds fall from the deity's hands and two priest-attendants flank the main figure on either side. Below this scene are many small human figures playing, singing, dancing, and swimming in a great lake. Because the painting appeared to conform to a well-known Aztec tradition of a paradise ruled over by the male rain god Tlaloc, and because the deity itself seemed to have some of Tlaloc's attributes, the late Mexican anthropologist Dr. Alfonso Caso identified the mural as Tlalócan, the Paradise of Tlaloc.

That identification has recently undergone major revisions. Several specialists in the art and iconography of ancient Mexico have come to recognize the central deity as not male but female, which eliminates the male Tlaloc of the Aztec pantheon. Instead, the deity of Tepantitla appears now to be an All-Mother or Mother Goddess, perhaps akin to the great Aztec fertility deity Xochiquetzal, Precious Flower, or another of her manifestations, Chalchiutlicue, Skirt of Jade, the Mother of Terrestrial Water. With the reinterpretation of the central deity has come a redefinition of the flowering plant that appears to tower tree-like above her. With Schultes's assistance, the "tree" has been identified by myself as none other than the morning glory *Rivea corymbosa*, clearly recognizable to the practiced eye of the botanist, despite an overlay of mythological elements and the adaptation of natural characteristics to the stylistic conventions of Teotihuácan (Furst, 1974a). Here then we perceive a direct association in an ancient work of art between a Mother Goddess, water, vegetation, and the divine morning glory, a plant that is well known to prefer the banks of streams as its natural habitat and that is still considered to be a messenger of the rainy season, because that is when it first begins to bloom—quite apart from its inherent magical powers of clairvoyance and transformation.

An intricate symbolic network linking the morning glory, fecundity, and the Virgin Mary, not only as the inheritor of the qualities of the pre-Hispanic Mother Goddess but specifically as the divine Mother of life-giving water, was first recognized by Dr. Gonzalo Aguirre Beltrán, a well-known applied anthropologist as well as medical doctor who at this writing is Undersecretary of Education for Cultural and Indian Affairs in the national government of Mexico.

According to some early Colonial sources, he wrote in *Medicina y Magia* (1963), a significant work dealing largely with the effects of acculturation on the religion, medicine, and magic of pre-Hispanic Mexico, the Indians of seventeenth-century New Spain thought of the male *ololiuhqui* as brother to a sacred but botanically unidentified plant called Mother of Water. Intimately related to the male morning glory, this female plant symbolizing a water goddess might have come to be syncretized as the result of Christian acculturation with the qualities of the Virgin Mary, who thereby assumed a Christopagan identity as "Mother of Water" or "Mistress of the Waters"—names by which she is actually still called in some villages of central Mexico.

One cannot help wondering to what degree these post-Hispanic folk traditions might actually reflect much older beliefs—such as those that more than a millenium earlier inspired the unknown master of the Tepantitla murals to link the Mother Goddess of Terrestrial Water and Fecundity with the sacred divinatory morning glory *Rivea corymbosa*.

God of Flowers and "Flowery Dream"

Recently, Wasson (1973), with the expert assistance of Schultes, has again contributed in a major way to our understanding of central Mexican symbolism with an analysis of the floral decorations on a famous stone sculpture of the Aztec God of Flowers, Xochipilli, in the Museo Nacional de Antropología in Mexico City, In addition to what he believes to be stylized depictions of the hallucinogenic mushroom *Psilocybe aztecorum*, he and Schultes identified flowers carved on the god's left leg as near-naturalistic representations of *R. corymbosa*. There is no doubt in my mind that he is correct. Still other flowers depicted on this magnificent fifteenth-century idol were recognized as those of *Heimia salicifolia*, the sacred auditory hallucinogen *sinucuichi* of the Nahua-speaking Indians of central Mexico, and of *Nicotiana tabacum*, one of the two principal sacred tobacco species (the other, as we recall, is *Nicotiana rustica*, *piciétl*).

The generic Aztec term for flower was *xochitl*. In Nahuatl, the language of the Aztecs, writes Wasson (1973: 324), the hallucinogenic experience was called *temixoch*, the "flowery dream," and the sacred mushroom, *teonanácatl* (*teo* = divine, god; *nácatl* = food or flesh), was also known as *xochinanácatl*.

"Flower," then, suggests Wasson, appears to have been used by the Aztec poets as a metaphor for the divine hallucinogens

I think Wasson is right: even now the Huichols, whose language, like Aztec, belongs to the Nahua family, employ "flower" as poetic metaphor for their sacred peyote cactus. I also think Wasson is correct in suggesting that Xochipilli himself was not just god of flowers, spring, and rapture, as he is usually defined, but patron deity of sacred hallucinogenic plants and the "flowery dream."

CHAPTER SEVEN

THE SACRED MUSHROOMS:
REDISCOVERY IN MEXICO

If true, surely one of the more significant developments in the study of the ritual use of plant hallucinogens in Middle America is the recent spate of reports that at least some individuals in two Maya populations in southern Mexico are employing the psychoactive mushroom *Stropharia cubensis** in the context of religious ceremony, divination, or curing. The two groups for which this has been reported—but not as yet wholly confirmed by scientifically trained observers—are the Chol, who live not far from the Classic Maya ceremonial and funerary center of Palenque, Chiapas (which, like other Maya lowland sites is thought to have been built and inhabited by Cholan-speaking Maya), and one small population of Lacandones, of whom only a few remnant groups survive today in the general area of the Usumacinta River near the border of Guatemala. Pending the necessary confirmation, the several accounts that have reached anthropologists and others in the recent past have already led to speculation that perhaps some other Maya-speaking

---

*Although the species name appears to identify this psychedelic mushroom with Cuba, it should not be taken to mean that it is, or originally was, native only to that island or the Caribbean in general. Rather, it was so designated because it was first described in 1906 by F. S. Earle after encountering it in Cuba. *S. cubensis* appears to be a New World variety found mainly—but not exclusively—in Mexico and parts of Guatemala; interestingly enough, a similar species, originally called *Naematoloma caerulescens* but subsequently assigned to the same genus as *S. cubensis*, was identified in 1907 in what is now North Vietnam. For the most recent discussion of the *Psilocybin* mushrooms, including *S. cubensis*, see Steven Hayden Pollock, M.D., "The Psilocybin Mushroom Pandemic," *Journal of Psychedelic Drugs*, Vol. 7, No. 1, pp. 73-84 (1975).

populations may also be found to have retained—or else re-adopted—mushroom rituals that were long thought to have died out among them centuries ago.

Considering the stream of non-Indian mushroom "devotees" that descended on the Mazatec Indians of Oaxaca after their mushroom rites were publicized in the 1950's and early 1960's, perhaps all that should be said for now about the Maya situation is that some reputable scholars have become convinced over the past several years that mushrooms are being employed ritually by at least some Chol and Lacandón Maya. It is true, however, that colleagues who sought to confirm this on the spot were unable to do so in the brief time available to them. At the very least, it seems, the local informants are more reticent on the subject now than even a few years ago. Whatever the reason, the most recent efforts to obtain first-hand information have proved unavailing. The problem is further complicated by a peculiarity of *S. cubensis*: it is a dung fungus that nowadays grows typically on the dung of cattle (as it does, for example, in the grassy meadows all around Palenque). This might lead one to think that it could not be a native New World species but must have been introduced together with cattle after the conquest. Against this, however, we have the fact *S. cubensis* has not been reported in Spain or southern Europe, and, in any event, as we shall see in another chapter, there is a native ruminant whose droppings are perfectly capable of playing host to *S. cubensis* and that played an extraordinarily prominent role in the cosmology of the Maya and other Indian peoples. That animal is the deer.

The use of an hallucinogenic mushroom in Chol country was first reported by a student of M. D. Coe at Yale University (Furst, 1972a:x); the existence of what appeared to be a well-integrated complex of mushroom intoxication, for the purpose of conversing with the deities, was first published by a specialist in Classic Maya art, Merle Greene Robertson (1972), in a paper on the carved monuments of Yaxchilán, an important Maya site on the Usumacinta River. In the course of her research, Mrs. Robertson said, she learned that some Lacandón priests consumed the mushrooms in ritual seclusion, sometimes within the ruins of the smaller temple or funerary structures at Yaxchilán. The mushrooms, she was told, are prepared in specially consecrated pottery bowls that are used for no other purpose and that differ from the so-called "god pots" with anthropomorphic decorations in which incense is burned.

The Lacandones have been subjected to anthropological inquiry for many decades, and it must be emphasized that although ritual intoxication is an essential aspect of their ceremonial life, not one of these investigators witnessed, or heard of, such mushroom rites. Nonetheless, Mrs. Robertson was told by her informants that the sacred mushrooms had served as a medium of communication with the gods for "as long as the oldest" member of that particular group could remember. One cannot help but feel that such information must be taken seriously; the Indians learned long ago—with good and sufficient reason—to conceal and disguise whatever they thought might provoke the wrath or disapproval of the ecclesiastical authorities and other outsiders. Besides, with the exception of peyote, the plant hallucinogens have only recently become the focus of anthropological inquiry in the Americas and elsewhere; field workers are only just beginning to learn to ask the right questions (or better, not to ask questions at all but wait patiently for the information to come naturally, which may, and often does, take many weeks or months of living with the people and convincing them that one means no harm nor desires to change their ways). So it should perhaps not surprise us that neither A. M. Tozzer (1907), author of a classic comparative study of the Lacandones, nor other students of Maya culture considered that ritual intoxication—which has been well-described—might have involved more than just alcohol.

However much it remains to be substantiated, the reported present-day existence of mushroom use among certain Maya groups should go a long way toward settling the question of mushroom "cults" among the ancient Maya, and the reasons for its apparent disappearance from the one area of Middle America where the archaeological evidence for such a cult has been most persuasive.

As Thompson (1970) noted, the Colonial sources on the Maya, which include several useful works on herbal medicines, are silent about intoxicating mushrooms, as well as about other botanically identified psychoactive plants (with the exception of tobacco), however much the sacred mushrooms and plant hallucinogens in general fascinated their contemporaries writing in sixteenth- and seventeenth-century central Mexico. Yet it has long been known that as long as 3000 years ago at least the inhabitants of the highlands and the Pacific slope of Guatemala, as well as some of their neighbors, held certain mushrooms to be so sacred and powerful—perhaps even divine—that they represented them in great number in sculptured stone. In fact, the production of mushroom images or idols of varying symbolic complexity endured in Mesoamerica for nearly two millennia, from ca. 1000 B.C. to the end of the Classic period, ca. A.D. 900, suggesting that a cult of sacred mushrooms not only lasted thousands of years but was anciently more widespread than the sixteenth-century chronicles would lead us to believe.

"Mushroom of the Underworld"

Actually, Thompson was only partly right when he said that the Spaniards were silent on the matter of hallucinogens among the Maya, for several of the early dictionaries compiled by Spanish priests in the Guatemalan highlands demonstrate considerable Indian knowledge of the intoxicating effects of a

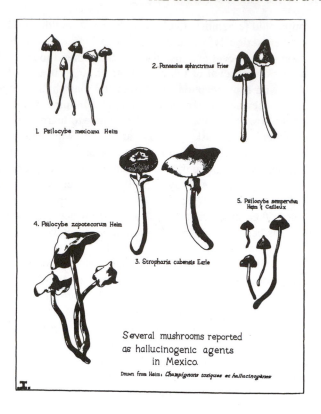

2. Panaeolus sphinctrinus Fries

1. Psilocybe mexicana Heim

5. Psilocybe sempervixa
Heim & Cailleux

4. Psilocybe zapotecorum Heim

3. Stropharia cubensis Earle

Several mushrooms reported
as hallucinogenic agents
in Mexico.

Drawn from Heim: *Champignons toxiques et hallucinogènes*

number of mushroom species.* One of the oldest of the Colonial word lists, the Vico dictionary, which was apparently compiled well before the 1550's, explicitly mentions a mushroom called *xibalbaj okox* (*xibalba* = underworld, or hell, realm of the dead; *okox* = mushroom), with the implication that this species is hallucinogenic. In fact, in this context *xibalbaj* refers not just to the Maya underworld, with its nine lords and nine levels, but also to having visions thereof, so that the name can be understood to mean "mushroom which gives one visions of hell" or "of the world of the dead." The same intoxicating mushroom is also mentioned in a later word list, Fray Tomás Coto's *Vocabulario de la lengua Cakchiquel*, dated ca. 1690 (manuscript in the library of the American Philosophical Society, Philadelphia), which pulls together much of the earlier material on Cakchiquel-Maya. According to the Coto dictionary, *xibalbaj okox*, mushroom of the under-

---

*My colleague Robert M. Carmack, one of the most knowledgeable of scholars in the field of highland Guatemalan ethnohistory and culture, to whom I am indebted for the mushroom references in early highland dictionaries, recently collected mushroom lore from a Quichean-speaking elder, confirming that some of the ancient knowledge continues to survive.

world, was also called *k'aizalah okox*, which can be translated as "mushroom that makes one lose one's judgment."

The Coto dictionary also describes a mushroom called *k'ekc'un*, which inebriates or makes drunk, and another, *muxan okox*, "mushroom that makes the eater crazy" (from *mox*, meaning "mushroom" in the Mixe-Zoque languages of southern Mexico, and "crazy," or "falling into a swoon," in Cakchiquel-Maya of the Guatemalan highlands). Lyle Campbell (personal communication) and Terrence Kaufman, two linguists who have recently investigated the problem of linguistic diffusion in Mesoamerica, believe *muxan okox* to be one of several cases of linguistic borrowing of ritual terms from Mixe-Zoque into Maya languages in ancient times, perhaps as early as 1000 B.C., or even before. Since they also postulate Mixe-Zoque as the language of the Olmecs—the "mother culture" of Mesoamerican civilization —it is tempting to suggest that the Olmecs might have been instrumental in the spread of mushroom cults throughout Mesoamerica, as they seem to have been of other significant aspects of early Mexican civilization.

Mushroom Stones and the Cult of Sacred Mushrooms

Mention in several of the early sources on Guatemalan Maya languages of a mushroom specifically named for the underworld—i.e. the realm of the dead—is especially interesting in light of the discovery of a ceremonial cache of nine beautifully sculptured miniature mushroom stones and nine miniature metates (grinding stones),dating back some 2200 years, in a richly furnished tomb at Kaminaljúyu, a late Preclassic and Early Classic archaeological site near Guatemala City. The coincidence of the number of mushroom effigy sculptures interred with a Maya dignitary and the number of rulers of the traditional Maya underworld immediately impressed archaeologist Stephan de Borhegyi (1961), who proposed that the mushroom idols were almost certainly connected with the Nine Lords of Xibalba, as described in the Popol Vuh, the sacred book of the Quiche-Maya.

Stone effigies of mushrooms have in fact been turning up in archaeological contexts in Guatemala and Mexico since the nineteenth century. Borhegyi, who until his untimely accidental death in 1969 was director of the Public Museum of Milwaukee, Wisconsin, described, classified, and tentatively dated some 50 of these. More recently, a botanist, Bernard Lowy (1971), augmented the list with another 50, mainly from the highlands and Pacific slope of Guatemala. At this writing, Richard M. Rose, an anthropologist working on a classification of all known mushroom effigies, has catalogued more than 200, many dating to the first millennium B.C. The majority were found on Guatemalan soil, but others come from as far south as El Salvador and Honduras, and as far north as Veracruz and Guerrero in Mexico. Unfortunately, with a few notable exceptions, such as the nine miniature sculptures from Kaminaljúyu, the majority of these interesting effigies was not recovered under scientifically controlled conditions, so that reliable information on provenance and context is not usually available (Richard M. Rose, personal communication).

Connection between these sculptures and the historic mushroom cults of Mesoamerica has not always been accepted. Though many mushroom stones are quite faithful to nature, they were, until recently, not even universally thought to represent mushrooms at all, and a few diehards even now, in the face of all the evidence, reject this interpretation. When first reported in the nineteenth century, the sculptures were thought to be phallic symbols only, a theory that still crops up occasionally but that must be rejected as one-sidedly male-centered. To have any validity at all, the phallic element would have to be seen as one half of a male-female unity, in that the arrangement or juxtaposition of stem (male) and cap (female) in the mushroom fits well into the traditional Mesoamerican system of complementary opposites and the synthesis of male and female elements as the essential precondition for fertility and fecundity. (It is this concept that is expressed so well in Mesoamerican cosmology in the merging of a primordial male and female pair of creator gods into a single bisexual being.)

It was Carl Sapper who in 1898 first identified archaeological mushroom stones from Guatemala and El Salvador as idols of deities in the shape of mushrooms, rejecting, on obvious morphological grounds, the notion that they had served as phallic symbols in a fertility cult. Even now one hears it said that perhaps they were used as seats, or as territorial markers, or even that they might have been potter's tools that served for the making of molds for ceramic bowls. Of these, only for the marker opinion could one make some kind of argument—but even if a mushroom idol served anciently to mark the boundary of a community's land holdings, which in any event were considered sacred, it could have done so as idol of a guardian deity rather than as a property marker in the modern sense. In any case, refusal to recognize the sculptures as what they obviously are—mushroom idols—is likely to be a function of R. G. Wasson's ingenious division of people into those who loathe mushrooms and those who like them (or, in his terminology, mycophobes and mycophiles), a dichotomy that he relates to the history of sacred mushrooms in the lives of different populations since remote antiquity. Even without the visual evidence, one would have to explain away the fact that many of these sculptures, especially those that date between 1000 and 100 B.C., not only represent a naturalistic mushroom but also incorporate a human face or figure, or some mythic or real animal—toads and jaguars in particular—that merge with or project from the stem. The jaguar-mushroom association is especially interesting in light of the mention, in the Coto dictionary, of a mushroom called "jaguar ear." One of the most intriguing of these mushroom "idols" depicts the fungus emerging from the upturned mouth of a toad, apparently *Bufo marinus*, the venomous amphibian that i much of Middle America, and also in the South American tropics, stands for the divine earth as Mother Goddess in her monstrous, devouring animal manifestation (e.g. Tlaltecuhtli, "Owner of the Earth," the earth monster in Aztec cosmology, or Toad Mother Eaua Quinahi, also meaning Owner or Guardian of the Earth, of the Tacana Indians of Amazonian Bolivia [Furst, 1972b].) Wasson (1967a), in his previously quoted discussion of the crucial role of the *doncella*, or maiden, in the preparation of ritual hallucinogens, has drawn attention to another interesting synthesis of naturalistic and symbolic elements in a mushroom stone in a New York collection:

The cap of the mushroom carries the grooved ring that according to Stephan F. de Borhegyi is the hallmark of the early pre-Classic[*] period, perhaps B.C. 1000. The stone comes from the Highlands of Guatemala. Out of the stipe there leans forward a strong, eager, sensitive face, bending over an inclined plane. It was not until we had seen the *doncella* leaning over a *metate* and grinding the sacred mushrooms in Juxtlahuaca in 1960, that the explanation of the Namuth artifact came to us. The inclined plane in front of the leaning human figure must be a *metate*. It follows that the face must be that of a woman. Dr. Borhegyi and I went to see the artifact once more: it was a woman! A young woman, for her breasts were only budding, a *doncella*. How exciting it is to make such a discovery as this: a theme that we find in the contemporary Mixteca, and in the Sierra Mazateca, and in the Zapotec country, is precisely the same as we find recorded in Jacinto de la Serna and in the records of the Santo Oficio. (p. 348)

Was the Fly-Agaric Sacred to the Maya?

Mushroom effigies of fired clay have also been found in Mexico, as well as South America. Wasson himself has in his collection a fine terracotta "mushroom priestess" in the Classic Veracruz style, probably from the middle of the first millennium A.D., and I have been able to identify a number of ceramic mushroom depictions in the 2000-year-old tomb art of western Mexico (Furst, 1973, 1974c).

Before we leave the archaeological evidence from Mesoamerica, there is one intriguing point to be made about the probable taxonomy of the various mushroom representations. The morphology of the west Mexican ones leaves little doubt that a species of *Psilocybe* is meant. Some of the clay effigies even emphasize the characteristic knob or bump in the center of the cap. Oddly enough, however—considering that there is no evidence that the genus *Amanita* was ever employed hallucinogenically in Mesoamerica—some Guatemalan mushroom stones seem less to resemble *Psilocybe* than *Amanita muscaria*, the fly-agaric of Siberian shamanism, which also grows in highland Guatemala and elsewhere in North America. On the other hand, the fact

---

*According to current terminology for the cultural phases of Mesoamerican prehistory this should be called Middle Formative. The dating is in any event only approximate.

that the stem or stipe of the mushroom stones is usually thick like that of *A. muscaria*, and not spindly like that of *Psilocybe*, might be a function only of the sculptor's material, especially where the stipe is combined with a human or animal effigy. Perhaps there were formerly also wooden mushroom idols that more closely approximated the characteristics of *Stropharia* or *Psilocybe* mushrooms. In any event, the Quiche-Maya of the Guatemalan highlands are evidently well aware that *A. muscaria* is no ordinary mushroom but relates to the supernatural, what with the fact that they have named it *cakuljá ikox* (*cakuljá* = lightning, *ikox* = mushroom) (Lowy, 1974, 188-191). *A. muscaria* is thus related to the Quiche-Maya Lord of Lightning, *Rajaw Cakuljá*, who also directs the dwarflike rain bringers, called *chacs* in former times but now generally Christianized (in name, not function) as *angelitos*, little angels.

The ceramic art of the Moche civilization of Peru (ca. 400 B.C.-A.D. 500) also includes a number of anthropomorphic mushroom effigies, as well as personages with mushroom headdresses, dating to the first centuries A.D. Even more interesting is a certain class of spectacular pendants of cast gold from northern Colombia and Panama, apparently representing a deity. Most are highly stylized, but they share one feature—a pair of hemispheric headdress ornaments that look vaguely like bells on an old-fashioned telephone. These had long mystified specialists in the prehistoric art of the region until André Emmerich (1965) published a convincing argument that they were pairs of mushrooms that had undergone a stylistic evolution from near-naturalism in earlier pieces to greater stylization, including loss of the stem, in the later ones. Paired mushroomlike head ornaments in fact also occur to the north, on archaeological figurines found in Jalisco, western Mexico. Little is known of pre-Hispanic mushroom use in South America, with the single exception of an early Jesuit report from Peru that the Yurimagua Indians, who have since become extinct, intoxicated themselves with a mushroom that was vaguely described as a "tree fungus."

It is fitting, in the developing story of the Mexican mushrooms, that recognition be given especially to the contribution of that scholarly *amateur* (in the original complimentary meaning of the word), R. Gordon Wasson. It was he and his late wife, Valentina P. Wasson, who in the mid-1950's rediscovered the living mushroom cult of Oaxacan Indians and brought it to the attention of the world, not only in the pages of *Life* and in scientific journals but in a remarkable book, *Mushrooms, Russia and History* (1957). In its pages Borhegyi and Wasson suggested a connection between the sacred mushrooms of Mexico and the prehistoric stone mushrooms of Guatemala— the first time that such a possibility had been considered in print. But this takes us slightly ahead of our story, which should properly begin in the sixteenth century when Sahagún first described slender-stemmed hallucinogenic mushrooms with small round heads that the Aztecs called *teonanácatl*, flesh or food of the gods, which he said were usually taken with honey (as the

Lacandón are also said to take them), and which could have either pleasant or frightening effects. Francisco Hernández (1651) was more specific; he mentioned three different kinds of intoxicating mushrooms that were revered by the people of central Mexico at the time of the Conquest. In the seventeenth century Jacinto de la Serna and Ruiz de Alarcón were still perturbed by the continued survival of such mushrooms in indigenous ritual, but thereafter they pass out of the literature, without a single one having been identified botanically—so much ignored that the economic botanist Safford (1915) decided they had never existed at all and that *teonanácatl* must have been peyote!

Safford's ethnocentric verdict came to be widely accepted although it flew in the face of some very specific historic references (e.g. Sahagún: "It grows on the plains, in the grass. The head is small and round, the stem long and slender"—a description that hardly fits the peyote cactus, which occurs only in the semi-arid northern high desert. One who disagreed was the aforementioned Dr. Reko, who insisted that the old sources were accurate and that the use of hallucinogenic mushrooms had in fact survived in remote mountain villages of Oaxaca.

Found at Last: A Living Mushroom Cult in Mexico

He was to be proved right in the late 1930's. In 1936 "Papa" Weitlaner encountered magic mushrooms for the first time in the country of the Mazatecs in Oaxaca. He sent a specimen to Reko, who forwarded it to the Harvard Botanical Museum, where unfortunately it arrived too badly deteriorated to be identified. In 1938, Weitlaner, his daughter Irmgard, and her future husband Jean Basset Johnson, on a field trip to Huautla de Jiménez became the first outsiders permitted to attend—though not participate in—an all-night curing ritual in which mushrooms were eaten. Johnson, who lost his life in North Africa in 1944, described the experience at a meeting of the Sociedad Mexicana de Antropología in August 1938 and in a more extensive paper published by the Gothenburg Ethnographical Museum (1939).

Mushroom use, he wrote, appeared to be widespread in Mazatec country; shamans, or curers, used them primarily for the purpose of divining the cause of an illness, and during the session it was the mushrooms, which were held in great reverence, that were believed to speak, not the curer. Johnson also confirmed that not just one but several kinds of intoxicating mushrooms were known to the Indians.

In August 1938, a month after the Weitlaner-Johnson experience at Huautla de Jiménez, Schultes and Reko received from Indian informants in the same village specimens of three different species they were told were revered by the people for their visionary properties. Schultes took careful notes of their morphology and in 1939 published the first scientific description. In 1956, the distinguished French mycologist Roger Heim, director of the Muse-

um d'Histoire Naturelle in Paris, identified one as *Psilocybe caerulescens*;
another was defined by the Harvard mycologist Dr. David Linder as *Panaeolus
campanulatus*, subsequently redefined as *P. sphinctrinus*; and the third by
Dr. Rolf Singer as *Stropharia cubensis*.

Schultes and Reko on their field trip in 1938 had also been able to extend
the area of sacred mushroom use beyond the frontiers of Mazatec country to
other Indian groups of southeastern Mexico. In the years since, more mush-
room-using populations have been added to the list, including, as recently as
1970-1971, the Matlatzinca of San Francisco Oxtotilpan, a small town
located about 25 miles southeast of Toluca in the state of Mexico, and possibly also the Chol and Lacandón in the Maya lowlands. The Matlatzinca, who belong to one of the oldest language families of Mexico, the
Otomian, are the first inhabitants of central Mexico to have been identified
with mushroom use since the sixteenth and seventeenth century, and the Chol
and Lacandón are, as already noted, the very first Maya populations for
whom sacred mushrooms have been reported in historic times. Altogether
we now know of about fifteen different Indian groups, each with its own
language, whose curers employ hallucinogenic mushrooms. There are likely
to be still others, including lowland and perhaps even highland Maya-speak-
ers, among whom the ancient practice will eventually be found to have
survived.

"Mycophiles" and "Mycophobes"

In the meantime Mexican mushroom research had entered an entirely new
and more public phase with the entry of the Wassons into the picture. Wasson
was a banker, a vice president of J. P. Morgan & Co. in New York; his wife,
Valentina Pavlovna (who died in 1958), was a Russian-born pediatrician.
Wasson has often told the story of their deep personal stake in mushroom
research, which received its initial impetus with his discovery, on their
honeymoon, that he and she had assimilated from their different parental
cultures very different—indeed, diametrically opposed—points of view toward mushrooms in general, and wild ones in particular:

A little thing, some will say, this difference in emotional attitude toward wild
mushrooms. Yet my wife and I did not think so, and we devoted a part of our leisure
hours for more than thirty years to dissecting it, defining it, and tracing it to its origin.
Such discoveries as we have made, including the rediscovery of the religious role of
the hallucinogenic mushrooms of Mexico, can be laid to our preoccupation with that
cultural rift between my wife and me, between our respective peoples, between
mycophilia and mycophobia (words we devised for the two attitudes), that divide the
Indo-European peoples into two camps. (1972a:186)

In 1952, the Wassons first learned of the early Colonial descriptions of
mushroom rites and their confirmation by Schultes and others in the late

1930's, and, simultaneously, of the remarkable archaeological artifacts called mushroom stones. In 1953 they plunged seriously into the problem, spurred on by a lengthy description of Mazatec mushroom practices they received from Miss Eunice Pike, a missionary linguist with the Wycliffe Bible Translators, who had spent several years among the Indians of Oaxaca. (See Pike and Cowan, 1939.) Belief in the sacred mushrooms was indeed widespread, she confirmed, but the Indians guarded their secrets well against strangers. As Johnson had reported in 1939, she wrote that pre-Christian and Christian religious concepts and terminologies were inextricably intermingled in the Oaxacan mushroom rites (as, indeed, they are everywhere else, with the exception of the Lacandón; Huichol peyote ritual is likewise essentially non-Christian in meaning and terminology). For example, the Mazatecs spoke of the mushrooms as the blood of Christ, because they were believed to grow only where a drop of Christ's blood had touched the earth; according to another tradition, the sacred mushrooms sprouted where a drop of Christ's spittle had moistened the earth and because of this it was *Jesucristo* himself that spoke and acted through the mushrooms. (Hofmann, 1964)*

"A Soul-Shattering Happening"

In 1953 the Wassons went to Oaxaca for the first time, but another two years passed before they were able to develop a sufficiently warm bond of trust with their Indian hosts to be permitted to partake of the sacred mushrooms. So, in 1955, Wasson and a companion, Alan Richardson, became the first outsiders to actually participate in a mushroom curing ceremony—an unforgettable experience, Wasson later reported, that was to profoundly affect him, who by his cultural inheritance had once utterly "rejected those repugnant fungal growths, manifestations of parasitism and decay" (1972a: 185).

In his enthusiasm for the extraordinary psychic effects of the mushrooms and other sacred halluginogens, Wasson would not be misunderstood as suggesting that these are, or were, the only means of attaining the ecstatic state. Clearly, poets, prophets, mystics, and ascetics

. . . seem to have enjoyed ecstatic visions that answer the requirements of the ancient Mysteries and that duplicate the mushroom agapé of Mexico. I do not suggest that St. John of Patmos ate mushrooms in order to write the Book of the Revelation. Yet the

---

*This belief seems to have its origin in indigenous shamanism. In Mexico, as everywhere else in shamanistic religion, supernatural and therapeutic power are attributed to the shaman's spittle, which is sometimes identified (as among the Papago of Arizona) as rock crystals in liquid form, rock crystals being near-universally regarded as crystallized spirits, usually of deceased shamans. Divine spittle is also related to the origin of the sacred mushroom in Siberia (see Chapter Eight).

succession of images in his vision, so clearly seen and yet such a phantasmagoria, means for me that he was in the same state as one bemushroomed. (1972a:196)

Nor would he suggest that Blake had to have taken mushrooms or some other natural hallucinogen in order to write that "he who does not imagine in stronger and better lineaments, and in stronger and better light than his perishing eye can see, does not imagine at all." Nevertheless,

. . . the advantage of the mushroom is that it puts many (if not all) within reach of this state without having to suffer the mortifications of Blake and St. John. It permits you to see, more clearly than our perishing mortal eye can see, vistas beyond the horizons of this life, to travel backward and forward in time, to enter other planes of existence, even (as the Indians say) to know God. . . . All that you see during this night has a pristine quality: the landscape, the edifices, the carvings, the animals—they look as though they had come straight from the Maker's workshop. (1972a:197-198)*

Wasson came away from what he later characterized as a profoundly soul-shattering happening, convinced that the magical powers the Indians had ascribed since ancient times to their revered mushrooms were very real indeed, and that chemistry alone could never fully account for the experience of an ineffable mystery, akin to those of the ancient Greeks, with the simultaneous participation of all the senses:

. . . the bemushroomed person is poised in space, a disembodied eye, invisible, incorporeal, seeing but not seen. In truth, he is the five senses disembodied, all of them keyed to the height of sensitivity and awareness, all of them blending into one another most strangely, until, utterly passive, he becomes a pure receptor, infinitely delicate, of sensations. (p. 198)

The Mosaic Completed

Nevertheless, Wasson was sufficiently a child of the scientific age not to leave it at that (he is, in fact, a meticulous and critical scholar and tireless researcher, as demonstrated by his extraordinary book on the identity of *Soma* [1968] and his latest work, the first definitive monograph on an Oaxacan mushroom rite [1974]). Even before his Mazatec mushroom experience he was in close contact with Roger Heim as one of the leading mycologists in the

---

*It is typical of the syncretistic nature of the present-day mushroom cult that some Oaxacan Indians say God gave them the sacred mushrooms because they could not read and it was necessary for him to speak to them directly through the mushrooms. Eunice Pike and her fellow missionary Florence Cowan (Pike and Cowan, 1959) have related how difficult it is to explain the Christian message to people who are convinced they already possess the means—the sacred mushrooms—to receive the word of God in immediate and vivid form, to visit heaven for themselves, and to establish direct contact with God. Readers interested in other sensitive accounts of the mushroom experience might consult, apart from Wasson's most recent work (1974), Henry Munn's essay in Harner (1973).

western world, and Heim now accompanied him on further expeditions into the mountains of Oaxaca, in consequence of which a dozen or so different mushrooms of the family Strophariaceae, mostly of the genus *Psilocybe*, but also of *Conocybe* and *Stropharia*, were identified. With the additional field work of Singer (1958) and the Mexican botanist Gastón Guzmán-Huerta (1959a, b), by the end of the 1950's the mosaic of the sacred mushrooms of Mexico, completely unknown only twenty years earlier, was reasonably complete.

According to Schultes's summary of 1972, and his and Hofmann's collaborative monograph on the plant hallucinogens (1973), species of *Psilocybe* and *Stropharia* are the most important, the most significant being apparently *Psilocybe mexicana*, *P. caerulescens* var. *mazatecorum*, *P. caerulescens* var. *nigripes*, *P. yungensis*,* *P. mixaeensis*, *P. hoogshagenii*, *P. aztecorum*, *P. muliercula*, and *Stropharia cubensis*. Singer (1958) reported that his own work in Oaxaca failed to find *Panaeolus sphinctrinus*—one of the three hallucinogenic species the Indians gave Schultes and Reko in 1938—in the Mazatec inventory of sacred mushrooms. But as Schultes (1972a) points out, different shamans have their own favorite species and also tend to vary these according to seasonal availability and the precise purpose for which the mushroom is intended. *Psilocybe mexicana*, a small, tawny inhabitant of wet pasture lands, he writes, is probably the most important species utilized hallucinogenically in Mexico, but the strongest psychedelic effects seem to belong to *Stropharia cubensis*.

Heim was able to propagate a laboratory culture of the sacred mushrooms in Paris, but when attempts to isolate the active principles of *Psilocybe mexicana* proved unsuccessful, he submitted several specimens, as well as other species, to Hofmann for analysis at Sandoz. Hofmann was almost immediately successful in discovering the agents responsible for the extraordinary psychic effects of the mushrooms, and, shortly afterwards, in reproducing the chemicals synthetically without the aid of the plants themselves. The principal active agent was identified to be an acidic phosphoric acid ester of 4-hydroxydimethyltryptamine, allied to other naturally occurring organic compounds such as bufotenine and serotonin, and probably derived biogenetically from tryptophane. This he named psilocybine. Also present as an unstable derivative was a compound he called psilocine. The same constituents have been isolated from several North American and European mushroom species that are not used as hallucinogens and for which we have no indication that they were ever so employed (Schultes, 1972a:10).

The active agents of the sacred mushrooms, Hofmann reported, amount to about 0.03% of the total weight of the plants; to achieve the effect of as many

---

*Schultes suggests that this might have been the species employed by the Yurimagua Indians of Peru.

as 30 mushrooms (only a few are actually used at a time in the rite) would require only 0.01 gram of the crystallized powder dissolved in water.

Hofmann (1964) has summarized the most important results of the phytochemical investigation of the sacred mushrooms as follows: Psilocybine and psilocine are chemically-structurally related to serotonin, a substance that occurs in the mammalian brain and that plays a role in the chemistry of brain function. The structural relationship of the active principles of the mushrooms with serotonin provides an explanation for their psychic effects, and offers insights into the biochemistry of the brain itself. The pharmacological phenomena are explainable in terms of central excitation of the sympathetic nervous system. In human subjects, doses of 6 to 20 milligrams bring about, without any physical symptoms worth mentioning, fundamental changes or transformations of consciousness, with wholly different perceptions of space, time, and one's psychic and bodily self. The sense of sight and also that of hearing are greatly heightened, to the point of visions and hallucinations. Not uncommonly, long-forgotten events, often those that belong to the realm of earliest childhood, manifest themselves with extraordinary clarity.

Although he was by no means finished with the phytochemistry of the mushrooms (for example, he himself, in the company of Wasson, was still to experience their wondrous mystical effects in a mushroom rite conducted by the famous Mazatec curing priestess María Sabina [Wasson et al., 1974]), for Hofmann the stage was now set for his discovery in the divine morning glories of lysergic acid derivatives closely related to LSD—just as the synthethis of LSD in 1943 had led to the isolation of psilocybine and psilocine in the sacred mushrooms.

CHAPTER EIGHT

THE FLY-AGARIC:
"MUSHROOM OF IMMORTALITY"

The Koryaks of Siberia have a marvellous tale in which the culture hero Big Raven has caught a whale but discovers that he cannot return him to his proper home in the sea because he is not strong enough to lift the grass bag with the provisions the whale requires to sustain himself on the long voyage. Big Raven appeals to the great deity Vahiyinin, which means Existence, and Vahiyinin tells him to go to a certain place where he will find spirit beings called *wapaq*. If he eats some of these *wapaq* spirits they will give him the strength he needs to gather the bag and assist the whale.

Vahiyinin spat upon the earth and where his spittle fell there appeared little white plants with red hats on which the god's saliva transformed into white flecks. It was these miraculous plants that were the *wapaq*. Big Raven ate some, as he had been told, and soon felt so powerful and exhilarated that he was easily able to lift the heavy grass bag, enabling the whale to return to his home. *Wapaq* showed Big Raven the path the whale was taking out to sea and the manner in which he would return to his comrades. When Big Raven saw all this he told the *wapaq*, "O *wapaq*, grow forever on this earth," and to his children, the people, he said that they should learn whatever *wapaq* had to teach them.

According to Waldemar (Vladimir) Jochelson (1905/1908), a Russian ethnologist who with his colleague Vladimir Bogoras contributed considerable data on the native peoples of Siberia to the American Museum of Natural History's Jesup North Pacific Expedition around the turn of the century, the Koryak believe that the *wapaq* would tell any man who ate them, even if he were not a shaman, "what ailed him when he was sick, or explain a dream to

him, or show him the upper world, or the underground world, or foretell what
would happen to him."

As the reader will undoubtedly have guessed, the *wapaq* of Koryak
mythology is none other than the familiar fly-agaric (*Amanita muscaria*)—the
spectacular red-capped and white-flecked "toadstool" whose renown among
Europeans has for so many centuries floated uncertainly between the realm of
magic and transformation, on the one hand, and death from its allegedly fatal
poison on the other. In reality, the fly-agaric is hallucinogenic rather than
deadly, having served for thousands of years as the sacred inebriant of the
shamanistic religions of the northern Eurasiatic forest belt, especially those of
Siberian hunters and reindeer herders. This enormous region, from the Baltic
Sea to Kamchatka, is the only area in the world outside Middle America
where mushrooms are known to have been employed extensively as sacred
vehicles of ecstatic intoxication in recent times (on a minor, and strictly
localized scale, hallucinogenic fungi have also been used in New Guinea and
Africa). Long ago, however, as Wasson has shown, the religious use of the
fly-agaric was far more widespread in the Old World; it was in fact this
remarkable "mushroom of immortality" that was the mysterious divine inebriating plant deity called *Soma* in the worship of the Indo-European peoples
who invaded India from the northwest ca. 1500 B.C. Of this identification
more later.

As early as the mid-1600's and with greater frequency and more detail
from the eighteenth century on, a variety of foreign travelers with unequal
gifts of observation and objectivity commented on fly-agaric as a ritual
inebriant among the tribesmen of Siberia. Depending on local custom and
tradition, the mushrooms might be eaten raw or cooked, fresh or dried, or in
liquid form either as an infusion or as a decoction of the juices of the
mushroom mixed with berries. Commonly the mushroom seems to have been
allowed to dry to some degree before it was consumed—a significant observation in relation to the psychoactivity of *Amanita muscaria* (p. 93, following).

With the advent of anthropology in the nineteenth century, at least some of
the descriptions of mushroom intoxication and their ritual and mythological
contexts take on a less ethnocentric flavor, but there are also older accounts
that seem remarkably modern in their approach to what must have seemed to
the average European very strange customs indeed. Outstanding in this
respect, as we shall see, was the German naturalist Georg Heinrich von
Langsdorf.

The Fly-Agaric and the Intoxicating Urine

There was one aspect of Siberian mushroom intoxication, reported even in
the earliest sources, that must have seemed singularly shocking to one who
encountered it for the first time—the drinking of the urine of a bemushroomed
person, and also the urine of reindeer that had browsed—as reindeer apparently like to do—on the fly-agaric.

By no means all the tribes that used *Amanita muscaria* also drank fly-agaric urine, but the custom was sufficiently well-developed and widespread to have drawn the attention of almost every observer—from Count Filip Johann von Strahlenberg, a Swedish colonel who spent a dozen years in Siberia as a prisoner of war and reported on his observations in the early eighteenth century, to the trained ethnographers of the late nineteenth and early twentieth centuries, when the Europeanization of Siberia, which had begun in the seventeenth century, was well underway, but before traditional tribal life began to be radically transformed even in the remoter hinterlands in the aftermath of the Russian Revolution.

As one might expect, not all the Europeans who saw the urine-drinking rite were able to report on it with detachment; and there are amusing instances in which the writer tries hard to hint at what he saw, or heard described, without being too specific, lest he offend the delicate sensibilities of his Victorian readers. As mentioned, a notably early exception was Langsdorf, who in 1809 published an extensive description of the fly-agaric among the Koryak, including the urine-drinking rite and at least its pharmacological, if not its ideological, foundation. He was also the only one of the early observers to inquire into the specific nature of the hallucinogenic drug contained in the mushroom—a question that was not to be definitively settled until the late 1960's, a full century after an alkaloid called muscarine, long credited as the main hallucinogenic agent in fly-agaric intoxication but now known to play only a minor role, was first isolated from *Amanita muscaria*.

After describing the psychic effects of the mushroom, which the Koryak took mainly in dried form or soaked in berry juices, Langsdorf turned to the phenomenon of urine-drinking:

The strangest and most remarkable feature of the fly-agaric is its effect on the urine. The Koryaks have known since time immemorial that the urine of a person who has consumed fly-agaric has a stronger narcotic and intoxicating power than the fly-agaric itself and that this effect persists for a long time after consumption. For example, a man may become moderately drunk on fly-agarics today and by tomorrow may have completely slept off this moderate intoxication and be completely sober; but if he now drinks a cup of his own urine, he will become far more intoxicated than he was from the mushrooms the day before. . . . (Langsdorf, quoted in Wasson, 1968:249).

The intoxicating effect on the urine, he continues, is found not only in those who actually eat the mushroom but in anyone who drinks the urine. Because of this peculiar effect the Koryaks could prolong their ecstasy for several days with a relatively small number of fly-agarics:

Suppose, for example, that two mushrooms were needed on the first day for an ordinary intoxication; then the urine alone is enough to maintain the intoxication on the following day. On the third day the urine still has narcotic properties, and therefore one drinks some of this and at the same time swallows some fly-agaric, even if only half a mushroom; this enables him not only to maintain his intoxication but also to tap off a strong liquor on the fourth day. By continuing this method it is possible, as can easily be seen, to maintain the intoxication for a week or longer with five or six fly-agarics. Equally remarkable and strange is the extremely subtle and elusive narcotic substance in the fly-agarics, which retains its effectiveness permanently and can be transmitted to other persons: the effect of the urine from the eating of one and the same mushroom can be transmitted to a second person, the urine of this second person affects a third, and similarly, unchanged by the organs of this animal secretion, the effect appears in a fourth and fifth person. (Langsdorf, quoted in Wasson, 1968:249-250)

Langsdorf, who seems to have been the only one of his time to whom such advanced questions occurred, wondered not only about the psychopharmacology of the fly-agaric drug, but also whether there was something about the mushroom that might impart a special, "possibly quite pleasant," smell and taste to urine, qualities that were known to adhere, for example, to asparagus and turpentine. By analogy, he writes—again considerably ahead of his time—it might be worth investigating whether other psychoactive substances, such as opium, digitalis, cantharides, and the like might also retain their properties in urine. In any event, he concludes, the nature of the fly-agaric

. . . offers the scientist, physician, and naturalist a great deal of food for thought: our *materia medica* might perhaps be enriched with one of the most efficacious remedies. . . .

Not, one would assume, in combination with urine, the very idea of which would have horrified the Europeans—as, indeed, it would shock many of us today. We have to remember, however, that (as Wasson, for whom the urine-drinking aspect of the Siberian fly-agaric rite was to prove of great significance to his identification of *Soma*, has pointed out) in the non-Occidental-ized East the attitude toward urine was very different from that prevailing in the West. In Asia, for example, urine was widely employed as a medicine and a sterile disinfectant and in certain areas served also in religious devotions. Likewise in Aztec Mexico—I have found several references to the therapeutic use of urine in Sahagún's *Florentine Codex*. Not only did Aztec physicians use urine externally to cleanse infections, but it was administered internally as a medicinal drink, particularly for disorders of the stomach and intestines. I hasten to add, however, that there is no hint that urine ever figured in ritual intoxication.

Chemistry and Effects

Wasson (1967b), who has tried the fly-agaric on himself, has summarized what limited knowledge can be gathered from the literature on the subjective effects of the mushroom:

a. It begins to act in fifteen or twenty minutes and the effects last for hours.
b. First it is soporific. One goes to sleep for about two hours, and the sleep is not

normal. One cannot be roused from it, but is sometimes aware of the sounds round about. In this half-sleep sometimes one has coloured visions that respond, at least to some extent, to one's desires.

c. Some subjects enjoy a feeling of elation that lasts for three or four hours after waking from the sleep. In this stage it is interesting to note that the superiority of this drug over alcohol is particularly emphasized: the fly-agaric is not merely better, it belongs to a different and superior order of inebriant, according to those who have enjoyed the experience.* During this state the subject is often capable of extraordinary feats of physical effort, and enjoys performing them.

d. A peculiar feature of the fly agaric is that its hallucinogenic properties pass into the urine, and another may drink this urine to enjoy the same effect. . . . This surprising trait of fly-agaric inebriation is unique in the hallucinogenic world, so far as our present knowledge goes.

Now, if it is not muscarine, which was isolated from *Amanita muscaria* in 1869, that was responsible for these effects, nor bufotenine, which has recently but mistakenly been reported to be an active constituent of fly-agaric, what is responsible?

Recent studies by Professors Conrad H. Eugster (1967) and Peter G. Waser (1967, 1971) of the University of Zurich, a chemist and a pharmacologist respectively, have demonstrated what it is. For while muscarine is present in *A. muscaria* as a minor constituent, not it but rather two isoxazoles, ibotenic acid and muscimole, constitute the principal psychoactive constituents, with others remaining to be studied (Schultes, 1970). It is muscimole that holds the pharmacological key to the urine-drinking custom. Muscimole, they discovered, is an unsaturated cyclic hydroxamic acid that secretes through the kidneys in basically unaltered form. It was this about which Langsdorf speculated as long ago as 1809. But there is more yet, for the investigators discovered that there is a natural conversion of ibotenic acid to the more stable muscimole. And this in turn relates directly to the preferred manner in which the mushroom was consumed. To quote Wasson (1972c:12):

Ibotenic acid is present in the fresh fly-agaric in widely varying amounts, ranging from 0.03% to 0.1%. When the fly-agaric dries, the ibotenic acid steadily disintegrates and disappears. Thus we have the unique situation where a psychotomimetic agent converts itself through simple drying into another active agent that is more potent and far more stable. In [the book] *Soma* I give *in extenso* (and in summary on pp. 153 ff.) the almost unanimous testimony, extending over two centuries and throughout almost the whole of the northern tier of tribes from the valley of the Ob to the Chukotka, that the fly-agaric must *not* be eaten fresh: it should be dried, preferably sun-dried. The empirical knowledge of the Siberian natives is now confirmed by Eugster.

---

*Langsdorf reported that the Koryaks greatly preferred fly-agaric to the vodka of the Russians, because mushroom intoxication was not followed by headache and other unpleasant symptoms.

Before turning to Wasson and *Soma*, let us look once more at the urine-drinking rite in Siberia. According to Strahlenberg (1736):

The Russians who trade with them [Koryak], carry thither a kind of Mushrooms, called, in the Russian Tongue, Muchumor, which they exchange for Squirrels, Fox, Hermin, Sable, and other Furs: Those who are rich among them, lay up large Provisions of these Mushrooms, for the Winter. When they make a Feast, they pour Water upon some of these Mushrooms, and boil them. They then drink the Liquor, which intoxicates them; The poorer Sort, who cannot afford to lay in a Store of these Mushrooms, post themselves, on these Occasions, round the Huts of the Rich, and watch the Opportunity of the Guests coming down to make Water; And then hold a Wooden Bowl to receive the Urine, which they drink off greedily, as having still some virtue of the Mushroom in it, and by this Way they also get Drunk. (Quoted in Wasson, 1968:234-235.)

Langsdorf, we recall, reported in 1809 that for inebriation the Koryak much preferred the fly-agaric to vodka. This would suggest that as early as the eighteenth century, and certainly by the nineteenth, what had formerly been purely religious-shamanistic mushroom intoxication was to some degree breaking down under the impact of the fur trade and the Europeanization of Siberia—akin to what happened in North America with the introduction of whiskey to Indians who had previously been accustomed to ecstatic or dream states as profound religious experiences. On the other hand, we cannot assume that the Europeans were really equipped to understand what they saw or heard. There are accounts from the nineteenth and twentieth century that leave no doubt that the mushrooms were widely regarded as sacred and that their primary purpose was magicoreligious, enabling shamans to communicate with the spirit world (e.g. Jochelson: "Many shamans previous to their seances eat fly-agaric in order to get into ecstatic states" [1908:583]). Jochelson also makes it clear that the eating of sacred mushrooms was not restricted to the rich or even to shamans, and that in any event the crimson *Amanita muscaria* was plentiful in Koryak territory, which contradicts Strahlenberg's claim that the poor had to rely on the fly-agaric urine of the rich in order to get intoxicated, even in the winter when the mushroom is not in season.

As a matter of fact, the way Langsdorf describes the urine-drinking rite suggests that his functional or economic interpretation, while certainly correct, tells only half the story. It seems to me that the sharing of the shaman's own intoxicating body fluid with his fellows, and theirs among themselves, beyond economizing on the supply of fly-agaric could have served to symbolize the total unification of the celebrants with one another and with the personified spirit power of the mushroom. If so, the real meaning of this curious rite is fundamentally the same as the ritual passing of peyote from one to the other on the Huichol peyote pilgrimage, when after the harvest of the sacred cactus, personified as Elder Brother, each pilgrim gives some of his or her peyote to each of the companions, customarily by placing a piece directly into the other's mouth. This giving is repeated several times in a counter-clockwise circuit. "One gives and one receives of the flesh of Elder Brother," intones the officiating shaman, "so that all are of one heart, so that all is unity."

Finally, it should be noted that muscarine, said to induce profuse sweating and twitching in some who take the mushroom directly, seems to be lacking in fly-agaric urine, so that those who drank their own or another's were spared these unpleasant side-effects of mushroom inebriation. One would assume that this too would have contributed far more to the popularity of the practice than economic considerations, aside from whatever symbolic meanings adhered to it.

CHAPTER NINE

R. GORDON WASSON AND THE IDENTIFICATION OF THE DIVINE *SOMA*

In the second millennium before our Christian era, a people who called themselves "Aryans" swept down from the Northwest into what is now Afghanistan and the Valley of the Indus. They were a warrior people, fighting with horse-drawn chariots; a grain-growing people; a people for whom animal breeding, especially cattle, was of primary importance; finally, a people whose language was Indo-European, the Vedic tongue, the parent of classical Sanskrit, a collateral ancestor of our European languages. They were also heirs to a tribal religion, with an hereditary priesthood, elaborate and sometimes bizarre rituals and sacrifices, a pantheon with a full complement of gods and other supernatural spirits, and a mythology rich with the doings of these deities. Indra, mighty with his thunderbolt, was their chief god, and Agni, the god of fire, also evoked conspicuous homage. There were other gods too numerous to mention here. Unique among these other gods was Soma. Soma was at the same time a god, a plant, and the juice of that plant.

So Wasson begins his remarkable work, *Soma: Divine Mushroom of Immortality*, first published in 1968 and republished in 1971 in a popular edition. The Soma sacrifice, in the words of the Vedic scholar Dr. Wendy Doniger O'Flaherty in her review of the post-Vedic history,

. . . was the focal point of Vedic religion. Indeed, if one accepts the point of view that the whole of Indic mystic practice from the Upanisads through the more mechanical methods of yoga is merely an attempt to replace the vision granted by the Soma plant, then the nature of that vision—and of that plant—underlies the whole of Indian

96

religion, and everything of a mystical nature within that religion is pertinent to the identity of the plant. (quoted in Wasson, 1968:95)

The Elusive *Soma* Deity

But that was just the problem—however many species different Vedic scholars have identified with *Soma* in the nearly two centuries since Sanskrit was first translated into European languages, its true identity proved elusive. *Soma* and its sacrifice are celebrated in many hymns, but the *Rig Veda* was sung by the ancient poet-priests for their contemporaries, who did not need to be told what *Soma* was precisely, and they obscured the mysterious plant god's natural morphology with all sorts of poetic imagery and inspired metaphors that hardly qualify, nor were intended, as botanical descriptions (e.g. "mainstay of the sky," with his foot at the earth's navel and his crown in the heavens; "divine udder," "he has clothed himself with the fire-bursts in the Sun," and the like).

Among the plants which Vedic scholars have put forward as *Soma* have been *Sarcostemma brevistigma* and related species; *Ephedra vulgaris*; *Ipomoea muricata*; different species of *Euphorbia*; *Tinospora cordifolia* (a climbing shrub an extract of which is used as an aphrodisiac and a cure for gonorrhea in Indian folk medicine); *Peganum harmala*, *Cannabis indica* (in the form of *bhang*), and even rhubarb. Others have suggested that *Soma* might have been a fermented drink or a distilled liquor. But there is nothing in the *Rig Veda* to suggest a process of fermentation, and distilled alcohol was as unknown in ancient India as it was in the New World before the coming of the Spaniards, not to mention that liquor would have been anathema to the devout Hindu. As a matter of fact, the *Rig Veda* informs us exactly how the marvellous drink was prepared: the dried *Soma* plants were moistened with water to make them swell up again and pounded with pestles. After being filtered through a fine woolen cloth, the tawny yellow inebriating juice was imbibed by the Vedic priests in their sacrificial rites. The effects, as these emerge from the poetic imagery of the hymns, were clearly what we would now call hallucinogenic or psychedelic.

Of the numerous species that have been proposed over the years the most persistent had been the aforementioned *Sarcostemma*, a leafless sprawling herb with a milky juice that is employed as an emetic in Indian folk medicine. It is true that the *Rig Veda* describes *Soma* as having no leaves, but unlike the red-flowered *Sarcostemma*, the mysterious *Soma* plant also lacked roots and blossoms. Nor is there evidence that *Sarcostemma* has psychoactive properties, particularly of the kind implied in such Vedic hymns as one that speaks of the priestly imbiber of the divine *Soma* having the power of flight beyond the limits of heaven and earth and feeling strong enough to pick up the earth itself and move it about wherever he desired.

Indeed, not one of the plants identified with *Soma* before Wasson's fly-agaric theory burst upon the scene of Vedic scholarship

. . . has carried any conviction, and all are implausible philologically, botanically, and pharmacodynamically. It is no wonder that most ranking twentieth-century scholars have come to regard the problem of *soma* as insoluble. (La Barre, 1970c:370)

Multidisciplinary Quest

Wasson initiated his quest for *Soma* in 1963, and he did so from entirely different points of view than had the Vedists. Above all, he recognized his own limitations and drew on a wide variety of disciplines and international experts in their respective fields to assist him. Basically his problem was this: *Soma* was clearly a hallucinogenic plant with certain well-defined subjective effects but lacking a botanical identity. As early as the first millennium B.C. the real *Soma* plant disappeared from Vedic ritual and the name came to be applied to various substitutes, of which none had the same psychic effects as the original *Soma* and all of which were known at least to the priestly caste to be substitutes. This assumption cannot be proven, admits Wasson, but must have been a fact from the very beginning:

The contrast between the ecstasy of *Soma* inebriation as sung in the hymns and the effects, often vile, of any of the many substitutes was always too glaring to be ignored. (1968:7)

But it is the substitutes with which the commentaries on the *Vedas*, the *Brahmanas*, written after 800 B.C., concern themselves, and it is they, not the original *Vedas*, that form the basis for all the plants that have been identified with *Soma* by western as well as Indian scholars. Wasson's methodological astuteness, writes La Barre (1970c),

has been to use the *Rig Veda* evidence alone, eschewing the tempting but wholly irrelevant prolixity of the *Brahmanas*. When taken all together and respected literally for what they say, the *Vedic* apostrophes to *Soma* turn out to be quite exact and mutually consistent botanical descriptions of the mushroom *Amanita muscaria*. . . the fly agaric. (p. 370)

Wasson proposed that the "Aryans" arrived in the Indus Valley from their homeland to the northwest with a well-integrated ancestral cult of the sacred fly-agaric, and that what remained of archaic Siberian mushroom ritual in the eighteenth and nineteenth centuries actually represents a kind of fossil of the ancient ecstatic-shamanistic stratum in which the Vedic rites of the early second millennium B.C. had their ultimate roots. If so, then the Vedic priests would from the start have had to wrestle with the problem of substitutes for the divine plant, for the fly-agaric is not always and everywhere available and like most mushroom species cannot be cultivated. It can, of course, be dried

Amanita muscaria. The divine *Soma* of the ancient Indo-Europeans and magic hallucinogenic mushroom of Siberian shamanism. *Courtesy R. Gordon Wasson.*

and preserved. And here the *Rig Veda's* description of *Soma's* preparation—a dried, leafless, rootless, blossomless plant to which water was added to make it swell up again—certainly suggests dried mushrooms. Similarly, the effects of the divine inebriant—including sensations of enormous strength, already mentioned in the Koryak myth, and of flight to the ends of the universe—fit precisely those of *Amanita muscaria*. Likewise, once one accepts the idea that *Soma* was the fly-agaric, many previously obscure Vedic passages that allude with poetic metaphors to *Soma's* appearance fit remarkably well those of the fly-agaric in its different stages.

But why would the priests have abandoned so miraculous and divine a plant in favor of substitutes that lacked the marvellous properties of the original *Soma*? Even this falls into place as a function of environmental adaptation once one accepts Wasson's thesis. The fly-agaric, as he points out, is a mycorrhizal mushroom which in Eurasia, including the ancient homeland of the Indo-European Vedic-speakers, grows only in an underground relationship with the pines, the firs, and above all, the birches. Where there are no such trees there is no fly-agaric. Stands of conifers were not inaccessible to the northern settlers of India but they were distant; the mushrooms could be dried and transported but the long distances and other factors, such as unpredictable seasonal availability, would have made substitution necessary and acceptable—certainly preferable to total abandonment of the traditional rituals themselves. Eventually, and perhaps even deliberately, the real *Soma* would have come to be forsaken altogether and its identity, though not its sacred meaning and its psychic effects, forgotten by all but the innermost privileged circle of priests.

I might add here that Wasson's thesis can be supported with an analogy from contemporary Mexico. At least two Indian populations that traditionally relied on peyote for their curing rites—the Tepehuanos of western Mexico and the (unrelated) Tepecanos of Veracruz—are known to have recently adopted a post-Hispanic import, a species of *Cannabis* (marihuana), as a substitute, because peyote has become too difficult and costly to obtain from its natural habitat in the north-central Mexican desert, several hundred miles distant from both these indigenous populations.

Fly-Agaric Urine and the Identity of Soma

With this we come to a crucial point in the development of the argument for *Amanita muscaria*, one that has predictably caused no end of debate among scholars. The psychoactive properties of the fly-agaric, we recall, are unique among the psychedelics in that they pass unaltered through the kidneys, which explains why in Siberia it was customarily taken in two forms:

First Form: Taken directly, and by "directly" I mean by eating the raw mushroom, or by drinking its juice squeezed out and taken neat, or mixed with water, or with water and milk or curds, and perhaps barley in some form, and honey; also mixed with herbs such as *Epilobium* spp.

Second Form: Taken in the urine of the person who has ingested the fly-agaric in the *First Form*. (Wasson, 1968:25)

Now, Wasson points out, the *Rig Veda* refers unmistakably to *two forms* of *Soma*. This in itself is not a new discovery, but as he notes, the interpreters of the sacred hymns, knowing nothing of the ethnobotany and chemistry of *Amanita muscaria*, always assumed that the first form was *Soma* juice alone and the second *Soma* mixed with curds or milk. Wasson demonstrates that the two forms parallel rather precisely the two forms of the fly-agaric in Siberian shamanism. For the god Indra and the priests are actually spoken of by the poets as drinking *Soma* and pissing it. One famous verse, cited by the noted Sanskrit scholar Daniel H. H. Ingalls (1971) of Harvard in a review of Wasson's *Soma*, addresses the god Indra thusly:

> Like a thirsty stag, come here to drink.
> Drink Soma, as much as you want.
> Pissing it out day by day, O generous one,
> You have assumed your most mighty force.

This cannot but remind us of the close association between fly-agaric and reindeer in Siberia. The same can also be said of passages that refer to the Rudras, zoomorphic storm deities that protected cattle, drinking and pissing *Soma* in the form of brilliantly shining and colored horses.

Wasson does not assert that the Vedic priests actually drank *Soma*-urine, but he cites passages from early sacred texts as well as later ones that at least allude to such a Siberian-like practice—e.g. Zarathustra's excoriation in the *Gatha* of the *Avesta*, *Yasna* 48.10: "When will you (O Mazdah) do away with the urine of this drunkenness with which the priests evilly delude the people?"

The Controversy Lives On

As might be expected, the identification of *Soma* as a mushroom was not greeted with equal enthusiasm among all Vedic scholars, nor has everyone who accepts his basic thrust—that *Soma* was the fly-agaric—agreed with each and every one of his interpretations of the ancient texts. Professor Ingalls, for example, fully agrees with the fly-agaric identification but not with his theory of urinated *Soma*. The most vehement criticism came from an eminent British scholar, John Brough, Professor of Sanskrit at the University of Cambridge (1971), who insisted that *Soma* cannot and must not be identified on any but internal evidence from the *Rig Veda* itself—a task that has proved insoluble to Vedic scholars—and that any parallel data from outside the Indo-Iranian sphere, such as those from Siberia, are extraneous and irrelevant. Wasson's detailed rejoinder (1972c) published in November by Harvard's Botanical Museum, makes a point that is as applicable to all the sciences—hard, social, natural, or humane—as it is to the discipline to which it is specifically addressed:

Let the Vedists leave off feeding exclusively on the *Rig Veda* and each other. Let them be on easy terms with the outside world, with botanists, chemists, pharmacologists, physiologists: with anthropologists, prehistorians, and students of religion among early cultures, living and moribund and dead. Brough's paper on every page shouts his need (unfelt by him) for those interdisciplinary contacts to which on principle he closes his eyes and ears. If the older generation of Vedists includes many for whom this expanded opportunity is disturbing, younger scholars will certainly seize on it with enthusiasm. (p. 41)

And not just younger scholars either. The greatness of a discovery, writes Professor Ingalls in the aforementioned comment on Wasson's book,

. . . lies in the further discoveries that it may render possible. To my mind the identification of the Soma with an hallucinogenic mushroom is more than a solution of an ancient puzzle. I can imagine numerous roads of inquiry on which, with this new knowledge in hand, one may set out. In a few paragraphs I shall indicate only one such road, a road on which I have traveled a short distance. (1971:190)

Reading Wasson, he writes, inspired him to study *Rig Veda* Book 9, which deals primarily with *Soma*. As a result he began to perceive a qualitative difference between the Soma hymns and certain other hymns of the *Rig Veda*:

The two poles seem to me to be the Soma hymns and the Agni hymns. The two gods represent the two great roads between this world and the other world. . . . They run straight through; they are the great channels of communication between the human and the divine: the sacred fire and the sacred drink.* Greatly to simplify matters, I would put the difference between the Agni hymns and the Soma hymns this way. The typical Agni hymn juxtaposes a given ritual with a mythical prototype, with the *"prathamani dharmani."* The ritual is intended to reactivate the prototype and to give to the participants the strength of their semi-divine ancestors. The Soma hymns, on the other hand, employ their imagery quite differently. The ascent of Soma to the river of heaven is not an act in the mythical past. It is happening right now, as the Soma juice cascades through the trough. (p. 191)

The Agni hymns are reflective, mythological, seeking for harmony between this world and the sacred but always aware of the distinction, while the Soma hymns concentrate on the immediate experience:

I am speaking of two sorts of religious expression and religious feeling, one built about the hearth fire, with a daily ritual: calm, reflective, almost rational; the other built around the Soma experience which was never regularized into the calendar, which was always an extraordinary event, exciting, immediate, transcending the logic of space and time. (p. 191)

Much of this parallels in the most exciting and specific way the peyote ceremony of the Huichols of Mexico. For there again we find the same juxtaposition: on the one hand, the fire god, at once sacred hearth and mediator between the everyday world and the world beyond, the great fire shaman who leads the *peyoteros* into the mythic past, and on the other the divine hallucinogen, Deer-Peyote, and the immediate, ecstatic experience that transcends the boundaries between the here and now and the there and then. But this takes us a bit ahead of ourselves (see Chapters Ten and Eleven).

---

*As the threefold fire god—earthly fire, lightning, and solar fire—Agni is second only to Indra in ancient Vedic and Hindu worship. He is the offspring of the vertical and horizontal sticks of the fire drill, sometimes called Agni's "two mothers." The Vedic word *Agni* is cognate to the Latin *ignis* = fire, and of course also to the English *ignite*.

A New Road of Inquiry

Wasson (1972b) himself also embarked on a "new road of inquiry" that led him to make the intriguing suggestion that the very concept of the Tree of Life and the Marvelous Herb that grows at its base in the folklore of many peoples might have had its genesis in the mycorrhizal relationship between the fly-agaric and certain trees, above all the birch and the pine. Throughout Siberia, he points out, the birch is revered as the shaman's sacred tree, which he ascends in his trance to reach the Upperworld:

Uno Holmberg, in the *Mythology of all Races*, has summarized for us the folk beliefs that surround the birch. The spirit of the birch is a middle-aged woman who sometimes appears from the roots or trunk of the tree in response to the prayer of her devotee. She emerges to the waist, eyes grave, locks flowing, bosom bare, breasts swelling. She offers milk to the suppliant. He drinks, and his strength forthwith grows a hundredfold. . . . In another version the tree yields "heavenly yellow liquor." What is this but the "tawny yellow *pavamana*" of the Rig-Veda? Repeatedly we hear of the Food of Life, the Water of Life, the Lake of Milk that is hidden, ready to be tapped near the roots of the Tree of Life. There where the Tree grows near the Navel of the Earth, the Axis Mundi, the Cosmic Tree, the Pillar of the World. What is this but the Mainstay-of-the-Sky that we find in the Rig-Veda? The imagery is rich in synonyms and doublets. The Pool of "heavenly liquor" is often guarded by the chthonic spirit, a Serpent, and surmounting the tree we hear of a spectacular bird, capable of soaring to the heights, where the gods meet in conclave. (pp. 211-213)

Wasson proposes that this well-known theme had its origin in the Eurasiatic forest belt and not, as has sometimes been suggested, in Mesopotamia and the ancient Near East, where it is found in the Sumerian Gilgamesh epic and, in somewhat different but obviously related form, the Book of Genesis. If his reconstruction holds good, Wasson concludes,

. . . the Soma of the Rig-Veda becomes incorporated into the religious history and prehistory of Eurasia, its parentage well established, its siblings numerous. Its role in human culture may go back far, to the time when our ancestors first lived with the birch and the fly-agaric, back perhaps through the Mesolithic and into the Paleolithic. (p. 213)

If it is indeed that ancient, it would also help explain why the same motif is found in strikingly similar form in Maya art as well as in shamanic tradition and ritual of other indigenous peoples of the New World.

Antiquity and Origins of the Mushroom Cult

It can of course be argued that the two great mushroom traditions, that of New World Indians and that of the peoples of Eurasia, are historically unconnected and autonomous, having arisen spontaneously in the two regions from similar requirements of the human psyche and similar environmental opportunities. But are they really unrelated?

A good though controversial case has been made by some prehistorians for sporadic early contacts across the Pacific between the budding civilizations of the New World and their contemporaries in eastern and southern Asia, perhaps as early as the second millennium B.C. The West, until very recently, consistently underrated the maritime capabilities of the early Chinese, whose ships more than 2000 years ago were not only already considerably larger and more seaworthy than those of medieval Europe but were equipped with an effective rudder of a type adopted by the Europeans only shortly before Columbus embarked on his first voyage of discovery. Moreover, it was the Chinese who invented the compass. So we must at least grant them the potential of having crossed the Pacific, whether they ever did so or not. Now *if*, as seems likely, the Chinese once worshiped an hallucinogenic mushroom and employed it in religious ritual and medicine,* and *if* some of their sages reached the New World, by accident or design, they could of course have introduced some of their own advanced pharmacological knowledge, or at least the idea of sacred mushrooms, to the ancient Mexicans. The same would apply to early India, whose calendrical system, like that of China, bears a perplexing resemblance to its pre-Hispanic Mexican counterpart. But these are very big *ifs* indeed.

Considering the proven antiquity of hallucinogens in the New World, it seems more reasonable to refer back to La Barre's argument and consider the problem in the context of the ecstatic-shamanistic phenomenon as a whole. The roots of the New World mushroom complex, as of the other ritual hallucinogens, would then have to be sought in a common pan-Eurasiatic-American Paleo-Mesolithic substratum, predating not just the evolution of advanced transoceanic sailing capabilities in ancient China or southern Asia, but even the first peopling of the New World. In that case, we could see the sacred mushroom of Paleo-Siberian tribes as prototype for all the ritual hallucinogens that proliferated so spectacularly among New World Indians, and the sacred mushrooms of Middle America as linear descendants of the fly-agaric.

This approach is the more plausible in that Wasson himself has traced some of the common names for the fly-agaric in Indo-European languages to Proto-Uralic, which ceased to be spoken around 6000 B.C. (the Proto-Uralic term was **panx*, ancestral to the Ob-Ugric *pango*, the Gilyak *pangkh*, as well as our *fungus* or *punk*). The seventh millennium B.C. is obviously substantially later than the major movements of the proto-American hunters who

---

*Wasson (1968:80-92) makes a persuasive case that the celebrated *Ling Chih*, the supernatural fungus of immortality and spiritual potency, endlessly represented in Chinese art from early times, had its genesis in the Eurasiatic cult of the divine hallucinogenic mushroom—i.e. *Soma* = *Amanita muscaria*—even through its abundant artistic forms came to be based on *Ganoderma lucidum*, an inedible species of woody fungus.

carried their north Asian intellectual and material heritage from Siberia to Alaska across the Bering land connection, the thousand-mile-wide corridor of low-lying tundra that was submerged when the sea level rose by 200-300 feet with the melting of the Pleistocene glaciers about 12,000 years ago.

But old though it is, we might imagine that Proto-Uralic was probably still a language of the distant future when the psychodynamic properties of the fly-agaric were first discovered by some venturesome shaman of an unknown Paleo-Eurasiatic hunting people exploring his environment not only for medicinal species but also for plants capable of transporting him to different, non-ordinary, planes of existence.

Discovery of Hallucinogens: Deliberate or Accidental?

Which brings up a point that was raised in the Introduction in relation to the plant hallucinogens in general: it is almost impossible to conceive that the discovery of the transformational qualities of certain acrid mushrooms that were clearly unsuitable as ordinary food could have been anything but the result of conscious search for psychodynamic agents and even deliberate experimentation for different ways to activate or heighten their effects. As we saw, this requirement applies especially to the fly-agaric, since it was dried, preferably in the sun, to have the desired effect.

That the Mexican mushrooms, on the other hand, can be eaten fresh* could, I suppose, mean that their magical properties were accidentally discovered when people already accustomed to wild mushrooms in their diet tried them as food. Perhaps so. Certainly it could have been the case in some very remote, primordial time. But to suppose this of the ancestors of the Indians of Oaxaca, one would have to conjure up a vision of the most primitive kinds of humans scavenging almost indiscriminately for anything that appeared edible—a picture that squares with absolutely nothing we know of the food-gathering behavior of the most technologically primitive hunters still left on earth and even less of incipient cultivators. Moreover, an environment in which mushrooms grow is not likely to have been deficient in all kinds of edible resources with far greater food value than the characteristically small and fragile sacred fungi.

What we must also remember is that traditional or pre-industrial people who live in harmony with their environment are the inheritors of a far more sophisticated level of knowledge than ours of the natural world on which their lives depend, and that they discriminate much more decisively and often more accurately than do we between its different phenomena. In the present case

---

*As was pointed out to me by Wasson, anciently a common method of consuming the sacred mushrooms was to press them out and drink their juice—i.e., the same way *Soma* was taken in Asia. However, they could also be eaten raw, often with honey, as indeed they often are today by Mexican Indians.

this reminder implies that ordinary and magic mushrooms should not even belong to the same category. And that is precisely the situation as we find it among present-day Indians.

As mentioned earlier, the Matlatzincas, who live about a hundred miles southwest of Mexico City, in a valley surrounded by pine forests and towered over by the majestic 15,000-foot-high Toluca volcano, have recently been added to the growing list of sacred-mushroom-using populations. Ordinary wild species also figure importantly in their diet, so that they would certainly fall into Wasson's category of "mycophiles." However, the sacred fungi and ordinary kinds are not simply lumped together under an all-embracing category of "mushroom." Rather, the hallucinogenic species is considered entirely separately, being grouped with such supernatural phenomena as God, the Virgin Mary, saints, ancestors, mountain spirits, and the like.

The Matlatzincas' highly complex mushroom taxonomy has been studied in detail by the Mexican linguist Roberto Escalante, and I am indebted to him for the data that follow. (Also see Escalante, 1973; Escalante and López, 1971.)

To the Matlatzincas, as to other Indians of Mesoamerica, edible mushrooms are of great dietary importance because they sprout during periods of scarcity, when the maize is growing in the fields but when it is still too early for the harvest. During the rainy season, when little work is required in the fields, mushroom gathering involves the entire family, regardless of sex or age, so that it is essential that the criteria of identification be thoroughly familiar to everyone.

A Mexican Indian Mushroom Taxonomy

No less than 57 different species or varieties are distinguished, named, and classified down to the last detail, including external characteristics and extending even to specific use or uselessness of each variety. Two principal nonhallucinogenic groups are recognized, one identified by the generic prefix *xi* (the smuts), the other by *chho*, followed by more specific phrases or terms that identify the species respectively by habitat, color, form, texture, similarity to other objects, and the like—for example, Green Mushroom of Maize, Mushroom (like) Gourd, Mushroom of the Birch. The Matlatzincas also know exactly which species are "companions"—i.e. sprout at the same time—which can contribute to identification where an edible species closely resembles a poisonous one. Over-all, mushrooms are considered to be formed of three parts—the cap, called "its little face," the stem or stalk, "its little foot," and the gills, "its inside," although some species utilized by the Matlatzinca may, like the puffballs, be recognized as consisting only of the "little face." In any event, in order to identify the mushrooms the Indians first observe the whole, then the "little face," then "the little foot," and finally the interior. Needless to say, such careful observation is especially important where an edible species is closely related and similar to a dangerously toxic one, as in the case of the edible *Amanita* species.

Now, in contrast to the edible species identified by the generic prefixes *xi* or *chho*, meaning mushroom, the sacred hallucinogenic species, *Psilocybe muliercula*—which are gathered near the river bank and which must always be replaced by an offering of wild flowers—are not called "mushroom" at all but are identified as divine personages: *ne-to-chu-táta* = (dear) little sacred lords, or, in Spanish, *santitos*, literally *saints* but also signifying ancestors, divine ancient ones, and the like.*

Matlatzinca mushroom taxonomy, which places edible mushrooms in one category and the hallucinogenic kind into a wholly different metaphysical one, alongside deities and spirits, illustrates not only how thorough must be knowledge of the plant world when survival itself depends on it, but also that we must not assume a functional relationship between mushrooms in the daily diet and mushrooms as divine beings or mediators between man and the supernatural. To most of us, all mushrooms, sacred or culinary, may look more or less alike, but to the Indians they are wholly different experiential phenomena.

Hallucinogenic Mushrooms North of Mexico

As a matter of fact, the ethnographic and ethnobotanical situation in North America proves just that. While we have as yet no conclusive evidence that any kind of psychoactive mushroom was employed by Native Americans north of Mexico, however important edible mushrooms might have been to their diet, it is a fact that, as was noted in a previous chapter, a number of varieties containing psilocybine and other hallucinogenic compounds occur in North America, including species of *Psilocybe*. Moreover, as La Barre (1970c) has pointed out, the flaming-red variety of *Amanita muscaria*—the sacred species of the northern Eurasians—is native not only to Asia and Europe but to British Columbia, Washington, Oregon, and Colorado, as well as the Sierra Madre of Mexico. The yellow variety occurs elsewhere in North America, including the northeast, especially in coniferous and birch forests— precisely the favorite habitat of *Amanita muscaria* also in the Old World.

We shall never know whether any memory of its wondrous properties remained with the first Americans to encounter the fly-agaric in their new northern environment, or indeed if any of their descendants ever tried it.

Ne-to-chu-táta, it is said, will diagnose the cause of the illness and prescribe the medicine, and even give a massage to the afflicted organ. Beautiful visions are also reported, including flowers, stars, and gardens, as well as terrible ones, such as blood oozing from cornstalks, serpents, skeletons, and dismembered bodies. The last is especially significant in that visions of dismemberment and skeletonization are related by the Matlatzincas—as by other traditional peoples—to shamanic initiation.

There is no direct mention of fly-agaric use in any of the oral traditions of which we have records. Yet in historic times the urine of shamans was considered to possess great magical and therapeutic powers by some of the Northwest Coast tribes; shamans preserved their urine carefully in containers reserved for that purpose and employed it to guard themselves and others against malevolent beings, by such techniques as blowing it through tubes in the direction of supernatural danger. Alaskan Eskimos, whose culture originated in Siberia some 13,000 years ago, likewise respect urine for its magical properties, and hold the bladder in high regard as the seat of special powers. Could such beliefs be survivals of a more ancient fly-agaric urine-drinking tradition?

If so, all knowledge of it has certainly long been lost, while in Mexico *Amanita muscaria's* Eurasiatic role as the mushroom of divine knowledge was assumed—when, we do not know—by fungi of very different appearance and pharmacology.

What we do know is that when the hunters of bison and mammoth in the Late Pleistocene reached and settled the country of the Rio Grande, they also discovered a new ritual inebriant, the highly toxic, red beanlike seed of *Sophora secundiflora*, which their descendants were to employ for the next 10,000 years in ecstatic-shamanistic medicine cults, until autonomous Indian culture succumbed to Anglo-American expansionism and the more benign peyote was adopted as the sacrament of a new, syncretistic pan-Indian religion.

CHAPTER TEN

THE "DIABOLIC ROOT"

The earliest hallucinogenic cactus depicted in ancient American art is a tall, columnar member of the *Cereus* family, *Trichocereus pachanoi*, the mescaline-containing *San Pedro* of the folk healers of coastal Peru (Sharon, 1972). *San Pedro* has been identified in the funerary effigy pottery and painted textiles of Chávin, the oldest of a long succession of Andean civilizations, dating to ca. 1000 B.C., and also in the ceremonial art of the later Moche and Nazca cultures, which gives this sacred psychedelic cactus of western South America a cultural pedigree of at least 3000 years.

But the most important, chemically and ethnographically most complex, hallucinogenic member of the cactus family—in terms of its history, the popular, scientific, religious, and legal attention it has drawn, and its cultural utilization from early times to the present—is a small spineless North American native of the Chihuahuan desert, *Lophophora williamsii*, better known as "peyote."

Despite its relatively restricted desert habitat, extending from the Rio Grande drainage basin in Texas southward into the high central plateau of northern Mexico between the eastern and western Sierra Madre mountains, to the approximate latitude of the Tropic of Cancer, peyote was held in great esteem over much of ancient Mesoamerica, where its earliest artistic representation—in mortuary ceramics found in western Mexico—dates to 100 B.C.-A.D. 200. It is still highly valued by many Indians, and for one indigenous population, the Huichols, it stands as it did in pre-Hispanic times at the very center of a shamanistic system of religion and ritual that has remained uniquely free of major Christian influences.

Finally, the divine cactus of the Huichols and of earlier peoples has evolved into the sacrament of a new religious phenomenon, the pan-Indian

Lophophora williamsii. Peyote in flower; cultivated material from the Río Grande of Mexico.

peyote cult which, born out of profound spiritual and sociocultural crisis in the nineteenth century, spread northward from the Texas border as far as the Canadian Plains. Now it is incorporated as the Native American Church, with an estimated 225,000 adherents. Its remarkable history, and that of the long struggle of Indians, anthropologists, and civil libertarians to win legal status for peyote in the face of scientifically absurd and constitutionally questionable state and federal narcotics laws, is documented by La Barre in *The Peyote Cult*. First published in 1938, this classic anthropological work has been repeatedly brought up to date and republished, most recently in 1969 and again in 1974.* In this chapter and the next, I will attempt from personal experience to convey something of the form and the meaning of "peyotism" in an aboriginal Mexican setting that certainly contributed, if it was not ultimately ancestral to, its North American manifestation.

---

*The anthropological literature is rich in North American peyote studies, outstanding among them the writings of Omer C. Stewart on Ute and Paiute peyotism, David F. Aberle's *The Peyote Religion among the Navaho* (1966), and J. S. Slotkin's *The Peyote Religion* (1956). The latter is especially interesting because Slotkin, an anthropologist, himself joined the Native American Church of North America and became one of its elected officials. His book was intended, he wrote (1956:v), as a "documented exposition of Peyotism for Whites, from the Peyotist point of view." For public support by anthropologists for religious freedom for Indian peyotists see, for example, La Barre *et al.*, "Statement on Peyote," in *Science* (1951:582-583).

A "Factory of Alkaloids"

Peyote is popularly identified with its best-known alkaloid, mescaline, but in fact mescaline is only one of more than thirty different alkaloids that have so far been isolated, together with their amine derivatives, from this remarkable plant, which Schultes (1972a) aptly calls "a veritable factory of alkaloids." Most of these constituents belong to the phenylethylamines and biogenetically related simple isoquinolines; and almost all are in one way or another biodynamically active, with mescaline as the principal vision-inducing agent (p. 15).* But peyote is a very complex hallucinogenic plant, whose effects include not only brilliantly colored images as well as shimmering auras that appear to surround objects in the natural world, but also auditory, gustatory, olfactory, and tactile sensations, together with feelings of weightlessness, macroscopia, and alteration of space and time perception. Because of the physiological interaction of the different alkaloids in the whole plant, Schultes cautions against too close an equation of the effects of synthetic mescaline, such as those described so eloquently by Aldous Huxley, with the psychic experiences of Indian peyotists.

Although the Church did not hesitate to employ the harshest measures to banish peyote from native use as "the diabolic root," at one point going so far as to equate its consumption with cannibalism (!), the cult of the sacred cactus survived Colonial repression; the supernatural and therapeutic powers anciently attributed to it remained intact. One reason certainly was the physical isolation of some of the groups that most esteemed peyote. The Huichols and their close cousins the Coras, for example, continued to enjoy relative freedom from Spanish overlordship even after their rugged territory in the western Sierra Madre was nominally brought under Colonial military and ecclesiastical sway about 1722. Missions were established but the Indians successfully resisted conversion. There was some acculturation, but ideologically and physically the Huichols continued to be relatively autonomous, a condition that became even more pronounced after Mexican independence. It is this isolation from the sociological and religious mainstream of post-Conquest Mexico that largely explains why the 10,000 Huichols preserved so

---

*The giant saguaro cactus (*Carnegiea gigantea*, also known as *Cereus giganteus*) of the Sonoran desert in Arizona and northern Mexico has been found to contain three alkaloids closely related to the tetrahydroisoquinoline alkaloids in *Lophophora williamsii* (peyote). These are carnegine, salsoidine, and gigantine, the latter said to cause hallucinogenic reactions (Bruhn, 1971:320-329). As noted elsewhere, dopamine has also been isolated in the stems of the saguaro. Saguaro fruit was a favorite food of the Indians of the region, who also used it to make a potent alcoholic beverage consumed at an annual festival called, in Pima, *Navaíta*, from *navaít*. intoxicating drink or wine (the Huichols call their fermented maize drink by the related term *nawá*). Whether the Pima, Papago and other peoples of the area, or their prehistoric ancestors, ever made use of the alkaloid-containing saguaro stem, for curing or other ritual purposes, is not known, but Mexican Indians to this day value close relatives of the saguaro for their curative powers.

much more of their pre-European religious heritage than did other Mesoamerican Indians.

In modern Mexico peyote has long been available in many herbal markets
as a highly esteemed medicinal plant. Nor do the Huichols (who more than
any other indigenous population consider peyote sacred—indeed, divine—
and who take it mainly in ceremonial contexts) have any sanctions, legal or
ethical, against its extraritual use. It is employed by them therapeutically
against a variety of physical ills, it is taken for relief from fatigue, and it is
often consumed just for its pleasurable psychic sensations. But it is never
regarded simply as a "drug," never deemed on a par with other chemicals
with which the Huichols have become increasingly familiar through the
Government's medical services to even the most remote Indians. A news-
paper reporter who made the mistake of calling peyote a "drug" while
interviewing a Huichol shaman in my presence was indignantly told, "*As-
pirina* is a drug, peyote is sacred," and warned not to confuse such important
matters.

"Mescaline": A Misnomer

I should mention here that not only "mescaline" but also "peyote" are
actually misnomers. *Lophophora williamsii*, sometimes called "mescal but-
ton" (hence "mescaline") has nothing whatever to do with the species of
agave from which the potent liquors known as mescal and tequila are
distilled. "Peyote" itself derives from the Aztec *peyótl*, a term that was
applied not just to *Lophopora williamsii* but also to several other unrelated
plants with medicinal properties. The Huichols call the sacred cactus *híkuri*,
and since they share this term with several other peoples belonging to the Uto-
Aztecan or Nahua language family, *híkuri* is probably the correct aboriginal
name.

That peyote, like coca (*Erythroxylon coca*) in the Andes, is an effective
stimulant against fatigue has been known for some time. For this we have,
among others, the testimony of Carl Lumholtz (1902), the Norwegian pio-
neer ethnographer of the Huichols and other Mexican Indians, who traveled
widely in the Sierra Madre in the 1890's. On one occasion, totally exhausted
at the bottom of a deep canyon after a long trek and unable to walk another
step (to make matters worse he had just recovered from a bout with malaria),
he was given a single *híkuri* by his Huichol friends:

The effect was almost instantaneous, and I ascended the hill quite easily, resting now
and then to draw a full breath of air. (pp. 178-179)

More interesting still are recent laboratory tests confirming that when the
Indians call peyote "medicine" it was not in terms just of supernatural power
("medicine power" in Plains Indian terminology) but rather of actual medication. Researchers at the University of Arizona isolated a crystalline substance
from an ethanol extract of peyote which, they found, exhibited antibiotic

activity against a wide spectrum of bacteria and a species of the imperfect fungi, including strains of penicillin-resistant *Staphylococcus aureus* (McLeary, *et al.*, 1960:247-249).

The Huichols, to whom peyote is synonymous with and qualitatively equivalent to the divine deer or supernatural Master of the Deer Species, take the hallucinogenic plant mainly in two forms. One is the fresh cactus itself, whole or cut into pieces, in which form it is equivalent to the flesh of the deer. The other is the cactus macerated or ground on a metate and mixed with water. The latter combination symbolizes, among other meanings, the symbiosis or interdependence of the dry season and the wet, hunting and agriculture, and male and female (cactus and deer being male and water female).

The Sacred Quest for Peyote

Peyote is not native to the Sierra Madre, so that the Indians have to travel long distances to obtain the necessary supplies—for the ceremonies, personal use, and trade to Indian neighbors. While this pilgrimage is by far the most sacred enterprise in the annual ceremonial cycle and also serves as a rite of initiation, not every Huichol adult has been a participant, nor can it even be said that everyone has tasted peyote. The pilgrimage is not required, but like that of the devout Moslem to Mecca, it is a sacred task, fraught with enormous potential benefit for one's own life and the welfare of one's kin, a task to which many Indians aspire at least once, to which would-be shamans must commit themselves a minimum of five times, and which some of the oldest and most traditional have repeated as many as ten, twenty, or, in rare instances, even thirty times over their lifetime.

For at the end of that long and arduous trail, 300 miles northeast of Huichol territory, in the high desert of San Luis Potosí, lies Wirikúta, the mythic place of origin. Here dwell the supernaturals known as the *Kakauyaríxi*, the Ancient Ones, divine ancestors, in their sacred places. Here the *híkuri*, the magic cactus, manifests itself as Elder Brother Deer, the mediator whose divine flesh enables not just the elect, the shaman, but also the ordinary Huichol to transcend the limitations of the human condition—"to find his life," as the Indians say.

Mythic Origins of Peyote

I remember one elderly *mara'akáme* (the Huichol term meaning both curing and singing shaman and sacrificing priest) of great renown, of whom it was said that he had made this difficult journey no less than 32 times—on foot! Walking in both directions was the traditional way, but nowadays most Huichol *peyoteros* make use of whatever transportation is available—autos, trucks, buses, horse-drawn wagons, even the train. This is acceptable so long as all the sacred places along the way are properly acknowledged with offerings and prayer, and all other ritual requirements are fulfilled. The pattern was established long ago, in mythic times, when the Great Shaman,

Fire, addressed as Tatewarí, Our Grandfather, led the ancestral gods on the first peyote quest. It is told that the fire god came upon them as they sat in a circle in the Huichol temple, each complaining of a different ailment. Asked to divine the cause of their ills, the Great Shaman, Fire, said they were suffering because they had not gone to hunt the divine Deer (Peyote) in Wirikúta, as their own ancestors had done, and so had been deprived of the healing powers of its miraculous flesh. It was decided to take up bow and arrow and to follow Tatewarí to "find their lives" in the distant land of the Deer-Peyote.

These gods were male, but true to Huichol belief that only unification and proper balance of male and female guarantees life, along the way, at the sacred water holes in the desert the Huichols call Tateimatinieri, Place of Our Mothers, they were joined by the female component of the Huichol pantheon, the Mother Goddesses of terrestrial water and rain, and of the fertility and fecundity of the earth and all the phenomena of nature, including humanity. In their animal aspect these mother goddesses are snakes, a symbolic identification the present-day Huichols share with pre-Hispanic peoples.

Every Huichol is completely familiar with this peyote tradition and the sacred itinerary. Each year, when the first ears of maize and the first young squashes have ripened in the fields, a lengthy ceremony is held for the youngest children, who are equated with the first fruits of agriculture, and for whom the shaman-elder of the kin group recites the story in repetitive song to the accompaniment of his magic drum.

I participated in two peyote pilgrimages, in 1966 and again in 1968. What follows is essentially based on the second of these, when we transported sixteen Huichols, including four women and three children, the youngest only seven days old at the outset, from Nayarit in western Mexico to Wirikúta in two motor vehicles.* Both these pilgrimages were led by the late Ramón Medina Silva, a charismatic, gifted artist and shaman who had lived for some years on the fringes of traditional Huichol subsistence-farming society but who was nonetheless firmly committed to the validity of Huichol religion and tradition. The 1968 pilgrimage was his fifth, culminating his self-training as a *mara'akáme*. He was to lead two more, one entirely on foot (in fulfillment of a commitment to the divine ancestors for curing his wife Lupe of rheumatoid arthritis), before his tragic death in June 1971 in a shooting incident during a

---

*For other first-hand data on the peyote pilgrimage see Barbara G. Myerhoff's *The Peyote Hunt* (1974), an excellent anthropological analysis of the whole deer-corn-peyote symbol complex, and Fernando Benítez, *In the Magic Land of Peyote* (1975), a sympathetic and insightful chronicle of the pilgrimage and its meaning by a well-known Mexican historian-journalist. Dr. Myerhoff's book deals with the 1966 peyote hunt, in which we were both privileged to be "participant observers."

fiesta to celebrate the clearing of Sierra forest land for a new maize plot. Such fiestas customarily involve much drinking and it was this that led to his death. He was then about 45 years old.

As the German ethnographer Konrad Theodor Preuss (1908) observed earlier in this century, Huichol shamanism and ritual, while sharing many basic elements, tend toward the idiosyncratic in actual performance, and no two shamans, even from the same community, are likely to agree entirely on a single rendition of a particular tradition. Nonetheless, the basic structure remains. So it was with Ramón's version of the peyote quest: here and there it differed from others that have been described to me, but in its essentials it

Ramón. The leader of the peyote quest described in these pages, using his hunting bow as ritual musical instrument. This is the same weapon with which the sacred cactus, identified with the deer deity, is "hunted" and sacrificially slain.

conforms remarkably well to those recounted, on the basis of informants' statements, by Lumholtz and more recent students of Huichol culture.

"We Are Newly Born"

Absolutely essential to the physical and metaphysical success of the sacred peyote enterprise is a rite of sexual purification, intended to return the pilgrims to a state of prenatal innocence. It requires all those present, men and women, to identify by name and in public each and every sexual partner since puberty. This applies even to those who will not actually make the journey but remain behind to keep the divine hearth fire—one of the manifestations of the fire deity—burning for the duration of the pilgrimage.

To appreciate this one has to know that the polygamous Huichols, while espousing the ideal of marital fidelity, are not especially noted for adhering to it, that the participants are usually drawn from the same small community, commonly from households more or less closely related by blood or marriage, and that the attentive audience more likely than not includes the very sexual partners whose names are publicly proclaimed. Yet it is an absolute require-ment that no one present, be it husband, wife, or lover, must show the slightest sign of anger or jealousy. Indeed, such feelings must be banished from one's innermost being—"one's heart," as the Indians say—and the confessions must be received with good humor, even high spirits. Hence, instead of recriminations or tears, in the two sexual purification rites which we attended there were laughter, shouts of encouragement, and sometimes joking reminders from husbands, wives, and other relatives of love affairs inadvertently or deliberately omitted.

As officiating shaman and manifestation of the old Fire God Tatewarí (who is also present in the ceremonial fire around which the group assembles as personators of the original, divine pilgrims of mythic times—for each peyote pilgrimage reenacts the first quest for the divine cactus), it was Ramón's task to accept the confession of sexuality and "unmake"—i.e. reverse—the pilgrim's passage through life to adulthood and return him or her symbolically to infancy and a state akin to that of spirit. The Huichols say: "We have become new, we are clean, we are newly born."

The tender state of the "newborn" pilgrims is also symbolized in a knotted string that ties the pilgrims symbolically to one another and, through their shaman, to the Earth Mother herself. As though tying off the umbilicus, the shaman ties one knot for each companion and then rolls the cord into a spiral which he attaches to the back of his hunting bow. This spiral is metaphor for the journey to "the place of origin" and the subsequent return to "this world"—i.e. death and rebirth.

The symbolic navel cord whose knots will be untied upon their return from Wirikúta must not be confused either with the knotted calendar cord men-tioned by Lumholtz (but omitted in our two pilgrimages), or with yet another knotted string that plays a crucial role in the obliteration of adult sexuality. This cord is one into which the shaman has "tied" everyone's sexual experience and whose sacrifice by fire completes the purification rite.

The Dangerous Passage

Having symbolically shed their adulthood and human identity the pilgrims can now truly assume the identity of spirits, for just as their leader is Tatewarí, the Fire God and First Shaman, so they become the ancestral deities who followed him on the primordial hunt for the Deer-Peyote. In fact, it is only when one has become spirit that one is able to "cross over"—that is, pass safely through the dangerous passage, the gateway of Clashing Clouds that divides the ordinary from the nonordinary world. This is one of several Huichol versions of a near-universal theme in funerary, heroic, and shamanistic mythology.

That this extraordinary symbolic passage is today located only a few yards from a heavily traveled highway on the outskirts of the city of Zacatecas seemed to matter not at all to the Huichols, who in any case acted throughout the sacred journey as though the twentieth century and all its technological wonders had never happened, even when they themselves were traveling by motor vehicle rather than on foot! Indeed, to us nothing illustrated more dramatically the time-out-of-life quality of the whole peyote experience than this ritual of passing through a perilous gateway that existed only in the emotions of the participants, but that was to them no less real for its physical invisibility.

We arrived at the outskirts of Zacatecas in midmorning. Assembling in their proper order as decreed in ancient times by Tatewarí, the pilgrims proceeded in single file to a grove of low-growing cactus and thorn bushes a few hundred feet from the highway. They listened with rapt attention as Ramón related the relevant passages of the peyote tradition and invoked for the coming ordeal the protection and assistance of Elder Brother Kauyumarie, a deer deity and culture hero who is the shaman's spirit helper. At Ramón's direction, each then took a small green and red parrot feather from a bunch attached to the straw hat of a *matewáme* (one who has not previously gone on a peyote pilgrimage, i.e. an unitiated neophyte), and tied it to the branches of a thorn bush in a propitiatory rite that has analogies among the Southwestern Pueblos.

Some distance up the road the pilgrims were led to an open space that commanded a fine view of the valley from which we had come. Here they formed a semicircle; men to Ramón's left, women and children to the right. Although they knew the peyote traditions by heart they listened carefully as he told them how, with the assistance of Kauyumarie's antlers, they would soon pass through the dangerous Gateway of Clashing Clouds. But from now until they arrived at the Place Where Our Mothers Dwell, the *matewámete* (pl.) among them would have to "walk in darkness," for they were "new and very delicate." Beginning with the women at the tail end of the line, Ramón proceeded to blindfold the novices. Even the children had their eyes covered, down to the baby.

Everyone took the blindfolding very seriously, some actually wept, but there were also the quick shifts between solemnity and humor that are so characteristic of Huichol ceremonial. Spirited and comical dialogues ensued between Ramón and veterans of previous pilgrimages: was the companion well fed, had he quenched his thirst? Oh yes, one's stomach was full to bursting with all manner of good things to eat and drink. Did one's feet hurt after so much walking? Oh no, one walked well, in comfort. (In reality none had had more than the most meager nourishment, only five dry tortillas per day and no water at all being permitted on the road to Wirikúta. As for walking, we were of course traveling by car, although the proper acknowledgement of various sacred places along the way repeatedly required single-file marches in and out of the desert).

Following the ritual blindfolding, Ramón led the pilgrims a few hundred years northeastward. Here, a place entirely unremarkable to the untutored eye, was the mystical divide, the threshold to the divine peyote country. The pilgrims remained rooted where they stood, intently watching Ramón's every move. Some lit candles they had stored in their carrying bags and baskets. Lips moved in silent or barely audible supplication. Ramón bent down and laid his bow and arrows crosswise over his oblong *takwátsi*, the plaited shaman's basket—bow and deerskin quiver pointing east in the direction of Wirikúta.

There are two stages to the crossing of the critical threshold. The first is called Gateway to the Clouds; the second, Where the Clouds Open. They are only a few steps apart, but the emotional impact on the participants as they passed from one to the other was unmistakable. Once safely "on the other side," they knew they would travel through a series of ancestral stopping places to the sacred maternal water holes, where one asks for fertility and fecundity and from where the novices, their blindfolds removed, are allowed to have their first glimpse of the distant mountains of Wirikúta. Of course, one would search in vain on any official map for places that bear such names as Where the Clouds Open, The Vagina, Where Our Mothers Dwell, or even Wirikúta itself, either in Huichol or Spanish. Like other sacred spots on the peyote itinerary, these are landmarks only in the geography of the mind.

Visually, the passage through the Gateway of Clashing Clouds was un-dramatic. Ramón stepped forward, lifted the bow and, placing one end against the mouth while rhythmically beating the taut string with a composite wooden-tipped hunting arrow, walked straight ahead. He stopped once, gestured (to Kauyumarie, we were later told, to thank him for holding the cloud gates back with his powerful antlers), and set out again at a more rapid pace, all the while beating his bow. The others followed close behind in single file. Some of the blindfolded neophytes held fearfully on to those in front, others made it by themselves.

"Where Our Mothers Dwell"

It was in the afternoon of the following day that we reached the sacred water holes of Our Mothers, the novices having remained blindfolded all the while. The physical setting again was hardly inspiring: an impoverished *mestizo* pueblo and beyond it a small cluster of obviously polluted springs surrounded by marsh—all that remained of a former lake long since gone dry. Cattle and a pig or two browsing amid the sacred water holes hardly helped inspire confidence in the physical—as opposed to spiritual—purity of the water the Huichols considered the very wellspring of fertility and fecundity. On the peyote quest, however, it is not what we would consider the real world that matters but only the reality of the mind's eye. "It is beautiful here," say the Huichols, "because this is where Our Mothers dwell, this is the water of life."

For some time, while the veteran *peyoteros* busied themselves in ritual activities, the blindfolded *matewámete* were made to sit quietly on the earth in a row, knees drawn up and arms held tightly against the body—the fetal position. Then at last the moment came when they could emerge into the light—i.e. be born—by the removal of their blindfolds. As Ramón did this in a separate ritual for each that included the same sort of jocular dialogue as had marked the dangerous passage, he also poured an ice-cold bowl of water taken from one of the springs over their heads, instructing them to rub the fecund fluid deeply into scalp and face. A second gourdful was handed them to drink, along with presoaked animal crackers and bits of tortilla, "for they are new, they can only eat tender food."

Offerings were left in the springs and numerous bottles and other containers filled with the precious water. The manner in which this filling was accomplished unmistakably celebrated the union of male and female, for Ramón and other *peyoteros* would dip a hunting arrow into a water hole and on its hardwood tip withdraw a few drops; the arrow would then be inserted into a waiting bottle and the drops shaken off in a motion simulating sexual intercourse. With this all ritual requirements preparatory to the actual hunt— bow and arrow in hand—for Elder Brother Deer-Peyote had been fulfilled. The water would first be taken to Wirikúta and then home, for use in the peyote rites and other ceremonies, and to be sprinkled with sprays of flowers over the women and even female livestock by the returning pilgrims, a symbolic act of fertilization that reminds one of the pre-Hispanic tradition in which the Toltec ruler Mixcóatl fathers the priest-king and culture hero Quetzalcóatl by impregnating his wife with the spray of flowers (an alternate version speaks of a jewel of jade). The contents of the springs of Our Mothers are thus seen to embody both male and female aspects.

CHAPTER ELEVEN*

"TO FIND OUR LIFE": PEYOTE HUNT
OF THE HUICHOLS OF MEXICO

Wirikúta is typical Chihuahuan-type desert, with an average altitude of 5000 feet, covered with creosote bush, mesquite, tar bush, yucca, agave, and many other kinds of cactus. It does the Huichols no favor to pinpoint the peyote country more precisely than to say that it overlaps more or less with the old mining *Real* of Catorce in northwestern San Luis Potosí; as it is, we were told by a railroad crew close to the sacred mountains that the year before a group of bearded young men and their girls had pitched tents nearby and lived there for several weeks, harvesting and eating peyote. This intelligence disturbed Ramón greatly, because the cactus grows slowly and such mass consumption by non-Indians was bound to have serious consequences for the success of future peyote hunts by those to whom the little cactus is, quite literally, the "source of life." Between the Place of Our Mothers and the peyote country proper there were to be two more camps. The second was only ten miles (in this rugged desert, two hours' driving time) from the area Ramón had selected in his mind for the hunt of Elder Brother Wawatsári, the "Principal Deer," who is animal avatar of peyote. We broke camp before dawn, in bitter cold, waiting only for the first red glow in the east so that the pilgrims might pay their proper respect to the rising Sun Father and ask his protection. There was little conversation on this final stretch. Everyone remained still, except for the times when the vehicles had to be emptied of

---

*The description of the peyote pilgrimage in Chapters Ten and Eleven appeared earlier in somewhat different form in *Flesh of the Gods: The Ritual Use of Hallucinogens*, Peter T. Furst, ed. (© 1972 by Praeger Publishers, Inc.), and in a briefer version in 1973 in *Natural History*, Vol. LXXXII, No. 4, pp. 34-43, and is included here with the permission of the publishers.

passengers to get past a particularly difficult spot in the trail. Even then there were few unnecessary words. Ramón's wife Lupe and her uncle José lit candles the moment we started out and held them the entire distance.

A Time to Walk

It was just past 7:00 a.m. when Ramón stopped the cars and told the Indians to get out and assemble in single file by the side of the trail. It was time to walk. For no matter how one had traveled thus far, one must enter and leave the "Patio of the Grandfathers" exactly as had Tatewarí and his ancient pilgrims—on foot, blowing a horn and beating the hunting bow. In former times, and occasionally today, the horn was a conch shell; José's was goat horn, and one of the others used a cow-horn trumpet.

As the *híkuri* seekers walked they picked up bits of dry wood and branches of creosote. Little Francisco, age ten, who was carrying his two-year-old brother, stopped to break off a green branch for himself and also stuck a long dry stick in the little boy's hand. This was the food of Tatewarí. It is another mark of the total unity of the *híkuritámete (peyoteros)* that each companion, down to the youngest, is expected to participate in the first "feeding" of the ceremonial Fire when it is brought to life by the *mara'akáme*.

This happened so quickly that we almost missed it. The line stopped, Ramón squatted, and seconds later there was a wisp of blue smoke and a tiny flame. Tatewarí had been "brought out" (fire is inherent in wood and only needs "bringing out"). Now more than at any other time on the pilgrimage, speed and skill in starting the fire are of the essence, for one is in precarious balance in this sacred land and urgently requires the manifestation of Tatewarí for protection. The fire is allowed to go out only at the end, when sacred water is poured on the hot ashes, after which the *mara'akáme* selects a coal, the *kupúri* (soul, life force) of Tatewarí, and places it in the little ceremonial bag around his neck. Since the ritual is repeated at each campsite there is an accumulation of magic coals, which become part of the *mara'akáme's* array of power objects.

Food for Grandfather

Chanting and praying, Ramón piled up bits of brush which quickly caught fire. The others, meanwhile, arranged themselves in a circle with their pieces of firewood and began to pray with great fervor and obvious emotion. We saw tears course down Lupe's face, and there was much sobbing also among the others. Such ritualized manifestations of joy mixed with sorrow were to recur several times during our stay in Wirikúta, especially at the successful conclusion of the "hunt," and again when we were getting ready to take our final leave. After much praying, chanting, and gesturing with firewood in the sacred directions, and a countersunwise ceremonial circuit around the fire, the individual gifts of "food" were given to Tatewarí and everyone went off to prepare for the crucial pursuit of the Deer-Peyote.

It was midmorning when Ramón signaled the beginning of the hunt. To my question how far we would have to walk to find peyote, he replied, "Far, very far. Tamatsí Wawatsári, the Principal Deer, waits for us up there, on the slopes of the mountain." I judged the distance to be about three miles.

Everyone gathered up his offerings and stuffed them in bags and baskets. Bowstrings were tested. Catarino Ríos, the personator of Tatutsí (Great-grandfather), one of the principal supernaturals, stopped playing his bow to help his wife Veradera (Our Mother Haramara, the Pacific Ocean) cut a few loose strings from the little votive design she had made from colored yarn on a piece of wood coated with beeswax, to be given as a petition to the sacrificed Deer-Peyote. The design depicted a calf. Catarino's bow music, we were told, was to make the deer happy before his impending death. Ramón conducted the pilgrims in another circuit around the fire, during which everyone laid more "food" on the flames and pleaded for protection. Ramón entreated Tatewarí not to go out and to greet them on their return. Then he led the companions away from camp toward the distant hills.

The Ritual Kill

About 300 feet from camp we crossed a railroad track and beyond it a barbed-wire fence. The men had their bows and arrows ready. Everyone had shoulder bags and some had baskets as well, containing offerings. We had walked perhaps 500 feet when Ramón lifted his fingers to his lips in a warning of silence, placed an arrow on his bowstring, and motioned to the others to fan out quickly and quietly in a wide arc. I pointed to the distant rise—was that not where we would find the peyote? He shook his head and smiled. Of course, I had forgotten the reversals of meaning that are a part of ritual language on the peyote pilgrimage. When he had said, "Far, very far," he really meant "very close." Ramón now crept forward, crouching low, intently watching the ground. Catarino's bow, which he had sounded by beating the string with an arrow along the route "to please Elder Brother," fell silent. The women hung back. Ramón halted suddenly, pointed to the ground, and whispered urgently, "His tracks, his tracks!" I could see nothing. José, personator of Tayaupá, Sun Father, sneaked up close and nodded happy assent: "Yes, yes, *mara'akáme*, there amid the new maize, there are his tracks, there at the first level." (There are five conceptual levels, corresponding to the four cardinal points—east, south, west, and north, with zenith and nadir combined into a single fifth direction rather than being counted separately as among the Zuñi. For a man to reach the fifth level, as Ramón was to do here in Wirikúta, means he has "completed himself"—i.e., become shaman.) The "new maize" was a sad little stand of dried-up twigs. The hunters look for any growth that can be associated with stands of maize, for the deer is not only peyote but maize as well. Likewise, peyote is differen-

"There, there, the deer!" A clone of peyote, the gray-green crowns barely
extending above ground. Photographed in the north-central desert of Mexico.

tiated by "color," corresponding to the five sacred colors of maize—blue,
red, yellow, white, and multicolored.

Ramón moved forward once more, José following close behind and to one
side, his face lit up with the pleasure of discovery and anticipation. All at
once Ramón stopped, motioning urgently to the others to come close. About
20 feet ahead stood a small shrub. He pointed: "There, there, the Deer!"
Barely visible above ground under the bush were some flecks of dusty
green—evidently a whole cluster of *Lophophora williamsii*. Although I have
seen peyote plants growing in full sunlight, more often it is found like

this—in a thicket of mesquite or creosote, shaded by a yucca or *Euphorbia* (especially *Euphorbia antisyphilitica*), or close to some well-armed *Opuntia* cactus, such as rabbit ear or *cholla*. Its broad, flat crown is usually almost level with the earth and so is easily missed by the inexperienced eye).

Ramón took aim, and the first of his arrows buried itself a fraction of an inch from the crown of the nearest *híkuri*. He let fly with a second, which hit slightly to one side. José ran forward and fired a third, almost straight down. Ramón completed the "kill" by sticking a ceremonial arrow with pendant hawk feathers into the ground on the far side, so that the sacred plant was now enclosed by arrows in each of the world quarters. The *mara'akáme* bent down to examine the peyote. "Look there," he said, "how sacred it is, how beautiful, the five-pointed deer!" Remarkably, every one of the peyotes in the cluster had the same number of ribs—five, the sacred number of completion! Later on, Ramón was to string a whole series of "five-pointed" peyotes on a sisal fiber cord and drape it over the horns of Kauyumarie mounted on the vehicles.

The companions formed a circle around the place where Elder Brother lay "dying." Many sobbed. All prayed loudly. The one called Tatutsí, Great-grandfather, unwrapped Ramón's basket of power objects, the *takwátsi*, from the red kerchief in which it was kept and laid it open for Ramón's use in the complex and lengthy rituals of propitiation of the dead deer (peyote) and division of its flesh among the communicants. Ramón explained how the *kupúri*, the life essence of the deer, which, as with humans, resides in the fontanelle, was "rising, rising, rising, like a brilliantly colored rainbow, seeking to escape to the top of the sacred mountains." "Do not be angry, Elder Brother," Ramón implored, "do not punish us for killing you, for you have not really died. You will rise again." Ramón was echoed by the pilgrims. "We will feed you well, for we have brought you many offerings, we have brought you tobacco, we have brought you water from Our Mothers, we have brought you arrows, we have brought you votive gourds, we have brought you maize and your favorite grasses, we have brought you *tamales*, we have brought you our prayers. We honor you and we give you our devotion. Take them, Elder Brother, take them and give us our life. We offer our devotion to the *Kakauyaríxi* who live here in Wirikúta; we have come to be received by them, for we know they await us. We have come from afar to greet you."

A Huichol Communion

To push the rainbow-*kupúri*, which only he could see, back into the Deer, Ramón lifted his *muviéri* (shaman's prayer arrow), first to the sky and the world directions, and then pressed it slowly downward, as though with great force, until the hawk feathers touched the crown of the sacred plant. In his chant he described how all around the dead deer peyotes were springing up, growing from his horns, his back, his tail, his shins, his hooves. "Tamatsí Wawatsári," he said, "is giving us our life." He took his knife from the basket and began to cut away the earth around the cactus. Then, instead of taking it out whole, he cut it off at the base, leaving a bit of the root in the ground. This is done so that Elder Brother can grow again from his "bones."* Ramón sliced off the tough bottom half of the cactus and peeled away the rough brown skin, carefully preserving the waste for ritual disposition later. Then he divided the cactus into five pieces by cutting along the natural ridges and placed these pieces in a votive gourd. The process was repeated by Ramón and Lupe with several additional plants, for there had to be enough to give each of the companions a part of "Elder Brother's flesh." Those who had made previous pilgrimages came first. One by one they squatted or knelt before Ramón, who removed a section of peyote from the gourd and, after touching it to the pilgrim's forehead (in lieu of the fontanelle hidden under the hat or scarf), eyes, larynx, and heart, placed it into his or her mouth. The pilgrim was told to "chew it well, chew it well, for thus you will see your life." Then he summoned the non-Huichol observers and repeated the same ritual for them (as he had also included them in the knotting-in ceremony).

In the meantime Ramón had gathered up all the tobacco gourds (yékwéte) belonging to the pilgrims and placed them near the sacred cavities from which the peyote had been taken. As Lumholtz (1900:190) noted, these gourds are an indispensable part of the outfit of the híkuri seeker, giving him, as it were, priestly status (the tobacco gourd was also a priestly insignia in Aztec times). I have heard it said that yé, tobacco, was once a hawk and the kwé, gourd, a snake. The tobacco is always the so-called wild species, Nicotiani rustica— the "tobacco of Tatewarí—which contains nicotine in far greater amounts than some domestic brands. Tobacco gourds are specially raised for the purpose. Those with numerous natural excrescences are highly valued, although smooth ones are also employed, sometimes with a covering of skin from the scrotum of a deer. This, of course, makes them especially powerful.

All the híkuri that had "grown from the horns and body of Elder Brother" had been dug up and set on the ground. Bows and arrows were stacked against

---

*Anderson (1969), who has been engaged in extensive field studies of Lophophora throughout its natural range from Texas to San Luis Potosí and Querétaro since 1957, reports that "injury or harvesting by man induces the formation of many stems from a single rootstock. Single clones of more than 1.5 m. across have been observed in San Luis Potosí, for example" (p. 302). The ritual practice of leaving part of the rootstock in the ground to induce new growth "from Elder Brother's bones" is common among Huichol peyote seekers. Clones growing from a single rootstock are considered especially sacred and powerful and are treated accordingly. Ramón, for example, would not allow anyone else to touch one such clone he had removed from the ground until it had been propitiated in the proper manner. Characteristically, he left part of the root where it grew.

a nearby cactus. Votive offerings and prayers addressed to the Deer and the *Kakauyaríxi* were placed in a pile in front of the holes where the peyote had been. The pilgrims were seated on the ground in a circle. Ramón touched the offerings with his *muviéri*, prayed, and set fire to one of the little wool yarn paintings he had made, depicting Elder Brother. As the wax melted, the flames licked at the ceremonial arrows, and soon the entire pile of offerings and the dry creosote bush itself were ablaze. Ramón muttered incantations and with his *muviéri* wafted some of the smoke toward the sacred mountains. Then he rose and with a gourd filled with peyote passed in a ceremonial circuit from right to left on the inside of the circle to give each his portion of "Elder Brother's flesh." Forehead, eyes, larynx, and heart were touched and the peyote placed into the mouth of each pilgrim in turn. The *matewámete* especially were exhorted over and over to "chew it well, brother [or sister], so that you will see your life, so that it will appear to you with clarity." When Ramón came to ten-year-old Francisco, all turned to watch. Peyote is not given in any quantity to young children, but after the age of three it can be a sign whether or not the child has the disposition to become a *mara'akáme*. If he or she likes the taste, which is exceedingly bitter and difficult to tolerate, it is taken as a positive omen. If it is rejected, it is a negative sign—though not necessarily definitive. Ramón touched Francisco on the head, eyes, throat, and heart and placed a small piece between his lips. "Chew, little brother," he admonished, "and we will see how you like it. Chew well, chew well, for it is sweet, it is delicious to the taste." There were smiles at this obvious reversal but no laughter—this was not a time for hilarity. After slight hesitation Francisco, who had not tasted peyote before, began to chew vigorously. He nodded—yes, he liked it. Later he participated with great enthusiasm in the search for peyote and that night ate a goodly amount himself, with no visible ill effect. He danced for hours, fell asleep smiling happily, and next morning was his old self. One *matewáme* who was obviously greatly moved by the whole experience was Veradera, a strikingly handsome young woman apparently under twenty. Veradera ate more peyote than anyone with the exception of Ramón and Lupe, and later that night fell into a deep trance that lasted for many hours and caused everyone to regard her as especially sacred.

"You Will See Your Life"

When every one of the companions had chewed a piece of the first sacrificial *híkuri*, Ramón took out his fiddle and one of the others a guitar (both homemade), and the veterans stood aside in a group to sing and dance the *matewámete* into a "receptive condition." In the meantime, another gourd had been filled with peyote cut into small pieces, and the initiates were not allowed to rise until they had emptied it. As the bowl was handed around, the others, led by Ramón, exhorted them over and over to "chew well, companion, chew well, for that is how you will see your life." Lupe then took a

Veradera. "We are all the children of a brilliantly colored flower, a flaming flower. . . ."

sizable whole plant, sliced off the bottom, lifted her long, magnificently embroidered skirt (like Ramón's clothes, it had been made specially for this journey), and rubbed the moist end of the cactus on her legs, especially on the numerous small scratches and cuts inflicted by spines and thorns during the trek through the desert. The others followed her example. Lupe explained that peyote not only discourages hunger and thirst and restores one's spirit but heals wounds and prevents infection.

Ramón having admonished the companions repeatedly to "be of a pure heart," the actual *híkuri* harvest was ready to commence, and the pilgrims went off into the desert, alone or in pairs. *Híkuri* "hides itself well," and several of the companions had to walk a considerable distance before seeing their first peyote. Lupe, on the other hand, almost at once discovered a thicket of cactus and mesquite so rich in peyote that in a couple of hours she had filled her tall collecting basket. Occasionally she would stop to admire and

"Our game bags are full." Lupe's carrying basket filled to the brim with mature peyote plants. In the foreground, peyote roots, called the "bones" of the sacred cactus, cut off to be ritually deposited in the desert in the hope that new plants will grow from them. This accords with the widespread belief of hunting peoples in rebirth from the bones, which are believed to contain the life force or soul.

speak quietly to an especially beautiful *híkuri* and to touch it to her forehead, face, throat, and heart before adding it to the others. We also saw people exchanging gifts of peyote. This seemed to us a very beautiful aspect of the pilgrimage. No ceremony in which peyote was eaten communally went by without this kind of ritual exchange, in which each participant is expected to share his peyote with every companion. A man or a woman would carefully divide a peyote, rise, and walk from individual to individual, handing over a piece and receiving one in return. Often an older participant would place his gift directly into the mouth of a younger one, urging him to "chew well, younger brother, chew well, so that you will see your life." But most often these ritual exchanges took place in silence as they were also to do in the concluding ceremony of "unknotting" that marked the formal end of the pilgrimage.

No *hikuri* was ever dug carelessly or dropped casually on the ground or into a basket or bag. On the contrary, it was handled with tenderness and respect and addressed soothingly by the *hikuri* seeker, who would thank it for allowing itself to be seen, call it by endearing names, and apologize for removing it from its home. As mentioned, small, tender, five-ribbed ("five-pointed") plants are considered especially desirable. Being young, they are also less disagreeable to the taste. Some plants were cleaned and popped directly into the mouth—after first being held to forehead, face, and heart. Lupe sometimes wept when she did this. She was also chewing incessantly, as was Ramón.

Toward four in the afternoon Ramón rose from where he had been digging peyotes and called out that it was time to return to camp. One of the *hikuri* seekers had just spotted a sizable cluster and was reluctant to abandon so rich a find. Ramón admonished him: "Our game bags are full. One must not take more than one needs." If one did, if one did not leave gifts and propitiate the slain Deer-Peyote (just as one should propitiate the spirits of animals one hunts, the maize one harvests, and the trees one cuts). Elder Brother would be offended and would conceal the *hikuri* or withdraw them altogether, so that next time the seekers would walk away empty-handed. We would call this practice conservation; to the Huichol it is part of the principle of reciprocity by which he orders his social relationships and his relationship to the natural and supernatural environment. So the pilgrims gathered their gear and their bags and baskets, now heavy with peyote, and after a tearful farewell returned to camp as they had come, walking single file to the sound of the bow. On the way they stopped here and there to pick up "food" for Tatewarí.

On arriving at camp they made the usual ceremonial circuit around the fire and offered thanks for its protection, without laying down their burdens. Again there was much weeping. Ramón's basket, held in one arm while he gestured in the sacred directions with the other, must have weighed a good thirty pounds. Though dormant, the ashes were still aglow, and new flames quickly licked through the growing pile of brush as each deposited some "food" for Tatewarí. The green branches, wet with dew, sent thick clouds of white smoke billowing to the leaden sky. It was turning cold and damp.

The night was passed in singing and dancing around the ceremonial fire, chewing peyote in astounding quantities, and listening to the ancient stories. Considering the lack of food, the long days on the road, the bitterly cold nights with little sleep (by now, Ramón had not closed his eyes to sleep for six days and nights!), and above all the high emotional pitch of the sacred drama, with its succession of increasingly intense and exalted encounters, one might have expected the pilgrims to feel some letdown now that they had successfully "hunted the deer" and to lapse into a dream state induced by the considerable quantities of *hikuri* they had already consumed. True, after their return from the hunt they were, for the most part, somewhat subdued and

Híkuri seekers. A Huichol peyotero and his wife searching the desert for the
sacred cactus.

quiet. Some had actually entered trances. Veradera had been sitting motion-
less for hours, arms clasped around her knees, eyes closed. When night fell
Lupe placed candles around her to protect her against attacks by sorcerers
while her soul was traveling outside her body. But most of the others were
wide awake, in varying states of exaltation, supremely happy and possessed
of seemingly boundless energy. If the dancing and singing stopped it was only
because Ramón laid down his fiddle to commune quietly with the ceremonial
fire or to chant the stories of the first peyote pilgrims and the primordial hunt
of the divine Deer-Peyote. It is also in this semi-conscious peyote dream state
that the *mara'akáme* "obtains" the new peyote names for the pilgrims in his
charge (e.g. Offering of the Blue Maize, Votive Gourd of the Sun, Arrows of
Tatewarí). These names, I was told, emerge from the core of the fire in the
manner of brilliantly colored, luminous ribbons, and it is in this form that
Ramón subsequently depicted them in his superbly fashioned "paintings" of
wool yarn, an art form for which the Huichols are justly famed and in which
he in particular excelled far beyond most other Huichol artists of his time.
The special peyote names are conferred on the *híkuri*-seekers on the last day
in Wirikúta and are evidently preserved by them at least until they are

formally released from their sacred bonds and restrictions by the ceremonial circuit to the sacred places and the deer hunt that follow their return to the Sierra.

Uniqueness of the Shaman's Visions

The Huichols say their peyote experiences are very private things and they do not often discuss them with outsiders except in the most general terms ("there were many beautiful colors," "I saw maize in brilliant hues, much maize," or simply, "I saw my life"). Under certain conditions the *mara'akáme* might be called upon to assist in giving form and meaning to a vision, especially for one who is a *matewáme* (novice) or in the context of a cure. This much is clear, however: beyond certain "universal" visual and auditory sensations, which may be laid to the chemistry of the plant and its effect on the central nervous system, there are powerful cultural factors at work that here as elsewhere influence, if they do not actually determine, both content and interpretation of the drug experience. Huichols told me they were convinced that the *mara'akáme*, or one preparing himself to become a *mara'akáme*, and the ordinary person have different kinds of peyote experiences. Certainly a *mara'akáme* embarks on the pilgrimage and the drug experience itself with a somewhat different set of expectations than the ordinary Huichol. He seeks to experience a catharsis that allows him to enter upon a personal encounter with Tatewarí and travel to "the fifth level" to meet the supreme spirits at the ends of the world. And so he does. Ordinary Huichols also "experience" the supernaturals, but they do so essentially through the medium of their shaman. In any event, I have met no one who was not convinced of this essential difference or who laid claim to the same kinds of exalted and illuminating confrontations with the Otherworld as the *mara'akáme*. In an objective sense his visions might be similar, but subjectively they are differently perceived and interpreted. Certainly this applies to the *mara'akáme* or aspiring *mara'akáme* who leads the *peyoteros* as the personification of Tatewarí, the First *Mara'akáme*, and who is so addressed by his companions for the duration of the pilgrimage.

However, a rather surprising number of Huichol adult men, and some women too, consider themselves, and are considered by their fellows, to be shamans, so that the more intense peyote experience attributed to shamans can be assumed to be relatively widely shared. The pervasiveness of shamanism among the Huichols was first noted by Lumholtz in the 1890's (Lumholtz, 1900). His estimate of perhaps half the adult males as shamans seemed to me at first improbably high for an agricultural people like the Huichols, however incipient and primitive their agricultural economy may be in comparison to that of other peoples with a longer tradition of farming and a more advanced agricultural technology. But Lumholtz turned out to be right, at least in the sense that all household heads really are family shamans, some with considerable prestige that extends far beyond their immediate kinfolk, and that at least half the men, and some women, possess a good deal of shamanic and ritual knowledge and presumably have had profound ecstatic trance experiences with peyote. Some shamans, of course, are considered to have much greater mystical powers than others, and their counsel carries correspondingly greater weight.

The Children of Peyote

The *híkuri* seekers left as they had entered—on foot, single file, blowing their horns. Their once-white clothing was caked with the yellow earth of the desert, for during the night it had begun to drizzle—an astonishing event at the height of the dry season and an auspicious omen. Behind them a thin plume of blue smoke rose from the ceremonial fire. They had circled it as required. They had made their offerings of tobacco and bits of food and sacred water from the springs of Our Mothers. They had purified their sandals. They had wept bitter tears as they bade farewell to Tatewarí, to Elder Brother, to the *Kakauyaríxi*. They had found their life. They had confirmed the sacred truths with their own senses, the inner vision that comes only when one eats the flesh of the divine Deer-Peyote. Now they were truly *Vixárika* (Huichol).

A few hundred yards down the trail they halted once more. Facing the mountains and the sun, they shouted their pleasure at having found their life, and their pain at having to depart so soon. "Do not leave," they implored the supernaturals, "do not abandon your places, for we will come again another year." And they sang, song after song—their parting gift to the *Kakauyaríxi*:

> What pretty hills, what pretty hills,
> So very green where we are.
> Now I don't even feel,
> Now I don't even feel,
> Now I don't even feel like going to my rancho.
> For there at my rancho it is so ugly,
> So terribly ugly there at my rancho,
> And here in Wirikúta so green, so green.
> And eating in comfort as one likes,
>
> Amid the flowers (peyote), so pretty.
> Nothing but flowers here,
> Pretty flowers, with brilliant colors,
> So pretty, so pretty.
> And eating one's fill of everything,
> Everyone so full here, so full with food.
> The hills very pretty for walking,

For shouting and laughing,
So comfortable, as one desires,
And being together with all one's companions.
Do not weep, brothers, do not weep.
For we came to enjoy it,
We came on this trek,
To find our life.

For we are all,
We are all,
We are all the children of,
We are all the sons of
A brilliantly colored flower,
A flaming flower.
And there is no one,
There is no one,
Who regrets what we are.

CHAPTER TWELVE

DATURA: A HALLUCINOGEN
THAT CAN KILL

There is another hallucinogenic plant in the mythology of the Huichols, anthropomorphized as Kieri Tewíyari, Kieri Person, whose special powers and relationship to the Sun deity are acknowledged with offerings of prayer arrows and other gifts. However, if Kieri (pronounced ki-yéri) is used at all, it is only rarely, in secrecy, and is generally disapproved. For many Huichols regard Kieri as a dangerous sorcerer whose effects, unlike those of peyote, may cause permanent insanity and even death.

Kieri, whose story "from ancient times" is recited by shamans especially in the context of the peyote ceremonies, grows in remote and rocky places in and about the mountainous Huichol country, with a prominent cluster of sharp rock pinnacles, rising precipitously at the edge of Cora territory in the foothills of the Sierra Madre Occidental, generally thought to be his proper home. It is said that Kieri established himself at this formidable redoubt—which, incidentally, also served as a last bastion of armed Indian resistance against the Spaniards in 1722—after his defeat by the deer god and culture hero Kauyumarie.

What does this Kieri look like? In his plant form, say the Huichols, Kieri has white, funnel-shaped flowers and spiny seed pods. With the enchanting music of his violin he lures the unwary and bids them taste of his leaves, his flowers, his roots, and his seeds. But whoever obeys his wiles suffers insanity or death: people bewitched by Kieri will believe themselves to be birds, for example, able to fly from the highest rocks, but unless they are saved by a shaman with the aid of peyote and Kauyumarie, they will dash themselves to death below. Or, if they heed Kieri's urgings and eat more and more of him, they will fall into a deep sleep and never awaken, because only the shaman knows in what manner to deal with such a sorcerer. Nevertheless, one must respect Kieri for his supernatural power, and when one encounters him one should deposit the proper offerings, such as prayer arrows, and when one passes his rocky abode in the distance, one should make appropriate ritual gestures in his direction. The peyote pilgrims whom we accompanied to Wirikúta in 1968 did in fact hold a special ceremony when they came within sight of the aforementioned rocky pinnacles in Nayarit, including the burning of candles (as miniature effigies of the fire deity), and propitiatory chants and gestures toward Kieri's dwelling place.

Conventional wisdom has long held that Kieri is *Datura inoxia* (*meteloides*). Robert Zingg (1938) identified it as such, and the descriptions of the plant collected by Barbara G. Myerhoff and myself in 1964/1966 accorded with most of its salient characteristics. These included, in particular, funnel-shaped flowers and the spiny seed pods from which "thorn apple," one of the popular names for two species, *D. inoxia* and *D. stramonium*, is derived (Furst and Myerhoff, 1966:3-39; 1972:53-106). ("Extract of Thorn Apple" is also the name under which medicinal *Datura* preparations were bottled and marketed by the Shakers in the nineteenth century). The identification of Kieri as *Datura* now appears to have been correct only for part of the Huichol country. While it accords with the probable ultimate origins of the ancestral Huichols in the Southwest, where *Datura* continues to play an important role, especially among the Zuñi, according to Timothy Knab (personal communication), a field worker in anthropological linguistics, Huichol informants in the region visited by him attributed the name Kieri to a species of *Solandra*, a genus closely related to and resembling to some degree the *Daturas* and probably chemically similar to them. While *Solandra* use in a strictly cere-monial context has not been previously reported, M. Martínez (1966) identi-fied *hueipatli*, said to have been a narcotic used in central Mexico at the time of the Conquest, as *Solandra guerrerensis*.* The same Mexican scholar, who also authored a classic modern work on medicinal plants, *Las Plantas Medi-cinales de México* (1959), notes that *S. guerrerensis* is still employed by some Indians in the state of Guerrero.

Although they make offerings to the plant, call it the "real Kieri," and express great awe, if not indeed fear, of it, no Huichols today appear to be using *Solandra* medicinally or hallucinogenically. But the mythic descrip-tions of the powers of Kieri to bewitch and transform are too specific not to be

---

*I am indebted to Timothy Knab (personal communication) for drawing my attention to this reference.

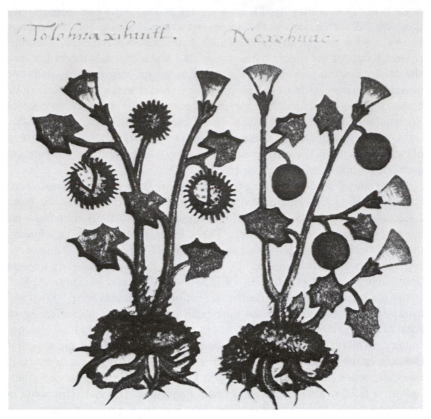

Datura. Two species, as depicted in the sixteenth-century Aztec herbal known as the *Codex Badianus*.

based on actual experience, presumably at some time in the past. If Kieri is *Datura* in one part of the rugged Huichol country and *Solandra* in another, or if, as well may be the case, there are two Kieris, in the main potentially malevolent, one manifesting himself in *Datura* and the other in *Solandra*, we are confronted with the phenomenon of a supernatural being who manifests himself in the same culture in two related but distinct solanaceous species. But considering that *Datura* and *Solandra* share similar potentially dangerous chemical properties, that would perhaps not be so strange.

The early chroniclers reported that the Aztec priests administered to those to be sacrificed an herbal anodyne, so that they did not feel the pain. Although the Aztec name for the unidentified plant was not one of those used for *Datura*, some botanists and pharmacologists have thought it might nonetheless have been a *Datura*, whose effects are known to be analgesic. But there was no certainty, and the real identity of the mysterious narcotic has remained in question since the sixteenth century. If *Solandra* turns out to possess the same analgesic properties as its close relative *Datura*, the mystery of the elusive hallucinogenic *yauhtli* may at last have been solved.

Myth as History

However this turns out, the Huichol tale of Kieri has a decidedly historical flavor. We hear of him acting like a shaman—curing, singing, playing his drum, conversing with the solar deity and seeking his aid. Kauyumarie watches and decides that Kieri is really an evil sorcerer who deceives the people. Only when he has learned all he can of Kieri's "secrets"—i.e. magic —does Kauyumarie decide to attack him. In the final struggle to overcome his adversary, he invokes the aid of the peyote cactus, which wards off Kieri's sickness projectiles, allowing Kauyumarie to shoot five arrows into the enemy's chest. Kieri falls, but instead of dying is allowed by his protector, the Sun, to transform into a flowering plant. In this form he flies away to his secret hiding place up in the rocks, where those who respect his magical powers pay him homage and often find themselves bewitched by his poison, which is proffered with such entreaties as, "Here, eat this, it is better than peyote."

One is tempted to read this as history couched in mythic terms because there must have been a time in Huichol prehistory when an ideological shift occurred among some of their Uto-Aztecan ancestors, away from the *Datura* cults characteristic of the Southwest to the more benign peyote, perhaps when they first came upon *Lophophora williamsii* in the course of their southward expansion from the original homeland of this important language family in the Arizona-Sonora desert. Since *Datura*, which can be fatal, and the more benign peyote are somewhat dissimilar experiential phenomena, such a change might have had some disruptive effects on the traditional magico-religious life of the society and its relationship with the supernatural. Perhaps the Kieri-Kauyumarie tradition recalls an actual rivalry between the two systems, symbolized by the priest-shamans of the competing sacred plants, or else the tradition collapses into manageable form a more gradual evolutionary transition from the one to the other after a period of coexistence, which has continued, at least in symbolic form, to the present day. Kieri's supernatural power (whether manifested in *Datura* or *Solandra* or both) is, after all, still acknowledged in prayer offerings, meant not only to ward off evil but also to to ensure fertility, rain, and other good things. To some degree this recalls the final displacement of the "mescal bean" by peyote among the Indians of the Southern Plains toward the end of the nineteenth century (a process that, considering the fact that peyote appears in the archaeological record in South Texas alongside the mescal bean as early as A.D. 800, may have had its beginning long ago). However, unlike *Datura*, the traditional *Sophora* bean was not consigned to the realm of sorcery but was incorporated into the new material culture of the peyote religion at least as an ornamental component.

Natural and Cultural History of *Datura*

Unlike peyote and other exclusively New World hallucinogens, the genus *Datura* is cosmopolitan and it and other members of the Solanaceae (potato or nightshade family) have played a role in religion, magic, divination, sorcery, and medicine in different parts of the world, apparently since ancient times. The family consists of more than 90 genera, with no less than 2400 species, including such disparate plants as the potato, eggplant, nightshade, peppers, tomato, tobacco, petunia, *Datura*, and many others. Only a few of these are known to be truly hallucinogenic, although Mesoamerican Indians, among others, attribute at least narcotic or medicinal properties to several solanaceous genera, among them *Solandra* and species of *Solanum*.

Apart from tobacco, which is in a class by itself, some of the Solanaceae are important only for nutrition (although even some of these, including the tomato and potato, contain toxic principles in the leaves or stalks but not in the edible fruit). But others, like the well-known *Atropa belladonna*, *Hyoscyamus*, and the *Daturas* are valued for psychotropic alkaloids, of which a number have passed from herbal into modern medicine.

Atropa belladonna, also called deadly nightshade and, in European folk usage, sorcerer's herb, is the source of several important drugs, of which atropine is the best known. The genus *Atropa*, whose prinicipal active alkaloid, scopolamine, occurs in four species in combination with other alkaloids, is native to the Old World and is found in Europe as well as Central and southern Asia. Henbane, *Hyoscyamus niger*, source of the important medical drug hyoscyamus, is one of about 20 species of the genus, which is native to Europe, northern Africa, and southwestern and central Asia.

The main tropane alkaloids in the famous mandrake, *Mandragora officinarum*, are hyoscyamine, scopolamine, and mandragorina. Six species of *Mandragora* are found from the Mediterranean to the Himalayas (Schultes, 1970; see also Schultes and Hofmann, 1973, pp. 161-191).

Both hemispheres share the genus *Datura*, and both have used it. Not surprisingly, however, in light of the stress on the ecstatic experience by most Native Americans, more species were utilized in the New World, and the genus achieved a much higher and more lasting status, being employed in divination, prophecy, ecstatic initiation, ritual intoxication, diagnosis, and medicine. It is also widely employed to give extra potency to ritual beverages, both of the hallucinogenic and the fermented variety. So, for example, the Tarahumara Indians of Chihuahua even now sometimes add *Datura inoxia* to *tesgüino*, a fermented drink made from sprouted maize which the Huichols call *nawá*, while in South America the Jivaro of Ecuador, for example, strengthen *natéma*, the hallucinogenic beverage made basically from a species of *Banisteriopsis*, by adding a species of *Datura* of the arborescent

SOPHORA **secundiflora** (Ort.) Lag.

subgenus *Brugmansia*, and sometimes also *guayusa*, a stimulating caffeine-containing tea made from *Ilex guayusa*, a species of holly.

In curing, *Datura* preparations served to place the doctor in touch with the supernaturals for the purpose of ascertaining the cause of the illness, but were also used as medicine for the patient, being applied both externally and internally. Not only the Aztecs but many other Indians were quite familiar with the analgesic effects of *Datura* and used it effectively to alleviate pain. Matilda Coxe Stevenson (1915), for example, reports that among the Zuñi of New Mexico, who ascribe divine origin to *Datura inoxia* and whose Rain Priest Fraternity has a special relationship to the sacred plant, the curer administers the root to

. . . render his patient unconscious while he performs simple operations—setting fractured limbs, treating dislocations, making incisions for removing pus, eradicating diseases of the uterus, and the like. (p. 41)

She also reports witnessing an operation in which the Zuñi curer used a flint knife to open the abscessed breast of a woman who had been placed into a deep sleep with *Datura inoxia* (then still called *D. meteloides*). When she awoke she said she had experienced only beautiful dreams but no pain whatever.

The principal alkaloids in the fifteen to twenty species that comprise the genus *Datura* and its four subgroups are hyoscyamine, norhyoscyamine, and scopolamine, all belonging to the tropane series. Depending on ecological factors, and possibly on genetic differences, there is considerable variation in the alkaloidal content even of the same species and their different parts. So, for example, scopolamine constitutes from 50 to 60 percent of the total base content of the arborescent *Datura candida* growing in the Andes, but only 30 to 40 percent for the same species cultivated in England or Hawaii (Schultes, 1970:584). Similar differences have been recorded for other alkaloids. Here again we find the Indians to have been careful observers. Schultes notes that the alkaloidal content of cultivated *D. candida* plants, for example, has been proved experimentally to correlate closely with accounts of their relative toxicity by the Indians of Sibundoy, Colombia, who certainly had no access to a chemical laboratory. The same kind of sophistication is also reflected in the selection of different parts of the *Daturas* (as of other hallucinogenic species) in accordance with their proven potency.

Effects of *Datura* Intoxication

The four subgroups of the genus are: (1) *Stramonium*, with three species in the two hemispheres; (2) *Dutra*, with six species; (3) *Ceratocaulis*, with only one, but very interesting, semiaquatic Mexican species whose supernatural spirit Indian curers invoke for the treatment of certain diseases; and (4) *Brugmansia*, a group of tree *Daturas* with often very showy flowers that were formerly exclusive to South America but are now found in many parts of the world as cultivated ornamentals.

Depending on dosage, the effects of the active alkaloids of *Datura*— scopolamine, for example—have been found experimentally to extend from a feeling of lassitude through hallucination to deep, dreamless sleep and loss of consciousness, with death possible in the absence of effective countermeasures. The early accounts are correct: *Datura can* kill, and it can apparently also be administered by an experienced person in such amounts and in such ways as to bring about temporary derangement and even permanent insanity, which is precisely why the genus has entered the practice of witchcraft.

In these respects the *Daturas* of course differ considerably from other hallucinogens, whose most drastic effects might be a "bad trip" but which are not known to be capable of physiological damage. The *Daturas* and the cytisine-containing "mescal bean" are thus in a very different class from other sacred plants in the psychedelic pharmacopoeia of American Indians. In this connection I recall a story I heard from a competent, well-educated, and trustworthy informant in Cuernavaca, Mexico, who had occasion to observe the disastrous effects of repeated, deliberate applications of *Datura* to an individual said to have been responsible for the betrayal and death of a popular peasant leader in the state of Morelos some years ago.

A quick death having been judged too benign a punishment by his captors, the wretched man was turned over to a local *bruja*—a word meaning "witch," but applied also to folk healers or *curanderas*. In my experience most Mexican folk healers are not only accomplished herbalists but generally effective psychologists, who might have much to teach their university-educated colleagues if these were only willing to listen. In any event, it seems that by a judicious combination of repeated infusions of *toloache* (*D. inoxia*) and a play on his guilt feelings, together with hypnotic suggestion, she brought the man to a state where for several months, until his death, he walked, barked, fed, and was treated like a dog—a fate some of the local people seemed to think he deserved only too well. Not only the proven veracity of my informant but the results of laboratory experiments with the chemicals in *Datura* lend weight to this tale of elementary justice derived from ancient knowledge of the properties of plants.

Datura among North American Indians

None of the above should be taken to mean that the negative potential of *Datura* in any sense, or anywhere, outweighed its positive role in the indigenous ritual and symbolic systems. On the contrary, most Indians in North and South America have used these plants solely for positive purposes, such as initiation of boys and their integration into adulthood and full participation in tribal culture through ecstatic confrontation of the truth of the ancestral ways; for individual and communal vision seeking and communication with ancestors, deities, and spirits of land, air, and water; and for divination, prophecy, curing, and the alleviation of physical and mental distress.

Apart from "thorn apple," a popular name for *Datura* in the United States has long been "Jamestown Weed," commonly shortened to "Jimsonweed." Properly, this refers only to the eastern species, *Datura stramonium*; the name itself stems from an incident involving some English soldiers on their way to quell a rebellion led by a Lieutenant Bacon, at Jamestown, Virginia, in the seventeenth century. Robert Beverly (ca. 1673-ca. 1722), in his *History and Present State of Virginia* (1705), describes what happened:

The *James Town Weed* (which resembles the Thorny Apple of *Peru*, and I take to be the plant so call'd) is supposed to be one the greatest Coolers in our World. This being an early Plant, was gather'd very young for a boil'd Salad, by some of the Soldiers sent thither, to pacify the Troubles of *Bacon*; and some of them eat plentifully of it, the Effect of which was a very pleasant Comedy; for they turn'd natural Fools upon it for several Days; One would blow up a Feather in the air; another would dart Straws at it with much Fury; and another stark naked was sitting up in a Corner, like a Monkey, grinning and making Mows at them; a Fourth would fondly kiss, and paw his Companions, and snear in their Faces, with a Countenance more antick, than any in a *Dutch* Droll. In this frantick Condition they were confined, lest they should in their Folly destroy themselves; though it was observed, that all their Actions were full of Innocence and good Nature. Indeed, they were not very cleanly; for they would have wallow'd in their own Excrements, if they had not been prevented. A Thousand such simple Tricks they play'd, and after Eleven Days, return'd to themselves again, not remembering any thing that had pass'd. (Quoted in Schleiffer, 1973:129-130)

The soldiers claimed they had picked *Datura stramonium* because they thought it might be a savory pot herb, but chances are that they had really learned of the intoxicating effects from the original inhabitants of Virginia, who used *Datura* in boys' initiation rites that resembled the *toloache* ceremonies of California Indians. The characteristic death-rebirth theme of rites of passage clearly emerges from Beverly's rather quaint but perceptive description of what he calls "the Solemnity of Huskanawing." When the time for initiation had been set by the elders, the young men and boys were taken into the forest, where they were kept in strict seclusion in a specially constructed hut of latticework. After long fasting and instruction, they were given repeated decoctions of *Datura* root, called *wysoccan*, which brought on a state of apparently violent intoxication that lasted from 18 to 20 days. During this crucial period the boys were supposed to shed themselves of all memory of their youth. When the shamans felt that the boys had drunk enough, the dosages were gradually reduced, and the initiates, carefully guarded, allowed to return to their homes. As they came out of their intoxication they had to watch themselves, and were watched by the shamans, lest there be any remembrance of their former state of childhood. If that happened they had to be "huskanawed" again, and since in that event even greater quantities of *wysoccan* were required, the second initiatory ordeal sometimes ended in death:

Thus they must pretend to have forgot the very use of their Tongues, so as not to be able to speak, nor understand any thing that is spoken, till they learn it again. Now whether this be real or counterfeit, I don't know; but certain it is, that they will not for some time take notice of any body, nor any thing, with which they were before acquainted, being still under the guard of their Keepers, who constantly wait upon them every where, till they have learnt all things perfectly over again. Thus they unlive their former lives, and commence Men, by forgetting that they ever have been Boys. . . .

Further, the rite of passage and the violent *Datura* intoxication was to undo whatever bonds or prejudices the initiates had formed toward "persons and things" during their childhood:

They hope by this proceeding, to root out all the prepossessions and unreasonable prejudices which are fixt in the minds of Children. So that, when the Young men come to themselves again, their Reason may act freely, without being bypass'd by the Cheats of Custom and Education. Thus also they become discharg'd from the remembrance of any tyes by Blood, and are establish't in a state of equality and perfect freedom, to order their actions, and dispose of their persons, as they think fit, without any other Controul, than that of the Law of Nature. By this means also they become qualify'd when they have any Publick Office, equally and impartially to administer Justice, without having respect either to Friend or Relation. (Quoted in Schleiffer, 1973: pp. 130-132)

Initiation Rites in California

An Indian so initiated would not likely have suffered an "identity crisis." Would that we and our parents had been so fortunate in knowing when the psychological boundary between childhood and adulthood had been crossed!

In California, the *toloache* initiation cult originated among the Shoshonean (Uto-Aztecan) peoples of the south, but some of its features spread as far north as the San Joaquin and Sacramento Valleys. The puberty-rite aspect with its prominent death-rebirth theme was especially well developed among such Southern Californians as the Diegeño and Luiseño, for whom the *Datura* cult stood at the very heart of the entire religious system (Kroeber, 1953). In the main, only boys were initiated with *toloache*, girls having their own puberty rituals, but among some tribes, especially in the north, girls could also take *Datura*.

Among the Luiseño, among whom the cult was especially well developed, the boys' puberty ceremony was not conducted annually, or even at a fixed season, but performed every few years—whenever a sufficient number of youths were judged to be ready for initiation. Also, any man, or even a visitor from some other group, who had never taken *toloache* (*Datura* was drunk only once in a lifetime), was given the drug along with the youngsters, to whom the drink was administered at night, in a specially consecrated secluded place, following a period of food restrictions and instruction. The dried roots of *Datura inoxia* were pounded in freshly painted mortars that were used for no other purpose and were kept in sacred hiding places. The powdered root, mixed with hot water, was drunk from the mortar itself, each boy in turn kneeling before it, with the ceremonial manager holding his head, to pull it back when it was thought he had had enough. Following the drinking the boys were taken charge of by men who assisted them in the processions and dances that followed, including ceremonial circuits around the fire.

Before long the drug took effect and the boys fell unconscious. They were then carried into a small enclosure where they lay stupefied, watched by some of the men. The duration of complete narcosis varied from group to group. The Diegeño gave warm water to the boys after one night to help them recover. Among the Luiseño the intoxication seems to have lasted longer, up to three nights, but there must have been considerable individual variation, since not all the initiates were of the same age and size, and there was no definite measure of the amount of root used. In any event, the effect of the drug was powerful and the Luiseño reported some fatal cases. Whatever the initiates experienced in the course of the trance,

> . . . becomes of lifelong intimate sanctity to them. This vision is usually an animal, and at least at times they learn from it a song which they keep as their own. It seems also that they will not kill any individual of the species. It is clear that the concept of the vision corresponds exactly with what among certain primitive tribes has been unfortunately denominated the "personal totem." It is certain that a special and individual relation of a supernatural kind is believed to exist forever after between the dreamer and the dream. The similarity to shamanism is also obvious; but it would be misleading to name the Luiseño institution outright "shamanistic" or "totemic." (Kroeber, 1953:669-670)

Nonetheless, the final ritual, which takes place about two months after the *toloache* drinking, is unmistakable in its similarity to shamanistic mythology the world over. The central figure in this ceremony is called *wanawut*, a man-sized animal-like effigy with a body, head, arms, legs, and sometimes a tail, made of mesh or netting of milkweed or nettle twine, that is laid in a trench, with three or four flat stones set upon it:

> Each boy in turn now enters the trench, supported by the old man who has acted as his sponsor, and at a signal leaps from stone to stone. Should he slip, it is an indication that he will die soon. Very small boys are partially assisted by the old men. When all have jumped, they help the old men push the earth into the trench, burying the figure. The symbolism of this strange rite clearly refers to life and death. The trench represents the grave: the Luiseño cremated their corpses over a pit which was filled when the embers and bones had sunk in. The figure is human. It is specifically said to denote the Milky Way—otherwise a symbol of the spirit or soul. There seems also to be present the idea that the spirit of the dead is to be tied, perhaps to the sky, at any rate away from the earth; and the cordage of the object is probably significant in this regard. (Kroeber, 1953:671-672)

After the burial of the *wanawut*, there was dancing through the night, ending with a fire dance and the destruction by fire of the brush enclosure in which the *toloache* drinking took place. The boys had now forever left their childhood days behind. The *Datura* had done its sacred work and they would never taste it again.

Transcending "Ordinary Reality"

The ritual use of *Datura inoxia* in boys' puberty rites of the southern California Cahuilla has been described by several anthropologists (e.g. Kroeber, 1908; Hooper, 1920; Strong, 1929; and, most recently, Bean, 1972); the most complete account is that of William Duncan Strong (1929: 173-175), who noted that the Cahuilla regarded *Datura* as a great shaman with whom they could communicate in the course of their ceremonies. There were special *manet* songs connected with the *Datura* rituals which only the shamans could understand, because they were not in the everyday Cahuilla tongue but in a special esoteric "ocean language" addressed to the shamans and supernatural beings that lived on the floor of the sea.

An extensive discussion of what has survived of the multiple meanings and uses of *Datura* among the modern Cahuilla, whose language belongs to the Shoshonean branch of Uto-Aztecan and who are historically related not only to their Shoshonean-speaking neighbors but also to the Hopi of Arizona, and, more distantly, to the Huichols, the Cora, and other speakers of Uto-Aztecan tongues in Mesoamerica, can be found in a recent work on Cahuilla ethnobotany by anthropologist Lowell J. Bean and Mrs. Katherine Siva Saubel, a member of the tribal council of Los Coyote Cahuilla Reservation and herself a noted authority on the traditions and culture of her people (Bean and Saubel, 1972). Apart from its crucial role in boys' initiation rites, which resemble those of the Luiseño, Gabrieleño and other desert and coastal tribes of southern California, the authors note (pp. 61-62) that *Datura* afforded the *puul* (shaman) a means of transcending ordinary reality and coming into contact with specific guardian spirits, as well as enabling him to go on magical flights to Otherworlds or transform himself into certain animals, such as the mountain lion or eagle. Such flights and transformations in the *Datura* trance were a necessary and routine activity of shamans, for such purposes as bringing back information about the Upper- and Underworld, visiting the dead, or retrieving lost or strayed souls.

Datura also played an important role in native medicine. As among the Zuñi and Aztecs, the plant was employed by Cahuilla shamans in the form of a paste or ointment as a highly effective pain killer in setting broken or dislocated bones, alleviating localized pain, and even relieving toothache. Depending on the effect desired, the Indians commonly used the root in a drink, generally smoked the leaves, and crushed both roots and leaves with other parts of the plant and mixed them into a medicinal paste.

At the same time, the authors stress that the Cahuilla are well aware of the very real dangers in using a plant that may cause serious mental disorientation, disorders in locomotor activities, acute cardiac symptoms endangering heart functions, and other severe physiological problems ranging from temporary psychosis to death. Despite their superior knowledge, even some shamans refrained from *Datura* use, preferring other techniques to achieve contact with the supernatural. All the Cahuilla who discussed *Datura* with them, Bean and Saubel write (p. 60),

. . . stressed that the plant is unpredictable and warned against its use by the casual experimenter.

No idle warning: in the past few years, the authors note, several young people in southern California have died after experimenting with *Datura*, and many others have required hospitalization.

CHAPTER THIRTEEN

HALLUCINOGENIC SNUFFS AND ANIMAL SYMBOLISM

Thus far we have encountered deer, jaguars, birds, snakes and toads in relation to the sacred hallucinogens, either in some symbolic association, or in the imagery of the ecstatic trance, or even as avatar of a particular plant. Animal symbolism is clearly inseparable from the traditional psychedelic complexes of the Old and New Worlds, and its investigation of great culture-historical and psychological interest. These final chapters will concern themselves with some of these questions, and they will lead us in some surprising directions.

But I want to back into that fascinating arena by returning once more to the potent snuffs that greeted the early Spanish explorers as the first manifestation of the New World hallucinogens. For it is above all in the technology and symbolism of snuffing that a whole complex of animal imagery manifests itself in archaeological and ethnographic art.

In considering the major hallucinogenic snuffs, we should not forget that many of the scores of psychoactive plants of the New World could at least theoretically be used in this way, and that especially in South America there is much evidence for such experimentation. Even *Ilex guayusa*, the caffeine-containing holly that, along with its sister species, is widely utilized as a stimulating tea (e.g., *maté* = *I. paraguayensis*), served as snuff, at least for some shamans of ancient highland Bolivia, judging from a recently excavated shaman's grave dated to ca. A.D. 500, that contained bundles of *Ilex* leaves together with a complete kit for preparing and taking snuff. The kit also includes clysters, so that the same plant might even have been employed as enemas (Schultes, 1972b).

146

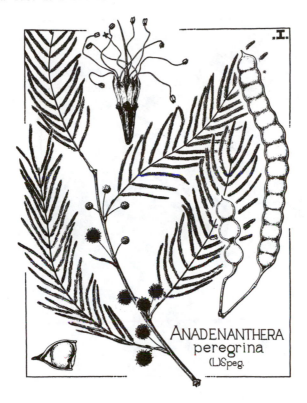

ANADENANTHERA
peregrina
(L)Speg.

The principal snuffs are now well known, their botany and chemistry having at last emerged from a long period of taxonomical confusion and uncertainty. At first, as was mentioned earlier, tobacco was thought to be the source of the hallucinogenic snuff of the West Indies. Then, for a long time—in fact, until just a few years ago—all intoxicating snuffs, from the Antilles through much of South America, were almost uniformly ascribed to one species of *Piptadenia*, *P. peregrina*, closely related to the acacias and mimosas. Now, thanks to plant taxonomist Siri von Reis Altschul (1964, 1972), a student of Schultes, *P. peregrina* has been removed from that genus and reclassified as one of two species belonging to a new, related, but clearly distinct hallucinogenic genus, *Anadenanthera*. The other is *A. colubrina*, a western South American species that is the source of the sacred *huilca* (*wilka*) seeds of the Andes, which were variously employed in the form of snuff, infusions, and even enemas.

The *Virola* Tree as a Source of Snuff

But even this corrected classification did not clear up all the confusion, because snuffs were attributed by many writers to *Anadenanthera*, whether or

VIROLA
theiodora
(Spr. ex Bth.)
Warburg

not that genus actually occurred locally, and even though the observed method of preparation suggested that several different and even unrelated species might be involved. The mystery was cleared up when several species of *Virola*, a tree belonging not, like *Anadenanthera*, to the Leguminoseae (pea family) but, like nutmeg, to the Myristicaceae, were confirmed as source of some of the snuffs once attributed solely to *A. peregrina*. Schultes was again prominently involved in settling this problem.

The principal hallucinogenic alkaloids in both *Anadenanthera* (*peregrina* and *colubrina*) and in the several species of *Virola* (*V. theidora*, *V. callophylla*, *V. callophylloidea*) are tryptamines, as they are also in one species of *Banisteriopsis*, and in the sacred mushrooms and other ritual hallucinogens of Mexico. In *A. peregrina* and *colubrina*, bufotenine (5-hydroxy-N,N-dimethyltryptamine) is present in large amounts, and for a time the central nervous activity of *Anadenanthera* snuffs was thought to be due mainly to this alkaloid, which these leguminous trees share with the toad (*Bufo* spp.). Recent analyses have shown, however, that other tryptamine derivatives are also present in the seeds—such as N,N-dimethyltryptamine, N-monomethyltryptamine, 5-methoxy-N, 5-methoxy-N-monomethyltryptamine, N,N-

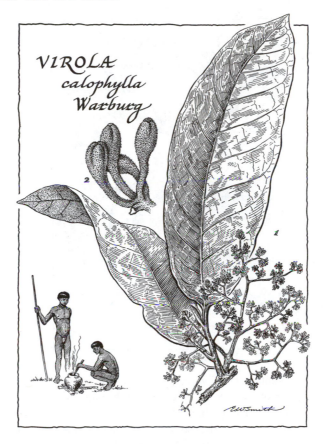

dimethyltryptamine-N-oxide,5-hydroxy-N, and N-dimethyltryptamine-N-oxide (Schultes, 1972a:28).

Snuff prepared from *Virola theidora* alone, without admixtures, contains 5-methoxy-N,N-dimethyltryptamine in concentrations of up to 8 percent, along with smaller amounts of N,N-dimethyltryptamine and related alkaloids. Alkaloid concentrations vary in different parts of the tree, but the bark generally contains the highest percentage.

Now, as we know, tryptamines require a monoamine oxidase inhibitor to become effective in man, a problem the Indians have solved in several known instances by mixing different hallucinogenic species together. For example, *Banisteriopsis rusbyana* is a chemical oddity among its sister species, in that in contrast to *B. caapi* and *B. inebrians*, whose active principles are *beta*-carboline harmala alkaloids, its active constituents are tryptamines! This explains why the Tukanoan Indians of Colombian Amazonia, for example, never take *B. rusbyana* by itself but mix it with *B. caapi* or *B. inebrians* into

an especially potent form of *yajé*, a method that allows the *beta*-carboline harmala alkaloids of the one to function as inhibitors for the tryptamines of the other. Thus not only the harmala alkaloids but also the tryptamines are able to play their part in the ecstatic intoxication. As Schultes (1972a) observes, here again one cannot help but wonder

how peoples in primitive societies, with no knowledge of chemistry or physiology, ever hit upon a solution to the activation of an alkaloid by a monoamine oxidase inhibitor. (p. 38)

Now, in the case of *Virola* snuffs, no such activating admixture seems to be absolutely required, since two new carbolines have recently been discovered in *V. theidora* itself (Schultes, 1970). Nevertheless, admixtures that can themselves be psychodynamically effective are frequently employed. Schultes (1972a), who visited the Waika (Yanomamö) in 1967 with the Swedish pharmacologist Bo Holmstedt, describes their technique as follows:

There are a number of methods of preparing the snuff, which is called *epená* or *nyakwana* by the many "tribes" which I include under the generic term *Waika*. Some scrape the soft inner layer of the bark of the tree, dry the shavings by gentle roasting over a fire, and store them until they are needed for making the snuff. They are then crushed and pulverized, triturated and sifted. The resultant powder is fine, homoge-

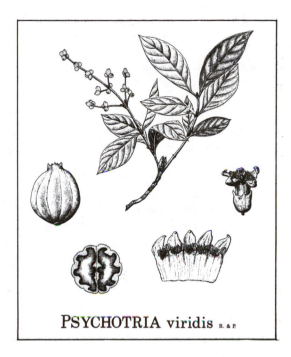

PSYCHOTRIA viridis R. & P.

neous, chocolate-brown, and highly pungent. Then, when the Indians desire it (but not always) a dust of the powdered dry leaves of the aromatic acanthaceous weed *Justicia pectoralis* var. *stenophylla* is added in equal amounts. The third, and invariable, ingredient is the ash of the bark of a rare leguminous tree, *Elizabetha princeps*. This tree is known as *ama* or *amasita* by the Waika. These ashes are mixed in approximately equal amounts with the resin, or resin and *Justicia* powder, to give a brownish-grey snuff.

Other Waikas follow a different procedure, at least when they are preparing the snuff for ceremonial purposes. The bark is stripped from the *Virola* tree, the strips laid over a gentle fire in the forest, and the copious blood-red resin is scraped into an earthenware pot. It is boiled down and allowed to sun-dry. Then, alone or mixed with the powdered *Justicia* leaves, it is sifted and is ready for use. (p. 43)

J. pectoralis appears to be itself a potent hallucinogen, containing, like *Virola*, tryptamine alkaloids. It is in fact cultivated by some of the Yanomamö groups studied by anthropologist Napoleon Chagnon and his colleagues on the Upper Orinoco and employed without any active admixtures in one variety of intoxicating *ebene* snuff (Chagnon *et al.*, 1971). (It should be noted here that *Justicia* and another tryptamine-containing South American genus, *Psychotria*, occur also in Mexico, a circumstance to which I will return in connection with the recent discovery of a very ancient snuffing complex in

Mexico that was apparently already long extinct at the time of the Conquest.)

Rapid Intoxication

Intoxication with snuffs prepared basically from the bark resin of *Virola theidora* or related species, or the seeds of *Anadenanthera peregrina*, is extremely rapid and powerful. Not only in the pre-European past but even today the snuffing technology of agricultural Indians is quite complex, and all sorts of decorated and undecorated nose pipes, snuffing tubes, mortars, containers and tablets abound in archaeological and ethnographic collections. Waika snuffing is much simpler, as is their material culture in general. The Waika, who are even today essentially hunter-gatherers with incipient tree- and root-crop cultivation, take the prepared snuff through very long bamboo tubes, one man blowing the charge into another's nostrils. Almost at once the mucous membranes are activated, the nose begins to run, and saliva flows copiously. There is also strong itching or tingling of the top of the skull, to which the Indians react by vigorous scratching. Schultes (1972a) himself experienced no extraordinary visual or auditory sensations, but for the Indians these occur within minutes of the *ebene* charge and are perceived as direct communication with the spirits of animals, plants, deceased relatives and other supernaturals. There is considerable variation between individuals in the degree of motor control, with experienced shamans apparently able to exercise much greater control over their movements than others. The intensity of the ecstatic trance also varies; the experience is usually of short duration, however, and in the course of ritual (and, nowadays, among more accultur- ated Waika, also recreational) intoxication repeated charges of snuff are customarily inhaled by the participants.

Addiction: Snuff, No; Tobacco, Yes

In light of the frequency with which these powerful tryptamine prepara- tions are employed and the intensity of the experience, it is worth quoting the following observation:

. . . none of the hallucinogens used by the Yanomamö are habit-forming, missionary opinions notwithstanding . . . Yanomamö can and do abstain from them for weeks and do not mention it or complain about it. Tobacco-chewing, on the other hand, is habitual: they cannot go several hours without it, and the entire village is in a state of crisis when the tobacco crop fails. In this connection the Yanomamö have discovered a number of tobacco substitutes, from both domestic and feral plant sources, to rely on when they run short of tobacco. When questioned on the possible substitutes for their hallucinogens, one informant summarized the drug-tobacco situation as follows:

"When we are out of tobacco we crave it intensely and we say we are *hōri*—in utter poverty. We do not crave *ebene* in the same way and therefore never say that we are "in poverty" when there is none. But *yakoana (Virola)* is everywhere, and we can always find some if we want to take *ebene*." (Chagnon *et al.*, 1971:74)

Snuffing and Animal Art

No one has contributed more to our knowledge of the symbolic content of Central and South American snuffing paraphernalia than the Swedish ethnologist S. Henry Wassén, recently retired director of the Gothenburg Ethnographical Museum. Wassén, to whose early studies of the ethnopharmacology and symbolism of South American frogs and toads we will shortly return in connection with what has recently been discovered about toad- and frog-poison intoxication, has over the past decade published several major studies on the use of Indian snuffs and the iconography of ornamented snuffing paraphernalia (Wassén, 1963-1967).

What has emerged from these studies is an unmistakable symbol complex that ties shamanism and the ecstatic experience to the already familiar bird-feline-reptilian configuration we find so prominently in Mesoamerican and Andean cosmology and iconography. The way this expresses itself in the paraphernalia of snuffing is in combinations or juxtapositions of elements representing the most important supernatural animals to which the South American shaman relates—the harpy eagle or king vulture (the condor in the Andes), the anaconda or boa constrictor, and above all, the jaguar, in styles that range from near-naturalism to geometric abstraction. Sometimes only one of these is clearly shown, or else a human being, representing the shaman himself, is depicted in juxtaposition with one or more of his principal zoomorphic allies or alter egos.

On occasion the complementary opposition of the bird and jaguar, or bird-jaguar-serpent, is symbolized not in the form of a two- or three-dimensional image but rather in the materials employed in the making or ornamentation of the implements—e.g. bird-bone snuffing tube juxtaposed with wooden snuff trays decorated with feline and snake motifs or else bird feathers and snake skin used as symbolic adornments (see Wassén, 1967, for numerous illustrations of these motifs).

The juxtaposition of bird and mammal in the material culture of snuffing has a respectable pedigree, since it is already evident in the oldest snuff paraphernalia thus far known—a bone tray and tubes which Junius B. Bird of the American Museum of Natural History excavated in the ancient Peruvian coastal site of Huaca Prieta, and which are dated to about 1600 B.C.

The point is that analogous arrangements of certain animals and human beings in the symbolic art of the snuffing complex are not limited to one region or one period but extend through space and time from the Caribbean to the Andes and from prehistory to the present.

Of special interest are decorated snuff containers, mortars, tubes, nose pipes, and related implements that depict the jaguar as guardian or alter ego of the shaman—a dominant theme, we recall, in tropical American shamanism that can be recognized in archaeological snuffing paraphernalia from Argentina and Chile as well as Mesoamerica (Wassén, 1967; Figures 8, 11, 13-14,

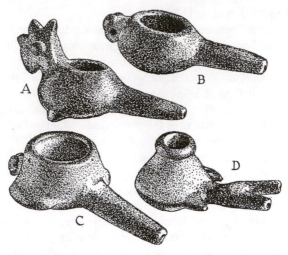

Bird-shaped snuffing pipes. Fired-clay objects from archaeological sites in Costa
Rica. *A*. Guanacaste; *B-D*, Linea Vieja. Average length, 5-6 inches. Collection
of the Gothenburg Ethnographic Museum. Drawing courtesy of S. Henry Wassén.

30-31). Not surprisingly we also find it symbolized in other artifacts connected with the practice of shamanism.

Quite apart from the frequent resort to bird bone for snuffing tubes (a
choice that must have been motivated at least as much by symbolic as by
practical considerations), the avian motif predominates also in the representational or abstract art of the snuffing complex. Where the bird motif is specific,
it usually represents the harpy eagle or its Andean cousin, the condor, or else
some other bird selected for special characteristics that relate it symbolically
to the phenomenology of shamanism. Typically these birds include waterfowl
or diving birds, presumably because their unique ability to transcend the
boundaries of different planes of existence is seen to be analogous to that of
the shaman. As a matter of fact, it is axiomatic of shamanic symbology that it
selects precisely those animals that can shift between different environments
or that by virtue of unusual life histories or habits are perceived as mediators
between disparate states. Where the bird motif is unspecific, it seems to stand
for the power of flight that is the shaman's special gift and that is activated by
the hallucinogen. It should also be noted that birds are often regarded as
guardian spirits or even manifestations of specific psychoactive plants, especially tobacco; this observation provides one clue for the meaning of bird-
shaped tobacco pipes in North American Indian art. Among the many known
archaeological examples of the bird motif in snuff paraphernalia are numerous
nose pipes of fired clay from archaeological sites in Costa Rica and a series of
small bird-shaped polished stone mortars from ancient shell middens on the
coast of Brazil. (See Wassén, 1967: Figures 4 and 12. Figure 34 in the same

publication depicts some interesting wooden or bamboo snuffing tubes from several South American localities with nose pieces shaped like bird's heads, which make them resemble the well-known bird-headed staffs associated with shamanism as symbols of the shaman's tree and his ascent to the Upperworld. Such a staff was also found in the shaman's burial in highland Bolivia. (Schultes, 1972b)

Snuffing in Mexico

Now we give attention to Mexico and the archaeological evidence for an ancient snuffing complex that dates back at least to the second millennium B.C., apparently became extinct as a major technique of ritual intoxication before A.D. 1000, and today survives only in remote mountain areas of Oaxaca and Guerrero, where some curers are said to inhale the pulverized seeds of the morning glory (T. Knab, personal communication, based on the unpublished field notes of the late botanist Thomas McDougall). It has always seemed puzzling that the early Spanish missionaries, who were certainly alert to the many manifestations of ritual intoxication, seem not to have seen any evidence of snuffing, even in areas adjacent to the well-developed snuffing complex of the Caribbean island cultures. Powdered tobacco is mentioned, but there is nothing to suggest that it, or any other hallucinogen, was inhaled as snuff.

Deer, holding peyote cactus in its mouth. A snuffing pipe about 2500 years old, from Monte Albán, Mexico. Length 5 inches; private collection.

The negative evidence from the sixteenth century notwithstanding, Mexico once did have a well-developed snuffing complex (Furst, 1974b). Individuals holding nose pipes to their nostrils are depicted in trance-like states in Colima mortuary art from western Mexico, dated ca. 100 B.C.-A.D. 200. Also, there are in the archaeological art of Oaxaca numerous small ceramic effigy bowls with short, perforated stems, dating from 500 B.C. to the first centuries A.D. Their purpose becomes obvious once one knows that snuffing was practiced: they are not "sacrificial" or "libation" bowls, as they are often described, but nose pipes, decorated with such typically shamanistic themes as flight and transformation.

The earliest Mesoamerican ceramic nose pipes, dating to about 1300-1500 B.C., were found at Xochipala, Guerrero, in association with finely made figurines of men and women in a remarkably sophisticated and naturalistic style. Among the Xochipala snuffers from this early site, one simple bowl with a hollow stem is virtually indistinguishable from many that have been found in Costa Rica. So also is a double-stemmed bird-effigy nose pipe from a deep shaft-and-chamber tomb in Nayarit, dated ca. A.D. 100.

Finally, there are the famous Olmec jade artifacts, nicknamed "spoons," that could have served as snuff tablets. Some of these finely carved and highly polished objects, sometimes decorated with incised bird-jaguar motifs in the typical Olmec style of 1200-900 B.C., resemble, with their long tails and slightly rounded bodies, stylized profile birds in flight—symbolism that would fit comfortably into the animal art of hallucinogens, and especially the flight motif in the iconography of shamanic snuffing (Furst, 1968:162-63).*

The cumulative evidence points to a southern origin—perhaps northwestern South America—for the early Mesoamerican snuffing complex. Why it should have disappeared from Mexico centuries before the Conquest while proliferating so spectacularly in South America and the West Indies is a mystery. Nor do we know the botany or chemistry of the Mexican snuffs. They could have been traded from South America (*huilca*, perhaps?), but as has been noted, various local hallucinogens could also have been utilized, including acacia-like trees native to Mexico that have not yet been tested for hallucinogenic alkaloids. Apart from these possibilities, Mexico shares with South America not only tobacco, which was and is used as snuff in South America, but also at least one tryptamine-containing genus, *Justicia*, from which Indians on the Upper Orinoco make an intoxicating snuff. Clearly, much ethnobotanical and phytochemical work remains to be done.

---

*A graduate student specializing in Olmec iconography, Anatole Pohorilenko, has suggested to me that these "spoons" may represent not conventionalized birds in flight but tadpoles. He could be right. As a transitional stage in an ongoing process of metamorphosis, and considering the importance of the frog/toad motif in Mesoamerican symbolism (see the next chapter), tadpoles would of course accord very well with the iconography of shamanism and hallucinogens.

Snuffing pipe in use. Ceramic tomb figurine of an "entranced" man with a snuff-ing pipe shows hallucinogenic snuff to have been used in Mexico 2000 years ago. From a shaft-and-chamber tomb in Colima, western Mexico, ca. 100 B.C.-A.D. 200. Height 10 inches. Collection of Kurt Stavenhagen, Mexico.

CHAPTER FOURTEEN

THE TOAD AS EARTH MOTHER: A PROBLEM IN SYMBOLISM AND PSYCHOPHARMACOLOGY

There is in North and South America a widespread mythic complex that links the toad to the earth as animal manifestation of a dualistic Earth Mother Goddess, at once destroyer and giver of life. Sometimes the toad is the earth, and from her body sprouted the first food plants—maize in Mexico, bitter manioc in Amazonia. She is also benefactress of the first people or culture heroes, teacher of the skills of hunting and the magic arts, and her dismemberment accounts for the origins of agriculture.

The most dramatic variation on this common theme is Tlaltecuhtli, "Owner (Guardian) of the Earth," the Mother Goddess in her monstrous, devouring form in the complex cosmological scheme of the Aztecs of central Mexico, in whose art she is depicted sometimes as a real toad, more commonly as a clawed, anthropomorphic being in the characteristic upright squatting position in which women in the traditional world customarily give birth. Her joints are adorned with human skulls, her fanged mouth is the maw of the Netherworld through which the human dead and dying Sun pass into her transforming womb in a never-ending cycle of destruction and rebirth.

In a somewhat fragmentary origin myth set down in Spanish in the sixteenth century, after the destruction of the world by water, the gods Quetzalcóatl and Tezcatlipoca (the one the bird-serpent, the other the magician who transforms into the jaguar) see Tlaltecuhtli floating alone in the primordial seas as sole survivor of the universal deluge. Transforming themselves into snakes, they take hold of the amphibian goddess and split her in half, one part becoming the heavens, the other the earth—the valleys, moun-

158

tains, lakes, rivers and other natural features being formed from different parts of her violated body. The wounded creature cries pitifully in the night, until the gods decree that she is to bring forth the useful plants to feed humanity, but that man in turn must guarantee her continued vitality by pledging his flesh and blood as her proper sustenance.

Toad as Mediator and Dualistic Mother

Tlaltecuhtli is of course not just toad. Rather, with her cavernous mouth and her delivery-like crouch, the toad is an archetypal form on which the characteristics of other life forms pertaining to different planes of existence (predators like the jaguar, for example) are often superimposed. She is thus an ideal image of the mediator, by which otherwise apparently disparate states are united—life and death, air and water, death and rebirth, and the like. The fact that the toad is at once impressively fertile and also cannabalistic, often feeding on smaller members of the same or related species, including her own offspring, almost certainly reinforced her role as metaphor for the earth as the Great Mother who is at once giver and taker of life, if it did not in fact inspire it in the first place.

In any event, there is clearly much more than only the "obvious" connection with rain to account for the importance of the toad-frog motif in the indigenous symbolic system, including its expression in the visual arts, where it appears both realistically and overlaid with mythic motifs. More than almost any other member of the animal kingdom, except perhaps butterflies, toads display a dramatic metamorphosis—from aquatic, gill-breathing, fish-like vegetarians into largely terrestrial, carnivorous quadrupeds, some of them equipped with powerful poisons capable of killing (i.e. transforming into another state of existence), with habitats ranging from the banks of streams and ponds to the crowns of the highest trees. Thus these creatures seem to embody some of the most fundamental principles of American Indian thought: transformation, rather than creation *ex nihilo*, to account for all phenomena in the natural and supernatural environment; dualism or complementary opposites; the cycle of death and regeneration.

Thus the gaping mouth of Tlaltecuhtli—the earth as the terrible devouring mother in her monstrous feline-toad form—becomes the proper symbol for the maw of the divine earth in the pictorial codices of ancient Mexico, swallowing the dead as she swallows the dying Sun—her own offspring—in a constant repetition of destruction and rebirth that will end only if humanity fails in its duty to feed her with its own flesh and blood. Actually Tlaltecuhtli is nothing else than the adaptation to complex Middle American civilization of an apparently very ancient concept—one we find to be fundamental even today in the origin myths of many peoples of the Amazon basin: the toad as dualistic, beneficent-devouring, transforming female shaman, owner of the earth and of fire, and originator of the magic arts as well as the useful arts of agriculture, of which she makes a gift to humanity through the agency of a culture hero, or more commonly, a pair of Hero Twins. These Twins are analogous to the Hero Twins of the Maya and other Middle and North American Indians.

Toad Mother and Culture Heroes

The following is a composite summary of the typical Toad Mother-Hero Twin myth whose distribution, in its essentials, extends from the Guianas in the east to the forested eastern slopes of the Andes in the west:

The twins are the offspring of a natural mother who is killed and eaten by the Jaguar People (paralleling the destruction of the first world era and its inhabitants by jaguars in Middle American cosmology). Toad Woman, or Toad Grandmother, who is also the supernatural Mother of the Jaguars, intervenes and rescues the pregnant uterus.* She keeps it near her life-giving maternal hearth until the embryonic twins grow to proper size and emerge. As befits culture heroes, they reach adulthood with miraculous speed, and are taught the skills of hunters and the arts of shamanism by their foster mother who, although agriculture has not yet been invented, feeds them baked cassava bread made from the flour of bitter manioc, the staple of root-crop agriculture in the tropical forest. Mystified, the Hero Twins, who have vowed to avenge their real mother's death, spy on their foster mother and discover that not only are the jaguars who killed their mother her children but she herself transforms into jaguar and squeezes cassava flour from her poison glands. They kill, dismember, and burn her in a part of the forest they have cleared for planting. From her ashes grow the first food plants, her milky poison transforming itself into the bitter, or poisonous, variety of manioc (*Manihot utilisima*).

The origin of manioc cultivation, which was already fully developed by 3000 B.C., is believed by some scholars to go back as far as 5000-7000 B.C. Bitter manioc, an exclusively New World member of the Euphorbiaceae that is much more nutritious than the sweet variety, in its untreated state contains a high concentration of hydrocyanic (prussic) acid. The Indians long ago learned to extract this poison in a complicated process by which the dangerous acid is either evaporated or, preferably, converted into sugars that serve to render other foods more palatable. Donald Lathrap (1970), one of the foremost students of tropical forest Indian culture, argues that the invention of these procedures must lie far back in prehistory, since archaeology has shown that bitter manioc was already the staple crop of flood-plain agriculture in

---

*It is interesting that in central Europe, in particular, the toad is identified with the womb or uterus, and toad effigies of metal and other materials are placed in churches as votive offerings to help women to conceive or get them through a difficult pregnancy. These beliefs of course predate the introduction of Christianity.

northern South America in the second millennium B.C. Since the genetic modification of bitter manioc from its wild ancestor probably took millennia, the whole process of manioc cultivation, so basic to tropical forest Indian culture, could well have had at least its tentative experimental beginnings seven thousand and more years before the present. The agricultural component of South American toad mythology obviously postdates the origins of bitter-manioc cultivation, which are here linked to the poisonous white secretion flowing from Toad Grandmother's parotid glands; on the other hand, this aspect of the toad as animal avatar of the Earth Goddess could have been superimposed upon a much older mythic complex. Considering the wide distribution of the Earth Mother-as-toad mythology in South America and the striking similarity of this mythic theme to Mesoamerican and even North American traditions, the Amazonian myth may ultimately derive from very ancient Paleolithic roots that extend beyond the New World into Asia.

Psychotropic Properties of Toad Poison

Myth is one thing, practice another. True, bufotenine occurs coincidentally in the skin glands of *Bufo marinus* and other species; and the related alkaloid, 5-methoxy-N,N-dimethyltryptamine, which is mainly responsible for the hallucinogenic activity of *Virola* and *Anadenanthera* snuffs, has recently been isolated from the North American desert toad, *Bufo alvarius* (Erspamer *et al.*, 1967; Daly and Witkop, 1971). But what actually is the evidence that the Indians themselves ever utilized such animal poisons for purposes that could be seen as magicoreligious?

Though widely scattered through the ethnographic literature, the evidence turns out to be surprisingly substantial, beginning with an early Colonial account by the English Dominican friar Thomas Gage, who reported in the mid-seventeenth century that the Pokoman Maya of Guatemala had the habit of not just adding tobacco to their fermented ritual drink but also poisonous toads to give it a special potency (Thompson, 1970)! This evidently ancient practice, which managed to survive into modern times, may explain the large quantity of skeletal remains of *Bufo marinus* which the Yale archaeologist Michael D. Coe found at the important Olmec ceremonial site of San Lorenzo, in Veracruz, Mexico, dating to 1250-900 B.C. (Coe, 1971). In view of the toad's high poison content and its sacred stature, *Bufo* would hardly have served the Olmecs as ordinary food. But as animal manifestation of the Earth Mother the toad could well have entered into magicoreligious inebriation—as much, perhaps, for symbolic as for pharmacological considerations.

Preparations of *Bufo marinus* poison apparently still play a role in the pharmacopoeias of some few indigenous *curanderos* (curers) in Veracruz, who claim that the secret techniques by which the venom is extracted and processed into pills and potions have been passed down to them through the generations from older masters, customarily their own fathers. It is said that the toad is never killed or harmed but only irritated gently to make it release its poison from the prominent parotid glands characteristic of the species. The poison is collected in small bowls and subjected to repeated treatment over fire to remove or reduce the harmful elements before being hardened. It is then rolled into pills for later use, love magic being one of the reported purposes. (T. Knab, personal communication)

Such surviving practices help to explain the purpose of small, toad-shaped effigy bowls that have been found in archaeological sites in Veracruz and adjacent parts of southeastern Mexico. On these the ancient ceramic artists customarily emphasized the parotid glands that contain the poison. The same emphasis marks a well-known monumental Aztec basalt sculpture of a toad (with the glyph of the Mother Goddess of Terrestrial Water Chalchiuhtlicue, Skirt of Jade, on her belly) in the National Museum of Anthropology in Mexico City.

Analogies in Asian Mythology

The use of *Bufo* poison as magical folk medicine in Mexico recalls Chinese Taoist and derivative Japanese traditions of the *Gama sennin*, a wise teacher and accomplished herbalist who lived alone in the mountains in the company of a giant toad. The toad, who in some versions is really the *Gama sennin* himself (*Gama* means "toad" in Japanese), taught him the magical and healing arts, including the making of pills that enabled him to transform at will into toad form. There are also Japanese and earlier Chinese traditions of toads capable of conjuring up the most exquisite visions, especially a vision that brought one face to face with the Taoist Islands of Paradise, in whose center stood a giant immortal pine amid the most beautiful flowers, trees, and animals that symbolized eternal life; among these is the fungus of immortality, the legendary Ling Chih, whose real ancestor may have been the fly-agaric of Eurasiatic shamanism. What is more, the dwellers of this blessed island stayed eternally young by drinking from the fountain of life at the foot of the enormous, never-decaying pine, which reminds one of similar references cited by Wasson in connection with *Soma* and the origins of the Tree of Life. (Volker, 1950:168-170)

Toad and Toadstool

Wasson (1968) also explored the whole problem of the toad's connection with *Amanita muscaria* in European folk usage. The English "toadstool" is a nonspecific term that now applies to all wild or inedible mushrooms, but Wasson showed that originally it referred to the fly-agaric, as in fact the rural French *crapaudin*, the toad's thing, still does. The ancient Finns also seem to have recognized a close affinity between *Bufo* and mushroom. In the *Kalevala*, the great national saga of Finland, the heroes are forever searching for the mysterious *sampo*, source of supernatural power. Just what *sampo* was has never been satisfactorily explained, but recently an anthropological linguist, Lyle Campbell (personal communication), discovered that in some Balto-Finnish dialects *sampo* stands for "mushroom" as well as "toad," raising the distinct possibility that the legendary *sampo* may be nothing else than the Finnish equivalent of *Soma* (see also Wasson, 1968:310-312). This possibility is all the more likely in that the fly-agaric is known to have been employed in Baltic shamanism as well.

Oddly enough, the toad-mushroom association, which in Europe seems to be very ancient, reappears in the New World in Preclassic highland Guatemala, where toads by themselves or toads with feline characters (the "earth monster" Tlaltecuhtli again), are depicted three-dimensionally on "mushroom stones" dating to the first millennium B.C. The most interesting of these is the already mentioned effigy with the mushroom emerging from the mouth of a toad with prominent poison glands that is unmistakably meant to be *Bufo marinus*. One would have to ignore some enormous gaps in space and time to suggest a direct connection with the Old World, but the coincidence is certainly striking.

Magical Uses of Frog and Toad Poison

Apart from the poison of *Bufo marinus*, which evidently does have what can be called hallucinogenic properties, the venoms of some other species of toads or frogs in South America have found uses that can only be described as magical, on occasion approximating the ecstatic state, even if from the point of view of pharmacology and toxicology their action belongs to a wholly different class. A good deal of the evidence then available from travelers, ethnologists, and other sources was brought together more than forty years ago by Wassén (1934), who came to the conclusion that the ubiquitous frog/toad motif in South American Indian mythology and art, including the great number of effigies of cast gold from pre-Hispanic Colombia and Panama, was inseparable from the practical use of frog venom for blowgun-dart poison (which in any event had a magical component), and from the widespread magicoreligious beliefs and practices involving the toxins of different species of these amphibians.

One of the most unusual of these—and one that certainly typifies transformation and the power of frogs to bring it about—is *tapirage*, a curious practice involving the use of frog or toad poison to cause a change in the natural plumage of parrots. As described in the *Handbook of South American Indians* (Steward, ed., 1963: Vol. 1, 265, 275, 424; Vol. 3, 102, 414; Vol. 6, 384, 397), in *tapirage* the feathers are plucked from a living bird and a small quantity of the extremely potent poison of *Dendrobates tinctorius* or some other venomous species is rubbed on the wound, which is then sealed with wax. When new feathers appear they do so in a color different from the original ones, yellow and red replacing green, for example. According to Gilmore (in Steward, ed., 1963: Vol. 6, 407-408), the poisonous secretion of the toad (*Bufo marinus*) is also used in this manner. *Tapirage* has been reported independently over the past two centuries from the Guianas, the Gran Chaco, Brazil, Venezuela, and Bolivia, but some zoologists have tended to doubt that the poison really plays any but a magical or symbolic role in the process. Instead they assume that a change in the diet of the captured birds is more likely to be responsible. Scores of Indian tribes from the Atlantic to the Andes believe otherwise.

On another level, as early as 1915 Walter E. Roth, colonial magistrate, medical officer and protector of the Indians in the Pomeroon District of British Guiana (now independent Guyana), reported in some detail on the magical use of the poisonous skin exudates and spawn of certain frogs. The Indians, he wrote, rubbed these poisons into cuts made in the skin, or else introduced them into the eyes, nose, mouth, and ears of men about to embark on a hunt. These curious practices received their charter in myths, clearly related to those of the Hero Twins, whose common theme is that a primordial hunter received his skill as gift from Toad or Frog Woman, who rubbed her venom into his sensory organs to heighten their acuity. After suffering drastic symptoms, including temporary loss of consciousness, the mythic First Hunter found himself imbued with miraculous skills in the pursuit of game. Likewise, Guyana Indian shamans employed toads and venomous frogs in ritual curing, rubbing the animals over the body of the patient or else introducing the poison directly into cuts.

In 1961, Drs. Gertrude Dole and Robert Carneiro (Carneiro, 1970) of the American Museum of Natural History observed somewhat the same rites among the Amahuaca Indians of the Peruvian Montaña. The Amahuaca believe that the strongest hunting magic of all is for a man to inoculate himself with an extremely potent frog poison. This is scraped off the back of the frog with a small stick and rubbed into self-inflected burns on the arms or chest. Within a short time the hunter becomes violently ill, suffering uncontrollable vomiting, diarrhea, convulsions, and loss of consciousness. For some time thereafter he experiences hallucinations which are interpreted as supernatural encounters with the spirits of the forest. Since this phase is accompanied by the drinking of *ayahuasca*, it is not clear how much of the actual ecstatic experience can be ascribed to the frog poison and how much to *Banisteriopsis*. Of course, the radical purging of the system through the action of the poison would tend to heighten the effects of the *ayahuasca*. In any event the two aspects of the ritual are conceptually and functionally related.

Carneiro and Dole were unable to identify the frog involved, but it was probably a species related to the *kokoi* frogs (*Phyllobates bicolor* and *Dendrobates tinctorius*) of Colombia, whose secretions the Choco Indians use to poison their blowgun darts.

These spectacularly colored frogs and their poisons have been well-studied by toxicologists and herpetologists (Daly and Witkop, 1971; Daly and Myers, 1967). Some species were found to be astonishingly venomous—the secretion of one tree frog measuring less than an inch in length was judged sufficient to kill a thousand mice! In fact the venoms of certain species utilized by the Indians were found to constitute the most powerful natural toxins known to man, and several species have turned out to be so potent that they cannot even be handled safely without causing severe physical discomfort, including extreme irritation to the eyes, nose, and throat. While none of these poisons should be called "hallucinogenic," even in the sense in which this can be said of bufotenine, some of their constituents are known to affect the central nervous system, which may contribute to the supernatural effects ascribed to them by some Amazonian Indians. For that matter, however a particular Indian interprets the experience with toad or frog poison, whether taken internally or rubbed into a wound, it is scientifically inexact in the extreme to equate these animal poisons, including the venom of *Bufo marinus*, with the botanical hallucinogens: the massive assault on the system brought on by bufotenine-containing *Bufo* venom is of a very different order than the shift from one state of consciousness to another triggered by bufotenine-containing snuff.

What should be stressed is that all these animal poisons, including that of *Bufo marinus* and its relatives, are extremely potent, and that for anyone outside the traditional world, with its great store of traditional knowledge, or outside strictly controlled scientific settings, to experiment on himself or herself with these dangerous substances would obviously be the height of folly.

CHAPTER FIFTEEN

HALLUCINOGENS AND THE SACRED DEER

Almost everywhere in the New World deer were important food animals. But almost nowhere were they only that. On the contrary, few animals were so universally revered as supernaturally endowed with a special power, and perhaps none was so widely associated with shamans and shamanism. Consequently, even where deer was favorite and frequent game, its hunt was never routine, its death never casual. To eat deer meat, it seems, almost always and everywhere was at least as much a matter of feeding the spirit as the body. If this was generally the case for everybody, it held even more for the shaman, so much so that in some societies (the Warao of Venezuela, to mention one), for the shaman to treat venison as ordinary food is still tantamount to cannibalism.

Deer deities or deer as divine beings occur prominently in the cosmologies and rituals of innumerable peoples, from the Far North deep into South America, as they also do in archaeological art. Sometimes the supernatural deer is male—Deer as patron of hunting, for example—sometimes female, as supernatural mistress of the species or even of all animals, or as animal wife to a primordial hunter and female ancestor of the human race.

Deer ceremonials to obtain supernatural power and other benefits—direct or indirect, physical or spiritual, from the spirit of a particular deer or from the species as a whole—are so widespread in North America as to be near-universal, not only among hunters but among agricultural Indians as well. Many of the latter regard the deer as master and protector of crops and fertility, invoking its spirit at every turn of the agricultural cycle, from the clearing of the forest for a new field to the first fruits at harvest time. Among the Huichols, whose culture hero Kauyumarie, we recall, is Deer and who have several other major deer deities, every important agricultural endeavor is

166

(or should be) preceded by a ceremonial deer hunt; in fact, deer are never hunted or eaten except in a ritual context. In many origin myths of North or South American Indians a supernatural Deer is directly associated with other major supernaturals in the establishment of the most important aspects of culture and the social order; so, for example, among the Gê-speakers of Brazil, one of the oldest American Indian language families, Sun, Moon, and Deer set up the system of age-graded societies.

Deer deities and ceremonialism were of overriding importance to the ancient Maya and other ancient Mesoamerican peoples (as they continue to be in some areas), and this outlook is of course reflected both in the complex calendrical system for which the Maya are rightly admired and in pre-Columbian art as a whole. In some areas deer were sacrosanct and could not be killed; Bernal Díaz del Castillo (1908:16), for example, reported that in the country of the Mazatecs (deer people) in Oaxaca, tame deer were venerated as deities and no deer could be hunted. From the enormous *corpus* of painted and carved Maya funerary pottery, it is quite evident also that the deer played an important role in Maya beliefs about the land of the dead, the Underworld; clearly the deer was intimately associated among the Maya and other Mesoamerican Indians with magic, transformation, death ritual and the Upper- and Underworlds, in particular the latter.

It is a reflection of the extraordinary status of the deer as divine being, the special animal of gods and shamans, in pre-Hispanic Mesoamerica that in the process of Christian acculturation Christ himself should sometimes have become identified with the deer—to the degree that in some Indianized Good Friday ceremonies in Mexico the Passion itself is treated like a sacrificial deer hunt. Among the Cora of Nayarit, for example, the symbolic hunt for the divine deer, which ends in the crucifixon and interment of the Christ-Deer, involves not just one animal but four, one each for the cardinal points, recalling the traditional non-Christian Deer Dance of the New Mexico pueblos of San Ildefonso and San Juan, which also culminates in the symbolic hunt and sacrificial death of four deer. There is little question that the present-day syncretistic Cora ceremony and that of the Pueblos ultimately derive from the same ancestral source.

The question is, how far back can we legitimately take this whole pan-American deer-shamanism complex? Can we in fact consider it solely in the context of American prehistory? I don't think so. American Indian deer-shamanism, with its particular emphasis on the deer as divine source of medicine and curing power, is too obviously analogous to the reindeer and deer shamanism of the Paleo-Siberians and their Eurasiatic Paleolithic and Mesolithic antecedents to be anything other than its linear descendant (for an illuminating discussion of antlered shamans and reindeer shamanism, see La Barre's chapter, "The Dancing Sorcerer," in his *The Ghost Dance: Origins of Religion* [1970d]).

Of particular pertinence to this problem is the deer's more or less intensive relationship to several New World hallucinogens, sometimes to the point of total qualitative identification between plant and animal. In these final paragraphs I would like to suggest this as a new focus of inquiry, in the hope that it may help shed light on the genesis of the widely held belief in the deer as source of supernatural power.

To the Huichols, we recall, the peyote *is* deer (and vice versa), whose inebriating flesh enables mankind to "find its life." Although this fundamental aspect of Huichol metaphysics is not theirs alone, it survives among them in its most dramatic and purest shamanistic form. Further, Elder Brother Deer is the Huichol shaman's guardian *par excellence*, his mount to the upper levels of the universe, and his indispensable spirit helper in curing. That the deer-peyote identification is of respectable antiquity in Mexico is at least suggested by a remarkable effigy snuffing pipe from Oaxaca, dating to ca. 400-200 B.C., which represents a reclining deer holding in its mouth a realistically modeled peyote cactus (see photo, p. 155). The upturned tail of the animal forms the perforated nosepiece (Furst, 1974b).

North of Mexico we find the deer widely associated with tobacco, and also with *Datura*; in the Andes, on the other hand, the deer seems to have been in some way identified with *Anadenanthera colubrina*, the principal hallucinogenic component of the divine compound known as *huilca* or *wilka*, judging from Moche vase paintings of the sixth century A.D. of ceremonial deer-hunt scenes, in which the animal is almost always flanked by *A. colubrina*, and sometimes also by free-floating *Anadenanthera* seed pods. In the Southern Plains, deer were very much involved in the ecstatic-shamanistic mescal-bean (*Sophora secundiflora*) medicine cults, among whose essential purposes was the securing of supernatural power ("medicine"), as well as sustenance, from the deer or from its larger cousin the elk. Indeed, in historic times at least, these rites were often referred to as "Deer Dance." In the ancient rock art of the Pecos River area of Texas, whose iconography seems to be related to early precursors of the historic mescal-bean ceremonies, the most common animals again are deer, sometimes depicted in association with mountain lions and anthropomorphic figures believed to be shamans (Newcomb, 1967).

Zuñi cosmology weaves the deer into an intricate symbol complex that is strikingly reminiscent of the deer-maize-peyote complex among the Huichols —not really surprising in light of the many other cultural parallels between Southwestern Pueblos and the Cora-Huichols of western Mexico. As was noted earlier, the sacred hallucinogenic plant of the Zuñi Rain Priest Fraternity is *Datura inoxia—aneklaka* in Zuñi—whose white, trumpet-shaped flowers stand for the East. However, there is also another divine plant, called *tenatsali*, never identified botanically, which stands for the Zenith and which the Zuñis say embodies all the sacred flowers or plants of the world directions (the four cardinal points plus zenith and nadir): the yellow sego lily

(*Calochortus nuttallii* var. *aureus*) for the north; the blue sego lily (*C. nuttallii*), and sometimes also lupine (*Lupinus palmerii* or *aduncus*) for the west; the red cardinal flower (*Lobelia cardinalis* or *splendens*) for the south; the white flower of *Datura inoxia* for the east; the "multicolored" flower, encompassing all of the other colors, of *tenatsali* itself for the zenith, and an unidentified root for the nadir, whose color is black.

Now, say the Zuñis, all these flowers, and the plants which bear them—including, of course, *Datura inoxia*, which is in a sense the most important because it stands for the east—have an irresistible attraction for deer, who "go crazy with them"; in the esoteric songs, therefore, we find the Zuñi hunter magically transforming into these flowers so as to draw deer toward himself and within range of his arrows. (Deer, by the way, move within an eternal closed cycle of death and rebirth, meaning that at death they travel to Katchina Village to be reborn as deer, whereas Zuñis who were members of the Katchina Societies go through three cycles of death and rebirth as spiritual beings but are reborn as deer when they die the fourth time).

It may be that *tenatsali* will never be specifically identified, for the reason that it may not be a botanical species at all but a compound representing a sacred concept—a symbol complex embodying all the sacred flowering plants of the world directions together with the deer, with *Datura* responsible for whatever psychoactivity figures in *tenatsali* medicine.* That, at any rate, is the preliminary conclusion of Barbara and Dennis Tedlock, anthropologists who have spent several years exploring the richness and sophistication of the traditional Zuñi world (cf. Tedlock, 1972, and personal communication).

American Indian Deer Symbolism: Asiatic Roots or Independent Origins?

The question, of course, is why of all possible animals the relatively gentle, herbivorous deer should recur over and over again as source of supernatural medicine power, and why it should so often be identified or associated with those plants that facilitate entry into the world of spirits. There are undoubtedly many levels of explanation for this phenomenon. But the fact remains that not only are deer considered to be closer to humans than any other animal by many American Indian societies, but where psychoactive plants are used, we often find deer closely associated with them—not, to be

---

*In addition, it may be that the cardinal flower (*Lobelia cardinalis* or *splendens*, which belongs to a genus from which lobeline, an alkaloid used in western medicine chiefly as a respiratory stimulant, has been isolated) also contributes some psychoactivity. Species of *Lobelia* have long been a part of the herbal pharmacopoeia of different Indian populations, including those of Mesoamerica, asthma being one of the afflictions which Aztec physicians treated with a *Lobelia* preparation. Indians of northeastern North America also smoke the cardinal flower as a substitute for tobacco (hence its popular but botanically erroneous name "Indian tobacco").

sure, always to the point of total identification and interchangeability, as between deer and peyote among the Huichols, but still closely enough to be impressive as a cultural phenomenon, and one, besides, that seems to have its counterpart, if not in fact its antecedents, in Paleo-Siberian mushroom shamanism. Here, again, Wasson's *Soma* is a rich source of information, as are Eurasian archaeology and ethnology.

It is evident from Neanderthal burials in central Asia and from mankind's earliest art in the great Paleolithic cave galleries of the Dordogne, as much as from the early rock art of western North America, that cervids of all kinds, and especially deer, were not merely an important food resource but a special font of metaphysical benefits, and that in Eurasia generally deer and shamans have apparently stood in a special relationship from very early times.

In northern Eurasia, wherever shamanism survived into recent times, the deer—specifically the reindeer—is still the shaman's animal. Among the Reindeer Tungus, for example, as among other tribes of Siberia, the deer is his spirit mount that carries him in his ecstatic trance to the realm of the sky people. The traditional shaman's costume of many Siberian tribes is festooned with deer symbolism, and the shaman's cap, without which he cannot properly shamanize, is frequently crowned by iron antler effigies or by real horns, for it is the animal horn that since time immemorial has embodied the concept of supernatural power and eternal renewal. (Early engravings showing antlered Siberian shamans in their full animal disguise are virtually indistinguishable from their Paleolithic counterparts in the cave sanctuaries of France). The northern forest and tundra people still live in an intimacy with the reindeer, wild and semidomesticated, that is hard for us to imagine, amounting almost to a symbiotic relationship, writes Wasson (1968:75). There is little doubt that this very ancient spiritual connection between man and the sacred deer, dating to a time long before reindeer were ever domesticated, inspired the horse nomads of central Asia to transform their mounts magically into stags by crowning them with antlers. Such antlered horses, presumably meant to carry their deceased Scythian riders into the Otherworld in the manner of Siberian shamans on their reindeer, were found by Russian archaeologists in the well-preserved "frozen tombs" of Pazaryk, in southern Siberia, dating to ca. 600-500 B.C. (Gryaznov, 1969).

The Reindeer and the Sacred Mushroom

Now, it happens that not only Siberian shamans but their reindeer as well were involved with the sacred mushrooms. Several early writers on Siberian customs reported that reindeer shared with man a passion for the inebriating mushroom, and further, that at times the animals urgently sought out human urine, a peculiarity that greatly facilitated the work of the herders in rounding them up—and that might just possibly have assisted their reindeer-hunting ancestors in early efforts at domestication:

. . . these animals (reindeer) have frequently eaten that mushroom, which they like very much. Whereupon they have behaved like drunken animals, and then have fallen into a deep slumber. When the Koryak encounter an intoxicated reindeer, they tie his legs until the mushroom has lost its strength and effect. Then they kill the reindeer. If they kill the animal while it is drunk or asleep and eat of its flesh, then everybody who has tasted it becomes intoxicated as if he had eaten the actual fly agaric. (Georg Wilhelm Steller, 1774, in Wasson, 1968: 239-240)

. . . in one of those open places in the woods we gathered twenty mushrooms, to the immense joy of the older of my companions who, as an enthusiastic devotee of this intoxicant, again praised its powers and its benefits. He affirmed, from his own experience, the most varied effects of this mushroom on herbivorous animals: wild reindeer that have eaten some of them are often found so stupefied that they can be tied with ropes and taken away alive; their meat then intoxicates everyone who eats it, but only if the reindeer is killed soon after being caught; and from this it appears that the communicability of the narcotic substance lasts about as long as it would have affected the animals' own nerves. (Adolph Erman, 1833:304-306, in Wasson, 1968:235)

As for the reindeer's longing for human urine, we are told by the distinguished Russian anthropologist Waldemar Jochelson (1905) that the Koryak had special sealskin containers, called "the reindeer's night-chamber," in which every herdsman collected his urine. This was used to attract refractory animals, who apparently required urine whenever they fed exclusively on certain lichens. So strong was this passion, he reports, that men urinating in the open ran a real risk of being run down by reindeer, who have a keen sense of smell, coming at him at full gallop from all sides!

From a strictly psychopharmacological point of view, Steller's and Erman's accounts are in one respect impossible, in that the tribesmen could not have become inebriated by eating only the meat of an intoxicated reindeer. But it is possible that the early writers missed something, and that the contents of the bladder were consumed for that purpose—perhaps in a hunting rite akin to the walrus-bladder ritual of Alaskan Eskimos. The urine of reindeer "drunk" with fly-agaric would of course be as hallucinogenic as that of humans.

On the other hand, what if to the Siberians the reindeer itself was fly-agaric, as to the Huichols deer and peyote are one? Then the killing and sacrificial eating of the inebriated deer would take on a very different and much more profound meaning, akin to the eucharistic implications of the Huichol Deer-Peyote sacrifice.

Whether or not such an interpretation has substance, the intimate relationship between the reindeer and the sacred mushroom is beyond question, as is the fact that this animal, which before the melting of the Pleistocene glaciers ranged much farther south than it does today, was one of the principal animals not only in the physical but also the spiritual universe of the Paleolithic ancestors of the first Americans. To some degree China is involved here as well, in light of the fact that according to Chinese mythology it is the deer that leads man to the legendary Ling Chih, the divine mushroom of immortality. Such a concept might, as Wasson (1968) has suggested, have diffused to China in the third century B.C. from India, but it could conceivably have come to the Chinese from western or southern Siberia, at an earlier time for which we have no written records, out of the same shamanistic stratum to which the Indian *Soma* rite ultimately owes its origin. The analogy between the Chinese tradition of the deer as a near-immortal precisely because of its association with a mushroom to which it points the way for man and the reindeer-mushroom identification in Siberia is strong enough to suggest something more direct than secondary diffusion northward across the Himalayas from a region in which all memory of *Soma* as mushroom had by then long disappeared.

All this brings us back to La Barre and the origins of the great hallucinogenic complex of Indian America. It is certainly tempting, on the basis of the above, to suggest that beyond the phenomenon of deer shamanism, the specific identification of the deer with plant hallucinogens also has its roots in an ecstatic Eurasian shamanism in which the reindeer's physical and metaphysical relationship to the sacred inebriating mushroom was an integral element. If so, the shamanistic deer-hallucinogen association that we now recognize in the Americas could have been already present in the ideational universe which the earliest Americans carried with them into the New World from the northeast Asian homeland, 15,000-25,000 or more years ago.

Proposing that possibility, of course, is assuming a great deal. But whether or not one is justified in postulating cultural survivals over such an enormous time span—and I, for one, would not reject this out of hand as at least a possibility—it is also conceivable that a deer-mushroom complex arose quite independently in the New World, out of the peculiar ecology of one of the principal species of psychoactive fungi employed in Mesoamerican ritual.

Deer-Mushroom Ecology in Mexico

As was noted in another chapter, *Stropharia cubensis*, reportedly the strongest hallucinogenically of all the psychoactive species found in Mexico, is a dung fungus; it is typically found growing on manure in open meadows. Like other mushrooms, *Stropharia* reproduces by releasing countless microscopic spores from its gills into the wind, which deposits them in the surrounding grassland.* Like those of other coprophyllic species, the spores of *S. cubensis* do not germinate directly when they reach a suitable environment but require passage through the digestive system of grazing animals; in other words, they are ingested with the forage, being subsequently deposited

---

*I am indebted to John Haines, mycologist for the New York State Museum in Albany, for clarifying the ecology of *Stropharia cubensis*.

as the animal evacuates. Not all herbivorous animals are capable of playing this essential symbiotic role, however; rather, it appears that to propagate, *Stropharia* requires the complex digestive system of ruminants. And indeed, the mushroom is today typically found on cow dung.

This curious circumstance has long worried those who, like Wasson, have studied Mexican mushroom cults in depth and been impressed with the important role *Stropharia* plays in these cults. The Mazatecs of Oaxaca, and perhaps some of the Maya of Chiapas and other Mesoamerican peoples to whom *Stropharia* is sacred, harvest the mushrooms in the rainy season in grassy meadows where cattle have been browsing. But cattle were unknown in the Americas before the coming of the Europeans. So the question naturally arises, in light of its apparent dependence on domestic ruminants, is *Stropharia* also a foreign import into Mexico? Or is there some indigenous species of animal that could have played the same essential role in pre-Hispanic times?

The answer is yes. And the animal is the deer. As a ruminant it is in fact the only species that could have served as *Stropharia's* host in Mexico and—assuming that the multichambered stomachs of ruminants are indeed the crucial factor—assured its survival as a species. In light of such an essential and easily observable relationship between deer and their preferred sacred psychoactive mushroom, the strict prohibition by the sixteenth-century Mazatecs of Oaxaca against the killing of deer in their country, and indeed their very name, which means "people of the deer," take on new significance.

To return to the question of Paleolithic or Mesolithic survivals, the discovery, by early migrants into Mexico, of a functional deer-mushroom relationship could, conceivably, have served to reinforce whatever ancient Asian traditions might then still have remained alive concerning the deer as source of supernatural power, and especially the visionary gifts of shamans. Thus, to borrow Albert Hofmann's imagery, another research series, culture-historical and ecological rather than strictly pharmacological, might be said to close like a magic circle.

LITERATURE CITED

Aberle, David F. 1966. *The Peyote Religion among the Navaho*. Chicago: Aldine.

Adovasio, J. M., and G. S. Fry. "Prehistoric Psychotropic Drug Use in Northeastern Mexico and Trans-Pecos Texas." *Economic Botany*, Vol. 30, No. 1, 1976 (in press).

Aguirre Beltrán, Gonzalo. 1963. *Medicina y Magia: El proceso de aculturación en la estructura colonial*. Mexico: Instituto Nacional Indigenista, Colección de Antropología Social, No. 1.

Altschul, Siri von Reis. 1964. "A taxonomic study of the genus *Anadenanthera*." Cambridge: Contributions of the Gray Herbarium, Harvard University, No. 193, pp. 3-65.

Altschul, Siri von Reis. 1972. *The Genus Anadenanthera in Amerindian Cultures*. Cambridge: Botanical Museum of Harvard University.

Anderson, Edward F. 1969. "The biogeography, ecology, and taxonomy of *Lophophora* (Cactaceae)." *Brittonia*, Vol. 21, No. 4, pp. 299-310.

Anonymous Conqueror, the. 1917. *Narrative of Some Things of New Spain and of the Great City of Temestitlán, Mexico*. Translated by Marshall H. Saville. New York: The Cortés Society.

Bean, Lowell J. 1972. *Mukat's People: the Cahuilla Indians of Southern California*. Berkeley and Los Angeles: University of California Press.

Bean, Lowell J., and Katherine Siva Saubel. 1972. *Temalpakh: Cahuilla Indian Knowledge and Usage of Plants*. Banning, Calif.: Malki Museum Press.

Benítez, Fernando. 1975. *In the Magic Land of Peyote*. Translated by John Upton. Introduction by Peter T. Furst. Austin: The University of Texas Press.

Beverly, Robert. 1705. *The History and Present State of Virginia*. London: R. Parker.

Blewett, Duncan B. 1969. Introduction to: *LSD in Action*, by P. G. Stafford and B. H. Golightly. London: Sidgwick and Jackson, pp. 17-23.

Bogoras, Waldemar G. 1904-1909. *The Chukchee*. Jesup North Pacific Expedition, Parts 1, 2, and 3. Memoirs of the American Museum of Natural History, Vol. 11.

Borhegyi, Stephan A. de. 1961. "Miniature Mushroom Stones from Guatemala." *American Antiquity*, Vol. 26, pp. 498-504.

174

Brecher, Edward M., and the Editors of *Consumer Reports*. 1972. *Licit and Illicit Drugs*. Boston: Little, Brown.

Brough, John. 1971. "Soma and *Amanita muscaria*." *Bulletin of the School of Oriental and African Studies*, Vol. 34, Part 2, pp. 331-362. University of London.

Bruhn, Jan G. 1971. "*Carnegiea gigantea*: The Saguaro and Its Uses." *Economic Botany*, Vol. 25, No. 3, pp. 320-329.

Carneiro, Robert L. 1970. "Hunting and Hunting Magic among the Amahuaca of the Peruvian Montaña." *Ethnology*, Vol. 9, No. 4, pp. 331-341.

Chagnon, Napoleon A., Phillip LaQuesne, and James M. Cook. 1971. "Yanomamö Hallucinogens: Anthropological, Botanical, and Chemical Findings." *Current Anthropology*, Vol. 12, No. 1, pp. 72-74.

Coe, Michael D. 1971. "The Shadow of the Olmecs." *Horizon*, Vol. 13, No. 4, pp. 67-74.

Daly, John W., and Charles W. Myers. 1967. "Toxicity of Panamanian Poison Frogs (*Dendrobates*): Some Biological and Chemical Aspects." *Science*, Vol. 156, pp. 970-973.

Daly, John W., *et al.* 1967. "Discussion on the Psychoactive Action of Various Tryptamine Derivatives." In Efron, ed., 1967, pp. 374-382.

Daly, John W., and Bernard Witkop. 1971. "Chemistry and Pharmacology of Frog Venoms." In: *Venomous Animals and their Venoms*, Vol. 2, pp. 497-519. New York and London: Academic Press.

Dobkin de Rios, Marlene, 1972. *The Visionary Vine: Psychedelic Healing in the Peruvian Amazon*. New York: Chandler Publishing Company.

Donaldson, Thomas. 1886. *The George Catlin Indian Gallery in the U. S. National Museum*. Annual Report of the Smithsonian Institution for 1885. Washington, D.C.: U.S. Government Printing Office.

Díaz del Castillo, Bernal. 1908-16. *The True History of the Conquest of New Spain*. Translated by A. P. Maudsley. 5 vols. London: The Hakluyt Society.

Durán, Fray Diego. 1971. *Book of the Gods and Rites and the Ancient Calendar*. Translated and edited by Fernando Horcasitas and Doris Heyden. Norman: University of Oklahoma Press.

Efron, Daniel H., ed. 1967. *Ethnopharmacologic Search for Psychoactive Drugs*. U.S. Public Health Service Publication No. 1645. Washington, D.C.: U.S. Government Printing Office.

Emboden, William A., Jr. 1972a. "Ritual Use of *Cannabis Sativa* L.: A Historical-Ethnographic Survey." In Furst, ed., 1972a, pp. 214-236.

Emboden, William A., Jr. 1972b. *Narcotic Plants*. New York: Macmillan.

Emmerich, André, 1965. *Sweat of the Sun and Tears of the Moon: Gold and Silver in Pre-Columbian Art*. Seattle: University of Washington Press.

Erspamer, V., T. Vitali, M. Roseghini, and J. M. Cei. 1967. "5-Methoxy- and 5-Hydroxyindoles in the Skin of *Bufo alvarius*." *Biochemical Pharmacology*, Vol. 16, pp. 1149-1164.

Escalante, Roberto. 1973. "Ethnomycological Data of the Matlatzincas." Paper read at the 72nd Annual Meetings of the American Anthropological Association, New Orleans.

Escalante, Roberto, and Antonio López. 1971. *Hongos Sagrados de los Matlatzincas*. Sección de Lingüística, 4. México, D.F.: Museo Nacional de Antropología.

Eugster, C. H. 1967. "Isolation, Structure and Syntheses of Central-active Compounds from *Amanita muscaria* (L. ex Fr.) Hooker." In Efron, ed., 1967, pp. 416-418, and 441.

Fernandez, James W. 1972. "Tabernanthe Iboga: Narcotic Ecstasis and the Work of the Ancestors." In Furst, ed., 1972a, pp. 237-260.

Furst, Peter T. 1968. "The Olmec Were-Jaguar Motif in the Light of Ethnographic Reality." In: *Dumbarton Oaks Conference on the Olmec*, Elizabeth P. Benson, ed., pp. 143-174. Washington, D. C.: Dumbarton Oaks Research Library and Collection, Trustees for Harvard University. Reprinted in: *Contemporary Archaeology*, Mark Leone, ed., 1972. Carbondale: Southern Illinois University Press.

Furst, Peter T. 1972a. *Flesh of the Gods: The Ritual Use of Hallucinogens*. New York: Praeger.

Furst, Peter T. 1972b. "Symbolism and Psychopharmacology: The Toad as Earth Mother in Indian America." In: *Religión en Mesoamerica, XII Mesa Redonda*, pp. 37-46. México, D.F.: Sociedad Mexicana de Antropología.

Furst, Peter T. 1973. "West Mexican Art: Secular or Sacred?" In: *The Iconography of Middle American Sculpture*, pp. 98-133. New York: The Metropolitan Museum of Art.

Furst, Peter T. 1974a. "Mother Goddess and Morning Glory at Tepantitla, Teotihuácan: Iconography and Analogy in pre-Columbian Art." In: *Mesoamerican Archaeology: New Approaches*, ed. Norman Hammond. Austin: The University of Texas Press.

Furst, Peter T. 1974b. "Archaeological Evidence for Snuffing in Prehispanic Mexico." Botanical Museum Leaflets, Harvard University, Vol. 23, No. 10, pp. 368 ff.

Furst, Peter T. 1974c. "Hallucinogens in Precolumbian Art." In: *Art and Environment in Native America*, ed. Mary Elizabeth King and Idris R. Traylor, Jr., pp. 55-102. Lubbock: Special Publications of the Museum of Texas Technological University.

Furst, Peter T., and Barbara G. Myerhoff. 1966. "Myth as History: The Jimson Weed Cycle of the Huichols of Mexico." *Anthropológica*, No. 17, pp. 3-39. Caracas.

Furst, Peter T. and Barbara G. Myerhoff. 1972. "El mito como historia: el ciclo del peyote y la datura entre los huicholes." In: *El Peyote y Los Huicholes*, by Salomón Nahmad Sittón *et al.*, pp. 55-108. Sep/Setentas No. 29. Mexico, D.F.: Secretaría de Educación Pública.

Gilmore, Raymond M. 1963. "Fauna and Ethnozoology of South America." In: *Handbook of South American Indians*, Julian H. Steward, ed., Vol. 6, pp. 345-464. Smithsonian Institution, Bureau of American Ethnology, Bulletin 143. Reprint Edition. New York: Cooper Square Publishers.

Gryaznov, Mikhail P. 1969. *The Ancient Civilization of Southern Siberia*. New York: Cowles Book Company, Inc.

Guzmán-Huerta, Gastón. 1959a. "Estudio Taxonómico y Ecológico de los Hongos Neurotrópicos Mexicanos," Tésis Profesional. México, D.F.: Instituto Politécnico Nacional, Ciencias Biológicas.

Guzmán-Huerta, Gastón. 1959b. "Sinopsis de los conocimientos sobre los hongos alucinogénicos mexicanos." *Boletín de la Sociedad Botánica de México*, No. 24, pp. 14-34.

Harner, Michael J. 1972. *The Jivaro: People of the Sacred Waterfalls*. New York: Doubleday/Natural History Press.

Harner, Michael J. 1973. "Common Themes in South American Indian Yage Experiences." In: *Hallucinogens and Shamanism*, Michael J. Harner, ed., pp. 155-175. New York: Oxford University Press.

Harner, Michael J., ed. 1973. *Hallucinogens and Shamanism*. New York: Oxford University Press.

Hernández, Francisco. 1651. *Nova Plantarum, Animalium et Mineralium Mexicanorum Historia. . . . Rome*: B. Deuersini et Z. Masotti.

Hofmann, Albert. 1964. "Die Erforschung der Mexikanischen Zauberpilze und das Problem ihrer Wirkstoffe." Basel: Basler Stadtbuch, pp. 141-156.

Hofmann, Albert. 1967. "The Active Principles of the Seeds of *Rivea Corymbosa* (L.) Hall F.(Ololiuhqui, Badoh) and *Ipomoea Tricolor* Cav. (Badoh Negro)." In: *Summa Antropológica en homenaje a Roberto J. Weitlaner*, pp. 349-357. México, D.F.: Instituto Nacional de Antropología e Historia.

Hooper, Lucille. 1920. "The Cahuilla Indians." University of California Publications in American Archaeology and Ethnology, 16 pp. 316-380.

Huxley, Aldous. 1954. *The Doors to Perception*. New York: Harper.

Ingalls, Daniel H. 1971. "Remarks on Mr. Wasson's *Soma*." *Journal of the American Oriental Society*, Vol. 91, No. 1, pp. 188-191.

Jochelson, Waldemar (Vladimir). 1905/1908. *I. The Koryak*. Jesup North Pacific Expedition, Vol. 6. Memoirs of the American Museum of Natural History, Vol. 10.

Johnson, Jean Basset. 1938. "Some Notes on the Mazatec." Paper read before the Sociedad Mexicana de Antropología, Aug. 4, 1938. *Revista Mexicana de Estudios Antropológicos*, 1939, pp. 142-156.

Johnson, Jean Basset. 1939. "The Elements of Mazatec Witchcraft." Ethnographical Studies No. 9, pp. 119-149. Gothenburg Ethnographical Museum.

Kinross-Wright, V. J. 1958. "Research on Ololiuqui: The Aztec Drug." Proceedings of the 1st International Congress of Neuro-Pharmacology, Rome (1958). In: *Neuro-Psychopharmacology*, P. B. Bradley *et al.*, eds., 1959, p. 453. Amsterdam and New York: Elsevier Publishing Company.

Koch-Grünberg, Theodor. 1917-1928. *Vom Roraima zum Orinoco*. Vol. III, 1923. Stuttgart: Verlag Strecker und Schröder.

Kroeber, Alfred L. 1953. *Handbook of the Indians of California*. Berkeley: California Book Co. Ltd.

Kroeber, Alfred L. 1953. *Handbook of the Indians of California*. Berkeley: California Publications in American Archaeology and Ethnology, 6, pp. 29-68.

La Barre, Weston. 1970a. "Old and New World Narcotics: A Statistical Question and an Ethnological Reply." *Economic Botany*, Vol. 24, pp. 368-373.

La Barre, Weston. 1970b. Film Review: "To Find our Life: the Peyote Hunt of the Huichols of Mexico." *American Anthropologist*, Vol. 72, No. 5, p. 1201.

La Barre, Weston. 1970c. Review of R. G. Wasson's *Soma: Divine Mushroom of Immortality*. *American Anthropologist*, Vol. 72, No. 5, pp. 368-373.

La Barre, Weston. 1970d. *The Ghost Dance: The Origins of Religion*. Garden City: Doubleday.

La Barre, Weston. 1974. *The Peyote Cult*. Revised and enlarged edition. Hampden, Conn.: The Shoestring Press. (Earlier editions 1938, 1969.)

La Barre, Weston, David McAllester, James S. Slotkin, Omer C. Stewart, and Sol Tax. 1951. "Statement on Peyote." *Science*, Vol. 114, pp. 582-583.

Lathrap, Donald W. 1970. *The Upper Amazon*. New York: Praeger.

Lewin, Louis. 1929. *Banisteria Caapi, ein neues Rauschgift und Heilmittel. Beiträge zur Giftkunde*. Berlin: Verlag von Georg Stilke.

López Austin, Alfredo. 1973. "Unas Ideas sobre el Tiempo Mítico entre los Nahuas Antiguas." Paper read at the XIII Mesa Redonda, Sociedad Mexicana de Antropología, Jalapa, Veracruz.

Lowy, B. 1971. "New Records of Mushroom Stones from Guatemala." *Mycologia*, Vol. LXIII, No. 5, pp. 983-993.

Lowy, Bernard. 1974. "*Amanita muscaria* and the Thunderbolt Legend in Guatemala and Mexico." *Mycologia*, Vol. 66, No. 1, pp. 188-191.

Lumholtz, Carl. 1900. *Symbolism of the Huichol Indians*. New York: Memoirs of the American Museum of Natural History, Vol. III.

Lumholtz, Carl. 1902. *Unknown Mexico*, Vol. 1. New York: Scribner.

McCleary, James A., Paul S. Sypherd, and David L. Walkington. 1960. "Antibiotic Activity of an Extract of Peyote *Lophophora williamsii* (Lemaire) Coulter." *Economic Botany*, Vol. 14, pp. 247-249.

Martínez, Máximo. 1959. *Las Plantas Medicinales de México*. Mexico, D.F.: Ediciones Botas.

Martínez, Máximo. 1966. "Las Solandras de Mexico Con Una Specie Nueva." *Anales de Instituto de Biología*, Vol. 37, Nos. 1 and 2, pp. 97-106. Mexico, D.F.: Universidad Nacional Autónoma de México.

Munn, Henry. 1973. "The Mushrooms of Language." In Harner, ed., 1973, pp. 86-122.

Myerhoff, Barbara G. 1974. *Peyote Hunt: The Sacred Journey of the Huichol Indians*. Symbol, Myth and Ritual Series, Victor Turner, ed. Ithaca: Cornell University Press.

Naranjo, Claudio. 1973. *The Healing Journey: New Approaches to Consciousness*. New York: Pantheon.

Newcomb, W. W., Jr. 1967. *The Rock Art of Texas Indians*. Paintings by Forrest Kirkland, text by W. W. Newcomb, Jr. Austin: The University of Texas Press.

Osmond, Humphrey. 1955. "Ololiuqui: the Ancient Aztec Narcotic." *Journal of Mental Science*, Vol. 101, pp. 526-527.

Pike, Eunice, and Florence Cowan. 1959. "Mushroom Rituals versus Christianity." *Practical Anthropology*, Vol. 6, No. 4, pp. 145-150.

Pollock, Steven Hayden. 1975. "The Psilocybin Mushroom Pandemic." *Journal of Psychedelic Drugs*, Vol. 7, No. 1, pp. 73-84.

Poma de Ayala, Felipe Guamán. 1936. *Nueva crónica y buen gobierno (Codex Peruvién illustré)*. Paris: Institute d'Ethnologie, Travaux et Mémoires, Vol. 23.

Pope, Harrison G., Jr. 1969. "*Tabernanthe iboga*: an African Narcotic Plant of Social Importance." *Economic Botany*, Vol. 23, No. 2, pp. 174-184.

Preuss, Konrad Theodor. 1908. "Die religiösen Gesänge und Mythen einiger Stämme der mexikanischen Sierra Madre." *Archiv für Religionswissenschaft*, Vol. 11, pp. 369-398. Leipzig: B. G. Teubner.

Reichel-Dolmatoff, Gerardo. 1971. *Amazonian Cosmos: The Sexual and Religious Symbolism of the Tukano Indians*. Chicago: University of Chicago Press.

Reichel-Dolmatoff, Gerardo. 1972. "The Cultural Context of an Aboriginal Halluci-nogen: *Banisteriopsis Caapi*." In Furst, ed., 1972a, pp. 84-113.

Reko, Blas Pablo. 1934. "Das Mexikanische Rauschgift Ololiuqui," *El México Antiguo*, Vol. 3, Nos. 3-4, pp. 1-7.

Robertson, Merle Greene. 1972. "The Ritual Bundles of Yaxchilán." Paper read at the Tulane University Symposia on the Art of Latin America, April 15, 1972. New Orleans.

Roth, Walter E. 1915. "An Inquiry into the Animism and Folklore of the Guiana Indians." 30th Annual Report of the Bureau of American Ethnology, 1908-1909, pp. 103-386. Washington, D.C.: U.S. Government Printing Office.

Rubin, Vera, and Lambros Comitas. 1975. *Ganja in Jamaica.* The Hague and Paris: Mouton & Co.

Ruiz de Alarcón, Hernando. 1629/1892. "Tratado de las Supersticiones y Cos-tumbres Gentilicas Que oy Viuen Entre los Indios Naturales Desta Nueua Espana." Francisco del Paso y Troncoso, ed. *Anales del Museo Nacional de México*, ep. I, VI, pp. 123-223.

Safford, William E. 1915. "Identification of the teonanácatl, or 'sacred mushroom' of the Aztecs, with the narcotic cactus, *Lophophora*, and an account of its ceremonial use in ancient and modern times." Paper delivered before the Botanical Society of Washington, May 4, 1915. Published as "An Aztec Narcotic (*Lophophora wil-liamsii*)" in *Journal of Heredity*, Vol. 6, 1915.

Safford, William E. 1920. "Daturas of the Old World and New." Annual Report of the Smithsonian Institution for 1916, pp. 537-567. Washington, D.C.: U.S. Government Printing Office.

Sahagún, Fray Bernardino de. 1950-1963. *The Florentine Codex. General History of the Things of New Spain.* Translated by Arthur J. O. Anderson and Charles E. Dibble. Santa Fe, New Mexico: The School of American Research and the University of Utah.

Santesson, C. G. 1937. "Piule, eine mexikanische Rauschdroge." *Archiv der Phar-mazie und Berichte der Deutschen Pharmazeutischen Gesellschaft*, pp. 532-537.

Sapper, Carl. 1898. "*Pilzförmige Götzenbilder aus Guatemala und San Salvador*." *Globus*, Vol. 73, p. 327.

Schleiffer, Hedwig. 1973. *Sacred Narcotic Plants of the New World Indians: An Anthology of Texts from the Sixteenth Century to Date.* New York: Hafner.

Schultes, Richard Evans. 1937. Peyote (Lophophora Williamsii [Lemaire] Coulter) and Its Uses. Senior Honors Thesis, Harvard University, Cambridge, Mass.

Schultes, Richard Evans. 1939. "Plantae Mexicanae II. The Identification of teo-nanácatl, the narcotic Basidiomycete of the Aztecs." Botanical Museum Leaflets, Vol. 7, pp. 37-54. Harvard University.

Schultes, Richard Evans. 1941. *A Contribution to Our Knowledge of* Rivea corym-bosa, *the Narcotic Ololiuqui of the Aztecs.* Cambridge, Mass.: Botanical Museum of Harvard University.

Schultes, Richard Evans. 1970. "The Botanical and Chemical Distribution of Hallu-cinogens." *Annual Review of Plant Physiology*, Vol. 21, pp. 571-598.

Schultes, Richard Evans. 1972a. "An Overview of Hallucinogens in the Western Hemisphere." In Furst, ed., 1972a, pp. 3-54.

Schultes, Richard Evans. 1972b. "Ilex Guayusa from 500 A.D. to the Present." *Etnologiska Studier*, No. 32, pp. 115-138. Gothenburg Ethnographical Museum.

Schultes, Richard Evans, and Albert Hofmann. 1973. *The Botany and Chemistry of Hallucinogens*. Springfield, Ill.: Charles C. Thomas.

Schultes, Richard Evans, William M. Klein, Timothy Plowman, and Tom E. Lockwood. 1974. "Cannabis: an Example of Taxonomic Neglect." Botanical Museum Leaflets, Harvard University, Vol. 23, No. 9, pp. 337-360.

Serna, Jacinto de la. 1892. "Manual de Ministros de Indios para el conocimiento de sus idolatrias y extirpación de ellos." *Anales del Museo Nacional de México*, 6, pp. 261-476.

Sharon, Douglas. 1972. "The San Pedro Cactus in Peruvian Folk Healing." In Furst, ed., 1972a, pp. 114-135.

Shulgin, Alexander T., Thornton Sargent, and Claudio Naranjo. 1967. "The Chemistry and Psychopharmacology of Nutmeg and of Several Related Phenylisopropylamines." In Efron, ed., 1967, pp. 202-222.

Singer, Rolf. 1958. "Mycological Investigations on Teonanácatl, the Mexican Hallucinogenic Mushroom. Part I. The History of Teonanácatl, Field Work and Culture Work." *Mycologia*, Vol. 50, pp. 239-261.

Singer, Rolf, and Alexander H. Smith. 1958. "Mycological Investigations on Teonanácatl, the Mexican Hallucinogenic Mushroom. Part II. A taxonomic monograph of Psilocybe, section Caerulescentes," *Mycologia*, Vol. 50, pp. 262-303.

Slotkin, J. S. 1956. *The Peyote Religion*. Glencoe, Ill.: Free Press.

Solecki, Ralph S. 1975. "Shanidar IV, a Neanderthal Flower Burial in Northern Iraq." *Science*, Vol. 190, pp. 880-881.

Stevenson, Matilda Coxe. 1915. "Ethnobotany of the Zuñi Indians." 30th Annual Report of the Bureau of American Ethnology, 1908-1909, pp. 31-102. Washington, D.C.: U.S. Government Printing Office.

Steward, Julian H., ed. 1963. *Handbook of South American Indians*. 6 vols. Washington, D.C.: Smithsonian Institution, Bureau of American Ethnology, Bulletin 143. Reprint edition: New York: Cooper Square Publishers.

Stewart, Omer C. 1944. "Washo-Northern Paiute Peyotism: a Study in Acculturation." University of California Publications in American Archaeology and Ethnology, No. 3, 40:63-141.

Stewart, Omer C. 1948. *Ute Peyotism*. University of Colorado Studies. Series in Anthropology, 1. Boulder, Col.: University of Colorado Press.

Strahlenberg, Filip Johann von. 1736. *An Historico-Geographical Description of the North and Eastern Parts of Europe and Asia; But more particularly of Russia, Siberia, and Great Tartary; etc. . . .* London. Cited in Wasson, 1968:234-235.

Strong, William Duncan. 1929. "Aboriginal Society in Southern California." University of California Publications in American Archaeology and Ethnology, 26, 329 pp.

Tart, Charles T. 1972. "States of Consciousness and State-Specific Sciences." *Science* 176:1203-1210.

Tedlock, Dennis. 1972. *Finding the Center*. New York: Dial Press.

Thompson, J. Eric S. 1970. *Maya History and Religion*. Norman: University of Oklahoma Press.

Tozzer, Alfred M. 1907. *A Comparative Study of the Mayas and the Lacandones*. New York: Archaeological Institute of America.

Tschopik, Harry, Jr. 1941. "Navaho Pottery Making. Part III. Pipes." Papers of the Peabody Museum of American Archaeology and Ethnology, Harvard University, Vol. 17, No. 1.

UCLA Weekly. 1975. "LSD May Provide Lead to Mental Illness." *The UCLA Weekly*, Vol. 5, No. 23, p. 4. University of California at Los Angeles Office of Public Affairs.

Volker, T. 1950. *The Animal in Far Eastern Art*. Leiden: Mededelingen van het Rijksmuseum voor Volkenkunde, Nos. 6 and 7.

Waser, Peter G. 1967. "The Pharmacology of *Amanita muscaria*." In Efron, ed., 1967, pp. 419-439, 441.

Waser, Peter G. 1971. "Pharmakologische Wirkungsspektren von Halluzinogenen." *Bull. Schweiz. Akad. Med. Wiss.*, Vol. 27, pp. 39-57.

Wassén, S. Henry. 1934. "The Frog-Motive among South American Indians." *Antropos*, Vol. 29, pp. 319-370. Part II: "The Frog in Indian Mythology and Imaginative World," *ibid*., pp. 613-658.

Wassén, S. Henry. 1965. "The Use of Some Specific Kinds of South American Indian Snuff and Related Paraphernalia." *Etnologiska Studier*, No. 28. Gothenburg Ethnographical Museum.

Wassén, S. Henry. 1967. "Anthropological Survey of the Use of South American Snuffs." In Efron, ed., 1967, pp. 233-289.

Wassén, S. Henry, and Bo Holmstedt. 1963. "The Use of Parica, an Ethnological and Pharmacological Review." *Ethnos*, Vol. 28, No. 1, pp. 5-45.

Wasson, R. Gordon. 1967a. "Ololiuhqui and the Other Hallucinogens of Mexico." In *Summa Antropológica en homenaje a Roberto J. Weitlaner*, pp. 329-348. México, D.F.: Instituto Nacional de Antropología e Historia.

Wasson, R. Gordon. 1967b. "Fly Agaric and Man." In Efron, ed., 1967, pp. 405-414.

Wasson, R. Gordon. 1968. *Soma, Divine Mushroom of Immortality*. Ethno-Myco-Sabina and her Mazatec Mushroom Velada. New York: Harcourt Brace Jovanovich.

Wasson, R. Gordon. 1972a. "The Divine Mushroom of Immortality." In Furst, ed., 1972a, pp. 185-200.

Wasson, R. Gordon. 1972b. "What was the Soma of the Aryans?" In Furst, ed., 1972a, pp. 201-213.

Wasson, R. Gordon. 1972c. *Soma and the Fly-Agaric: Mr. Wasson's Rejoinder to Professor Brough*. Cambridge, Mass: Botanical Museum of Harvard University.

Wasson, R. Gordon. 1973. "The Role of 'Flowers' in Nahuatl Culture: A Suggested Interpretation." Botanical Museum Leaflets, Harvard University, Vol. 23, No. 8, pp. 305-324.

Wasson, R. Gordon, and Valentina P. Wasson. 1957. *Mushrooms, Russia and History*. New York: Pantheon Books.

Wasson, R. Gordon, George and Florence Cowan, and Willard Rhodes. 1974. *María Sabina and Her Mazatec Mushroom Velada*. New York: Harcourt Brace Jovanovich.

Weil, Andrew T. 1967. "Nutmeg as a Psychoactive Drug." In Efron, ed., 1967, pp. 188-201.

Weil, Andrew T. 1972. *The Natural Mind*. Boston: Houghton Mifflin.

Wilbert, Johannes. 1972. "Tobacco and Shamanistic Ecstasy among the Warao Indians of Venezuela." In Furst, ed., 1972a, pp. 55-83.

X, Malcolm, with Alex Haley. 1964. *The Autobiography of Malcolm X*. New York: Grove Press.

Zigmond, M. L. 1941. *Ethnobotanical Studies among California and Great Basin Shoshoneans*. Ph.D. dissertation, Yale University. Ann Arbor, Mich.: University Microfilms.

Zinberg, Norman E. 1974. *"High" States: A Beginning Study*. Washington, D.C.: The Drug Abuse Council.

Zinberg, Norman E. 1975. *Altered States of Consciousness*. Washington, D.C.: The Drug Abuse Council.

Zingg, Robert. 1938. *The Huichols: Primitive Artists*. New York: Stechert.

INDEX

Aberle, David F., 110n
Achillea, 4n
addiction:
  alcoholism, 18
  heroin, 17-18
  tobacco, 24-27, 30-31, 152
  tryptamines vs. tobacco, 152
adenyl cyclase, 58
Adovasio, J. M., 8
Africa, 39-42
age regression, 38
Agni, 96, 102
Aguirre Beltrán, Gonzalo, 72
alan (Alchornea floribunda), 41n
Alaska:
  drug law, 16n
  land bridge to Asia, 3, 8, 105
Alchornea floribunda, 41n
alcohols, 17-18, 34
Althea, 4n
"alternate states," 10-14, 15n
Altschul, Siri von Reis, 147
Amahuaca, 164
Amanita muscaria:
  illustration, 99
  see fly-agaric; Soma
Amazonia, *yajé* in, 51
America:
  Asiatic migration into, 3, 8, 105
  deer symbolism, 169-172
  hallucinogens in, 2-4
  Indians, *see* Indians; *also see names of tribes and cultures*

religions, 5-7
anacondas, 49, 50, 153
Anadenanthera, snuffs, 20, 48, 161
Anadenanthera colubrina, 147, 149, 156
  deer association, 168
  enemas, 27
Anadenanthera peregrina, 20n, 147, 149, 152
analgesics:
  Datura as, 136, 139, 144, 145
  manufactured in human body, 12n
Anderson, Edward F., 125n
aneklaka (Datura inoxia), 168
angelitos, rain bringers, 82
angiosperms, psychoactive, 33
animals:
  snuffing and, in art, 153-155, 168
  supernatural, 153-155
  symbolism, 146-157
Anonymous Conqueror, 28
Apocynacae, 39
Arabs, nutmeg and, 36-37
arbol loco, 66
"archetypes," 14, 50-56
Argentina, snuffing in, 153
Argyreia spp., 66n
Ariocarpus retusus, 49n
Army, United States, LSD and, 59-60n
art:
  animal, snuffing and, 153-155, 168
  Aztec, 73-74
  Chinese, 56
  mushrooms in, 79-82, 163

Teotihuácan, 71-72
yajé and, 54-56
Aryans, *Soma* and, 96, 98
Asia:
  Cannabis origin in, 35
  deer symbolism, 169-172
  overland migration to America from, 3,
    8, 105
  religions, 5-7
  toad in mythology, 162
  use of urine in, 92
Atropa belladonna, 25, 138
ayahuasca (Banisteriopsis caapi), 27, 29,
    50, 164
  also see Banisteriopsis; yajé
Aztecs:
  art, 73-74
  cosmology, 158
  Datura use, 136, 145
  herbal *(Codex Badianus)*, 21
  medicine, 169n
  morning glories and, *see* morning glories;
    ololiuhqui
  ololiuhqui and, *see* ololiuhqui
  origin myth, 158
  religion, 6, 21, 23, 72
  shamanism, 6
  teotlacualli and, 13-14

badoh negro, 62, 65
balché, sacred beverage, 28
Banda (Nutmeg) Islands, 37
banisterine, 45
Banisteriopsis, 138, 164
  species of, 45
  transcultural phenomenon, 51-56
  tryptamines in, 148, 149
  also see ayahuasca; yajé
Banisteriopsis caapi, 22, 39, 42-49, 149
  beverage *(ayahuasca)*, 27, 29, 50, 164
  illustration, 43
  as "vine of souls," 44-49
Banisteriopsis inebrians, 44, 45, 149
Banisteriopsis muricata, 44
Banisteriopsis rusbyana, 44, 45, 149
Bean, Lowell J., 16, 145
Benítez, Fernando, 114n
beta-carboline harmala alkaloids, 149-150
Beverly, Robert, 141-143
bhang, 97
Big Raven, 89
birch tree, 103
Bird, Junius B., 153

birds, 153-154
Blake, William, 85-86
bleeding, religious, 11
Blewett, Duncan B., 59
Bogoras, Vladimir, 89
Bolivia, 155
Borhegyi, Stephan F. de, 79, 81, 82
borrachera, 66
Brahmanas, 98
brain, biochemistry of, 1, 15, 51-52, 88
Brecher, Edward M., 18, 25, 35
Brough, John, 101
Brugmansia, 139, 140
Bruhn, Jan G., 58, 111
Bufo alvarius, 161
Bufo marinus, 80-81, 161, 163, 165
  also see toad
bufotenine (5-hydroxy-N,N-dimethyl-
    amine), 87, 93, 148, 161-162
Bwiti ancestor cult, 39, 41, 42

caapi (kahpi, gahpi), 44
Cabeza de Vaca, Álvar Núñez, 8
Cabi paraensis, 45
cacti, 109
caffeic acid, 1
Cahuilla, 16, 144-145
Cakchiquel, 78-79
cakuljá ikox, 82
Calochortus nutallii, 169
Campbell, Lyle, 79, 163
Canada, Native American Church in, 63
cannabinols, 34, 35
Cannabis spp. 16, 33-36
  Bwiti use, 41n
  decriminalization, 16-17n
  supplanting peyote, 100
  supplanting *Psilocybe*, 16
  also see marihuana
Cannabis americana (gigantea), 34
Cannabis indica, 34, 35, 97
Cannabis ruderalis, 34
Cannabis sativa L., 34-35
cardinal flower, 169
Carib, 26
Carmack, Robert M., 78
Carnegiea gigantea, 58, 111n
carnegine, 111
Carneiro, Robert, 164
Casas, Bartolome de Las, 21
Catlin, George, 10-11
Central Intelligence Agency, 59-60n
Ceratocaulis, 140

Cereus giganteus, 58, 111n
Chaco, 164
chacs, rain bringers, 82
Chagnon, Napoleon, 29, 151, 152
Chalchiutlicue, 72, 162
Chávin, 109
chho, 106, 107
Chile, 153
China/Chinese, 56, 104, 162, 172
Chinantecs, 62
Chol, 75-76, 84
cholla, 124
Christ, deer association, 167
Christianity:
    fanaticism in, 6-7
    Indian religions and, 19-22
    morning-glory acculturation, 70
    mushroom rites and, 85
    peyote religion and, 111-112
    syncretism and, 42-43
cigarettes, 26, 29, 32
cigars, 26, 29
Clashing Clouds, Gateway of, 117, 118
Claviceps, 33, 65
Claviceps purpurea, 58
coatl-xoxouhqui, 62
coca *(Erythroxylon coca)*, 112
Codex Badianus, 21
Coe, Michael D., 28, 76, 161
Colima, tomb object from, 157
Colombia, 82, 140
Columbus, Christopher, 20
Comitas, Lambros, 17
condor, 153, 154
Congo, 40
Conocybe, 87
consciousness:
    altering, 7
    "alternate states" of, 10-14, 14n, 15n
    biochemistry of, 14-15
Convolvulaceae, confusion, 66
Coto, Tomás, 78, 80
Coras, 111, 134, 167-168
Costa Rica, 154
Cowan, Florence, 85, 86n
creation and origin myths, 46-48
    Aztec, 158
culture heroes, 160-161
cultures:
    prehistoric American, 8
    "primitive," 5
curing:
    eboka cult, 39, 40, 42

in Mexico, 53-54
    also see medicine
cytisine, 8

Daly, John W., 161, 165
dapa, 44
dart poison, frog venom as, 163
Datura, 16, 21, 25, 134-145
    analgesic effects, 136, 139-140, 144, 145
    deer association, 168
    illustration, 136
    intoxication, 140-145
    lethal quality, 140-141, 144-145
    peyote rivalry, 135-137
    subgenera, 140
    toxicity, 9
    uses, 138-145
Datura candida, 140
Datura inoxia (meteloides), 41, 135, 169
    anaesthetic, 139-140
    synergism, 138
    Zuñi and, 168
    also see toloache
Datura stramonium, 141-143
deer:
    associations with, 168-169, 171-172
    Christ identification, 167
    as divinities, 166-173
    Elder Brother, 67, 95, 113, 117, 119,
        121-132, 168
    hallucinogens and, 166-173
    mushroom association, 170-173
    peyote association, 13, 67, 112-125, 130,
        132, 164, 168, 170, 171
    in snuffing pipe, 155, 168
    symbolism, 169-173
    tobacco association, 168
    also see Kauyumarie
"Deer Dance," 168
Dendrobates tinctorius, 163-165
Desana, 45, 47
Devil, 19-20
Díaz del Castillo, Bernal, 167
dictionaries, Maya, 77-79
Diegeño, 143, 145
directions, 122, 168-169
d-isolysergic acid amide (isoergine), 65
d-lysergic acid amide (ergine), 65
d-lysergic acid diethylamide (LSD), 58, 65,
        69
    also see LSD
DMT, 16
Dobkin de Rios, Marlene, 50

Dole, Gertrude, 164
doncella, 70, 81
dopamine, 57-58, 111n
dragon, 56n
Drug Abuse Council, Inc., xii,n
drugs, hallucinogens distinguished from, 112
d-tetrahydroharmine, 45
Durán, Diego, 13-14
Dutra, 140

Earth Mother, toad as, 158-165
Eaua Quinahi, 81
ebene (epená), 150-165
eboka (iboga), 40-42
   also see iboga; Tabernanthe iboga
Elaeophorbia drupifera, 41
Elder Brother (deer/peyote), 67, 94-95, 113,
   117, 119, 121-132, 168
Eliade, Mircea, 5
Elizabetha princeps, 151
Elkes, Joel, 15n
El Salvador, mushroom stones, 79, 80
Emboden, William A., Jr., 35, 66n
Emmerich, André, 82
enemas, psychedelic, 27-29, 146
Ephedra, 4n
Ephedra vulgaris, 97
ergine, 65
ergolines, 39
ergot *(Claviceps)*, 33, 58, 59
Erman, Adolph, 171
Erspamer, V., 161
Erythroxylon coca, 112
Escalante, Roberto, 106
Eskimos, 171
eucharistic practices:
   hallucinogens and, 42-43
   in peyote religion, 42-43, 171
Eugster, Conrad H., 93
Euphorbia, 97, 124
Euphorbiaceae, 160
Eurasia:
   mushroom traditions, 103-105
   shamanism in, 2-4
Europe, toad myths, 160n

Fang, 40, 41, 42
Feathered Serpent, 56n
Fernandez, James W., 40, 41, 42
Fire:
   as Great Shaman, 113-114, 117
   in peyote pilgrimage, 121, 129, 132

First Hunter, 164
First Shaman, 26
5-hydroxy-N,N-dimethyltryptamine (bufotenine), 87, 93, 148, 161-162
5-methoxy-N-monomethyltryptamine, 148
5-methoxy-N,N-dimethyltryptamine, 149,
   161
Florentine Codex, 92
flower:
   meaning of, 73-74
   in peyote pilgrimage, 127, 132-133
"Flowery Dream," 73-74
fly-agaric *(Amanita muscaria)*, 33, 89-95,
   96-105
   cults, in Siberia, 3
   deer association, 101, 171-172
   growth in North America, 81, 107-108
   habitat, 99-100
   illustration, 99
   in mushroom effigies, 81-82
   names, 104
   preparation and use, 90, 94, 97, 99, 100,
      105
   reindeer and, 101
   as *Soma*, 1, 96-108
   toad association, 162-163
   trees and, 99-100, 103
   use in America, 81-88
   use in Siberia, 89-95
food plants, origin, 158, 160
4-hydroxymethyltryptamine, 87
Fox, 24
Francisco, peyote pilgrim, 121, 126
frogs:
   archetypes, 52
   venom, 163-164
frog-poison ordeals, 13
frog/toad motif, 156n, 163
Frog Woman, 164
Fry, G. S., 8
fungi, psychoactive, 33
Furst, Peter T., 48, 76, 81, 120n, 135, 156,
   168

Gabon, 40, 41n
Gabrileleño, 145
Gage, Thomas, 161
ganja (Cannabis), 17n
Ganoderma lucidum, 104n
Genista canariensis, 8
gigantine, 111
Gilgamesh epic, 103

Goldstein, Avram, 12n
Gran Chaco, 164
Great Shaman (Tatewarí), 113-114
Gryaznov, Mikhail P., 170
Guatemala, 77, 79, 80, 82, 163
guayusa, 139
Guerrero, 135, 155, 156
Guyana, 164
Guzmán-Huerta, Gastón, 87
gymnosperms, 33

Haines, John, 172n
hallucinogens, 1 *et passim*
  categories of, 33-34
  deer and, 166-173
  discovery of, 105-106
  drugs distinguished from, 112
harmala alkaloids, 39-40, 43-49, 149-150
  archetypes and, 51-56
  brain and, 51-52
  in psychotherapy, 39
harmaline, 39, 43-49, 51, 52
harmalol, 43
harmine, 43, 45
Harner, Michael J., 47n, 50-51, 86n
harpy eagle, 153, 154
Harvard Botanical Museum, xi
hashish, 34
Hawaiian wood roses, 66n
Heim, Roger, 63, 83-84, 86-87
Heimia salicifolia, 73
hemp *(Cannabis)*, 34, 41
  also see Cannabis *entries*; marihuana
henbane *(Hyoscyamus niger)*, 138
Hernández, Francisco, 60, 61, 67, 83
heroin, 17-18
Hero Twins, 26, 160, 164
híkuri (peyote; *Lophophora williamsii*),
  112, 121-133
  also see peyote
Hill, Diane F., 58
Hofmann, Albert, 57-60, 63, 65-66, 85-88,
  173
Holmstedt, Bo, 150
Honduras, mushroom effigies, 79
Hooper, Lucille, 144
Huaca Prieta, 153
Huastec, 28
Huautla de Jiménez, 65, 83
hueipatli (Solandra guerrerensis), 135
Hughes, John, 12n
Huichols, 12, 13, 16, 53, 74, 94-95, 120-

133, 166, 168, 170
  on "bad trips," 49n
  Datura and, 134-140
  Desana compared to, 47
  directions, 122
  nawá drink, 111n, 138
  peyote and, *see* peyote *entries*
  resistance to acculturation, 111-112
  tobacco uses, 26
huilca (wilka; Anadenanthera colubrina),
  27, 147, 156
  also see Anadenanthera *entries*
Humboldt, Alexander von, 22
Hunger, Kern von, 58
hunting, toad/frog venom and, 163-165
hunting and gathering cultures, and New
  World religions, 6
huskanawing, 142-143
Huxley, Aldous, 5, 111
hydrocyanic acid, 160
hyoscyamine, 138, 140
Hyoscyamus, 138

iboga *(eboka)*, 40
  also see Tabernanthe iboga
ibogaine, 39-41
  psychoactivity, 39, 40
ibotenic acid, 93
"idolatry," 19-22
Ilex guayusa, 139, 146
Incas, 28
incest, "bad trips" and, 49
India, 96, 104
Indians:
  origin of, 3-4
  religions, 19-22
"Indian tobacco," 169n
Indo-European languages, fly-agaric in, 104
indole alkaloids, 15, 39-40
Indra, 96, 100
Ingalls, Daniel H. H., 100-102
initiations:
  Datura in, 142-145
  of shaman, 53
Ipomoea muricata, 97
Ipomoea rubro-caerulea, 66
Ipomoea sidaefolia, 66
Ipomoea tricolor, 66
Ipomoea violacea, 62-66
  illustration, 64
  varieties, 62, 66
  also see morning glories

Iraq, 4-5n
Islam, 6
isoergine, 65
isoquinolines, 39, 111
isoxazoles, 39

jaguars:
    in art and symbol, 153
    mushroom association, 80
    shaman as, 153
    transformation, 48-49
    in *yajé* experiences, 51
Jaguar People, 160
Jalisco, 82
Jamaica, 17n
Japanese, toad myths, 162
Jesup North Pacific Expedition, 89
Jimsonweed, *see* Datura
Jivaro, 138
Jochelson, Waldemar (Vladimir), 89, 94,
    171
Johnson, Irmgard Weitlaner, 65, 83
Johnson, Jean Basset, 83
José, peyote pilgrim, 121-123
Jung, C. G., 14
Justicia, 156
Justicia pectoralis, 151

Kamerun, 40
Kakauyaríxi, 113, 124, 132
Kalevala, 162-163
Kaminaljúyu, 79-80
Kaufman, Terrence, 79
Kauyumarie, 117, 118, 124, 134, 137, 166
    also see deer
k'ekc'un, 79
Kieri Tewíyari, 134-137
king vulture, 153
Kinross-Wright, V. J., 64
Kiowa, 2
Knab, Timothy, 28, 135, 155, 162
Koch-Grünberg, Theodor, 26, 47n, 48, 50
kohobba (Anadenanthera peregrina), 20
Koryaks, 89-92, 93n, 94, 99, 171
Kosterlitz, H. W., 12n
Kroeber, Alfred L., 143, 144
kupúri (soul), 121, 124

La Barre, Weston, xii, 53, 98, 104, 167
    on hallucinogens and history, 1-2, 6-8,
        172
    on peyote religion, 110-111

Lacandones, 27, 75-76, 83-85
lagochiline, 34n
Lagochilus inebrians, 34
Langsdorf, Georg Heinrich, 90-92, 94
Lathrap, Donald, 160
L-dopa, 58
Leroi-Gourhan, A., 4n
Lewin, Louis, 45
Linder, David, 84
Ling Chih, 104n, 162, 172
Lobelia cardinalis or *splendens*, 169
lobeline, 169n
López, Antonio, 106
López Austin, Alfredo, 54
Lophophora williamsii, 109-119, 120-133
    illustrated, 110
    also see peyote *entries*
Lowy, Bernard, 79, 82
LSD (*d*-lysergic acid diethylamide), 1, 57-74
    bad experiences with, 38
    discovery of, 1, 58-59
    manner of use, 16
Luiseño, 143, 144, 145
Lumholtz, Carl, 112, 116, 125, 131
Lupe, peyote pilgrim, 121, 125, 130
lupine, 169
Lupinus palmerii or *aduncus*, 169
lysergic acid, 58
    derivatives in morning-glory seeds, 57, 65

McCleary, James A., 112
McDougall, Thomas, 155
magic, frog/toad motif in, 163-165
maize, origin, 158
Malcolm X, 36n
Malpighiaceae, 39
Mandan, 10-11
Mandragora officianarum, 138
mandragorina, 138
mandrake *(Mandragora officianarum)*, 138
Manihot utilisma (manioc), 160
mara'akame, 113-114, 121-132
marihuana *(Cannabis)*, 16n, 17, 34, 100
    also see Cannabis *entries*
Marmor, Judd, 59n
Martínez, Máximo, 135-137
Mary, the Virgin, 19, 70, 72
maté (Ilex paraguayensis), 146
matewámete, peyote pilgrims, 117, 119,
    126-132
Matlatzincas, 84, 106-107
Maya, 26, 27, 161

blood rites, 11-12
  deer role among, 167
  enema in art of, 28
  fly-agaric and, 81-83
  mushrooms and, 75-77, 78-81, 173
  tobacco use, 29-32
Mazatec:
  deer deities, 167
  mushroom use, 81, 83-85, 88, 173
  ololiuhqui and, 62, 65
MBieri curing cult, 39, 40, 42
MDA (methylene dioxyamphetamine), 36-
    38
mediator, toad as, 159-160
medicine:
  Aztec, 169n
  Cannabis in, 35
  Datura in, 139-140
  nutmeg in, 36-38
  peyote as, 112-113
  also see curing
Medína Silva, Ramón, 114-119, 120-133
"mescal bean" *(Sophora secundiflora)*, 7-9,
    41, 108-109, 137, 168
mescaline, 1, 5, 109
  misnomer, 112-113
Mesoamerica:
  religions in, 6
  snuffing paraphernalia, 153-155
Mesolithic survivals, 2, 3, 173
Mesopotamia, 103
Mexico:
  curing in, 54
  deer-mushroom ecology, 172
  morning glories in, 57-74
  mushroom effigies, 79
  mushrooms in, 74-88, 103-108
  peyote in, 109-119, 120-133
  psychopharmacopoeia, 21
  snuffing in, 151-152, 155-157
  tobacco in, 23, 26-28
Mictlan, 54
mihi, 44
Mixcóatl, 119
Mixtecs, 62, 81
MMDA (3-methoxy-4,5-methylene dioxy-
    phenyl isopropylamine), 36-38
Moche, 28, 32, 109, 168
monoamine oxidase, inhibitor, 149-150
Monte Albán, 155
morning glories, 1, 21, 57-74
  Christian acculturation, 70

seeds, 1, 54
snuff, 155
  also see Ipomoea violacea; ololiuhqui;
    Rivea corymbosa
Mother Goddesses, 72, 73, 81, 162
  toad as, 158-165; *also see* Toad Mother
  also see Tlaltecuhtli
Mother of the Jaguars, 160
Mother of Water, 72, 162
Munn, Henry, 86n
muscarine, 91, 93, 95
muscimole, 93
"Mushroom of the Underworld," 77-79
mushrooms:
  in American Indian art, 79-82
  animal associations, 80, 162-163, 170-173
  cults, 1, 103-105
  as divinities, 67
  in Mexico, 1, 21, 33, 63, 74-88, 103-108
  names, 107
  preparation, 81, 105
  sacred, 21, 33, 74-88, 104, 105, 107,
    148, 170-173
  stones, 79-81, 163
  tryptamines in, 148
  also see fly-agaric; teonanácatl
mutilation, religious practice of, 10-13
muviéri (prayer arrow), 124, 126
muxan okox, 79
mycophiles/mycophobes, 80, 84, 85
Myerhoff, Barbara G., 114n, 135
Myers, Charles W., 165
Myristica fragrans, 36-38
myristicine, in nutmeg, 36
mythic time, 23, 53-54

Naematoloma caerulescens, 75n
Naranjo, Claudio, 37-40, 50-54
natéma, 44, 138
Native American Church, 8, 9, 63, 110
Navaho, pipe making, 30
nawá, 111n, 138
Nayarit, 157
Nazca, 109
N-dimethyltryptamine-N-oxide, 149
Neanderthals, 4, 4-5n
Neolithic Revolution, 6
ne-to-chu-táta, 107
neurotransmitter agents, 57-58
newborn, Huichol peyote pilgrims as, 116-
    117
Newcomb, W. W., 168

New World, *see* America; Mesoamerica;
    North America; South America
New York, drug law, 16n
Nicotiana spp., 23, 25
Nicotiana attenuata, 25
Nicotiana bigelovi Watson, 25
Nicotiana glauca Graham, 25
Nicotiana rustica, 13, 23, 25, 54
    cultivation of, 27
    religious use, 25-27, 29-32
    "tobacco of Tatewarí," 125
    also see piciétl; tobacco *entries*
Nicotiana tabacum, 25
    cultivation of, 27
Nicotiana trigonophylla, 25
nicotine, 25, 26
Nine Lords of Xibalba, 79
nitrogenous hallucinogens, 33
N-monomethyltryptamine,5-methoxy-N,
    148
N,N-dimethyltryptamine-N-oxide,5-
    hydroxy-N, 148-149
non-nitrogenous hallucinogens, 33-34
noradrenaline, 1
norepinephrine, 1, 58
norhyoscyamine, 140
North America, overland migration to, from
    Asia, 3, 8, 105
Northwest Coast, shamans, 108
nutmeg *(Myristica fragrans)*, 36-38
Nyingwan Mebege, 42

Oaxaca, 83, 85-87, 155, 156
O'Flaherty, Wendy Doniger, 96-97
Oglala, 10
Old World, hallucinogens in, 2-4
Olmecs, 79, 156, 161
ololiuhqui, 2, 13, 14, 54, 60-74
    in art, 71-72
    as divinity, 67-72
    identification of, 61-64
    illustrated, 64
    preparation of, 64-65
    also see Ipomoea *entries*; morning glories;
        Rivea corymbosa
ololuc, 60-62
Opuntia, 124
Oregon, drug law, 16n
Osmond, Humphrey, 63
Otherworlds, 14, 15, 31, 41, 145, 170
Our Grandfather, 26
Our Mother Haramara (Pacific Ocean), 122

Our Mothers, places, 114, 117
Owner (Guardian) of the Earth, 158

Palenque, 75-76
Paleolithic:
    deer in, 170
    psychedelic phenomena in, 2-4
    survivals from, 2, 3, 173
Panaeolus campanulatus, 84
Panaeolus sphinctrinus, 84, 87
Panama, 82
Pané, Ramón, 20
Papagos, 85n
Parkinson's disease, LSD and, 57-58
Pasternak, Gavril, 12n
"Patio of the Grandfathers," 121
Pazaryk, 170
Peganum harmala (Syrian rue), 39, 43-44,
    97
Peru, 29, 82
petúm, see Nicotiana rustica
peyote *(Lophophora williamsii)*, 21, 26, 54,
    102, 111-119, 120-133
    cultural history, 9
    Datura rivalry, 135-137
    deer association, 13, 67, 112-125, 130,
        132, 164, 168, 170, 171
    "diabolic root," 109-119
    as divinity, 67
    enemas of, 28
    as "flower," 74
    growth habit, 125n, 127
    habitat, 119, 123-124
    harvest, 125-129
    healing use, 112-113, 127
    hunt for, 120-133
    illustrated, 110, 123
    marihuana supplanting, 100
    medical use, 112-113, 127
    preparation, 112
    Soma parallels, 102
    Sophora supplanted by, 108
    teonanácatl confusion, 61, 83
    strict meaning, 112
    also see híkuri; Lophophora williamsii
peyote names, for pilgrims, 130
peyote pilgrimage, 12-13, 47n, 49n, 94-95,
    113-119, 120-133
    Kieri and, 135
peyote religion, 2, 8, 9-10, 102, 109-119,
    120-133
    Christianity and, 111

eucharistic element, 171
  also see Native American Church
peyote ritual, *Soma* parallel, 102
phenylethylamines, 39, 111
Phyllobates bicolor, 164-165
piciétl (Nicotiana rustica), 21, 25, 54
  also see Nicotiana rustica; tobacco *entries*
Pike, Eunice, 85, 86n
Pima, 111
pindé, 44
pipes:
  sacred, 29-30
  snuffing, 154, 155, 157, 168
Piptadenia, 147
Place of Our Mothers, 114
Place Where Our Mothers Dwell, 117
Pohorilenko, Anatole, 156n
Pokoman, 161
Pollock, Steven Hayden, 75n
Poma de Ayala, Felipe Guamán, 27
Pope, Harrison G., Jr., 40n
Popol Vuh, 26, 79
Portuguese, nutmeg and, 37
Preuss, Konrad Theodor, 115
"primitive" societies, social-psychological
    context, 15-16
prussic acid, 160
psilocine, 63, 87, 88
Psilocybe:
  in mushroom effigies, 81-82
  species, 87
  supplanted by *Cannabis*, 16
Psilocybe aztecorum, 73, 87
Psilocybe caerulescens, 84, 87
Psilocybe hoogshagenii, 87
Psilocybe mexicana, 87
Psilocybe mixaensis, 87
Psilocybe muliercula, 87, 107
Psilocybe yungensis, 87
psilocybine, 1, 63, 87, 88
psychoactive plants:
  culture content and, 15-16
  number of, 33
psychotherapy, hallucinogens in, 37-49
Psychotria spp., 151
Psychotria viridis, 151
puberty ordeals, 53
pulque, 28
purification, for peyote pilgrimage, 116
Pygmies, 41, 42

Quetzalcóatl, 54, 119, 158

Quiche, 26, 82

Rain Priest Fraternity, 168
Rajaw Kakuljá, Lord of Lightning, 82
Ramón (Medína Silva), 114-132
Reichel-Dolmatoff, Gerardo, 45, 51, 54, 55
reindeer, fly-agaric and, 90-92, 101
  also see deer
Reko, Blas Pablo, 60-62, 65, 83-84
religions:
  in Africa, 39
  in America, 5-7
  Aryan, *see* Rig-Veda; Soma
  Asian and American, 4-7
  Aztec, 6, 21, 23, 72
  mushroom, *see* mushrooms
  ololiuhqui in, *see* ololiuhqui
  peyote, *see* peyote religion
  shamanism, *see* shamanism
  spirit quest, 10
  vision quest, 11
  yajé and, *see* yajé
  see also names of religions
rhubarb, 97
Richardson, Alan, 85
Rig-Veda, 97, 99, 101-103
Ríos, Catarino, 122
Rivea, species, 66
Rivea corymbosa, 60-74
  in Aztec art, 73
  illustrations, 61, 62, 63
  synonyms, 66
  also see morning glories; ololiuhqui
Roberts, Sidney, 58
Robertson, Mark Green, 76-77
Rose, Richard M., 79, 80
Roth, Walter E., 164
Rubin, Vera, 17
Ruiz de Alarcón, Hernando, 20, 21, 54, 60,
    83
  on *ololiuhqui*, 67-69

Sabina, María, 88
Safford, William A., 60-61, 83
safrol, in nutmeg, 36
saguaro cactus (*Carnegiea gigantea; Cereus
    giganteus*), 58, 111n
Sahagún, Bernardino de, 21, 28, 61, 82-83,
    92
salsoidine, 111
sampo, 163
San Bártolo Yautepec, 65

San Francisco Oxtotilpan, 84
San Ildefonso pueblo, 167
San Juan pueblo, 167
San Lorenzo, Veracruz, 161
San Pedro cactus, 29, 109
Santesson, C. G., 61
Sapper, Carl, 80
Sarcostemma brevistigmata, 97
sassafras, 37
Saubel, Katherine Siva, 16, 145
schizophrenia, 52n, 57
Schleiffer, Hedwig, 142-143
Schultes, Richard Evans, xi, xii, 1, 2, 33, 87
  on alcohols, 34n
  on Aztec art, 73-74
  on *Cannabis*, 34-35
  on Convolvulaceae, 66
  on *Datura*, 140
  on hallucinogenic alkaloids, 148-149
  on harmala alkaloids, 45
  on *Ilex*, 146
  on *Mandragora*, 138
  on mushrooms, 83-84, 87
  on *ololiuhqui*, 61-62, 64
  on *P. harmala*, 44
  on peyote, 111
  on "primitive" chemistry, 150
  on *Psilocybe*, 87
  on *Rivea* and *ololiuhqui*, 61-62, 64
  South American work, 22
  on *T. iboga*, 40
  on *Virola* snuffs, 150-152
scopolamine, 138, 140
semilla de la Virgen, 70
sego lily, 168-169
Seneca, 26
Senecio, 4n
Serna, Jacinto de la, 21, 83
serotonin(e) (5-hydroxy-tryptamine), 1, 52n, 58, 87
Shafer, Raymond P., 17n
shamanism/shamans, 48-49
  birch tree and, 103
  deer and, 170
  ecstatic, as *ur*-religion, 4-7, 8
  Eurasiatic origin, 2-4
  female, 159
  initiation of, 53
  as jaguar, 48, 153
  Northwest Coast, 108
  in peyote religion, 113-119, 121-132
  Siberian, 2-7, 170

smoking and, 30-32
snuffing and, 153-156
spittle of, 85n
tobacco, 30-32
Shanidar cave, 4-5n
Sharon, Douglas, 29, 109
Shen Nung, Emperor, 35
Shiriana (Yanomamö), 29, 150-151
Shulgin, Alexander T., 37
Siberia:
  migration from, to America, 3, 8, 105
  mushroom use, 89-95, 98, 100-101
  shamanism in, 2-7, 170
Sibundoy, 140
Singer, Rolf, 84, 87
sinucuichi, 73
Sioux, 10
Skirt of Jade, 162
Slotkin, J. S., 110n
smoking, 26, 29, 32
  Bwiti, 41
  hedonistic vs. religious, 23, 25-26
  pipe, 29-30
  medical effect, 17
  shamanistic, 30-32
  also see Cannabis *entries*; tobacco *entries*
snakes, 49-52
snuffing/snuffs, 48
  Anadenanthera, 20, 161
  and animal symbolism, 146-157
  hallucinogenic, 146-157
  pipes for, 154, 155, 157, 168
  in South America, 29
  tobacco, 48
  Virola, 150-152
Snyder, Solomon H., 12n
society, mythic origin, 46-48
Solanaceae, 25, 138
Solandra, 135-137
Solanum spp., 138
Solecki, Ralph S., 5
Soma, 90, 92
  hymns, 102
  identification of, 1, 96-104
  meanings, 96
  peyote parallels, 102
  preparation, 97, 99
  rite, 172
  toad association, 163
Sophora secundiflora (mescal bean), 7-9, 41, 108-109, 137
  deer association, 168
South America, 3

deer in, 167
enemas in, 28
mushrooms in, 82
psychoactive plants in, 21-22
religions in, 6
snuffing in, 29, 153-156
tobacco use in, 29
Spaniards:
Indian religions and, 10, 19-22
tobacco and, 23
spirit-quest religions, 10
spittle, 85, 89
Spruce, Richard, 22, 44, 45
Stavenhagen, Kurt, 157
Steller, Georg Wilhelm, 171
Stevenson, Matilda Coxe, 139
Steward, Julian H., 163
Stewart, Omer C., 110n
Stoll, A., 58
Strahlenberg, Filip Johann von, 91, 94
Stramonium, 140
Strong, William Duncan, 144
Strophariaceae, 87
Stropharia cubensis, 75-76, 84, 87, 172-173
symbolism:
animal, 51-53, 146-157
male-female, 42-43
transcultural, 51-56
Syrian rue *(Peganum harmala)*, 39, 43-44, 97

Tabernanthe iboga, 39-41
Tacana, 81
tadpoles, 156n
Taino, 20
Tajik, 34n
takwátsi, 118, 124
Tamatsí Wawatsári (Principal Deer), 121-132
Taoism, toad in, 162
tapirage, 163-164
Tarahumara, 138
Tart, C. T., 14n
Tartar, 34n
Tatewarí (Great Shaman; Our Grandfather), 113-114, 116-117, 122-125, 129, 131, 132
Tatutsí (Great Grandfather), 122, 124-125
taxonomy, primitive, 5
Tayaupá (Sun Father), 122
Tedlock, Barbara, 169
Tedlock, Dennis, 169
telepathine, 45, 51n

temíxoch, 73
tenatsali, 168
10-methoxyharmaline, 51
teonanácatl, 60, 61, 63, 73-74, 82-83
Teotihuácan, art in, 71-72
teotlacualli, 13-14
Tepantitla, art in, 71-72
Tepecanos, 100
Tepehuancos, 100
Terenius, Lars, 12n
tesgüino, 138
tetrahydroisoquinoline, 111n
Tezcatlipoca, 13, 158
THC (tetrahydrocannabinol), 17
Thompson, J. Eric S., 27, 29, 31-32, 77, 161
thorn apple, *see* Datura
tigers, 50, 52-53
Tinospora cordifolia, 97
Tlaloc, 71-72
Tlaltecuhtli, "Owner of the Earth," 81, 158-160, 163
tlitiltzin, 62
toad/toads:
archetypes, 52
as earth mother, 158-165
as female shaman, 159
fly-agaric association, 162-163
mushroom association, 80-81, 162-163
Soma association, 163
toad-frog motif, 159
Toad Grandmother, 160-161
Toad Mother, 81, 158-165
toadstool, fly-agaric as, 160-163
Toad Woman, 160-161, 164
tobacco, 19-32, 48, 168
also see Nicotiana *entries*; piciétl
tobacco gourd, 125
toloache (Datura inoxia), 41, 141-144
also see Datura
torture, religious, 10-13
Tozzer, A. M., 77
traditional societies, context of hallucinogens in, 15-16
transcultural phenomena, in *yajé* experiences, 50-56
Trichocereus pachanoi, 29, 109
tropanes, 39, 140
tryptamines, 33, 45
activity, 149
sources of, 148-149
tryptophane, 33, 87
Tschopik, Harry, Jr., 30

Tukano, 16, 45, 46, 48, 49, 53-55, 149
Tungus, 170
Turbina corymbosa, 66
Turkoman, 34n
Tzotzil, 26-27

Underworld, 145
   "Mushroom of the," 77-79
   tobacco and, 27
Ungnadia speciosa, 8
United States Pharmacopoeia, *Cannabis* in,
   35
Upperworld, 48, 145, 155
urine:
   deer and, 90, 171
   fly-agaric and, 90-95, 100-101
   intoxicating, 90-95
   magic and therapeutic power, 108
   medicinal use, 92
   Soma and, 100-101
uterus, toad identified with, 160
Uzbek, 34n

Vagina/vagina:
   in Huichol pilgrimage, 47n, 118
   in *yajé* ritual, 46-47
Vahiyinin, 89
Vaupés, 47
Veradera, peyote pilgrim, 122, 126-127, 130
Vico, dictionary, 78
"vine of souls" *(Banisteriopsis caapi)*, 44-49
   healing via, 50
Virola, snuffs, 48, 147-152, 161
Virola callophylla, 148, 149
Virola callophylloidea, 148, 149
Virola theidora, 148, 149, 150, 152
vision-quest religions, 11
Volker, T., 162

Waika (Yanomamö), 29, 150-151
wanawut, 144
wapaq, spirits/plants, 89
Warao, 24, 30-32, 166-173
Waser, Peter G., 93
Wassén, S. Henry, 153-155, 163
Wasson, R. Gordon, xii, 1, 3, 63
   on *Amanita* intoxication, 93-94
   on Aztec art, 73-74
   on *doncella*, 70, 81
   on deer and *Soma*, 170
   mushroom research, 80, 82, 84-88, 105,
      173

on *ololiuhqui*, 64-65, 69-70
on sacred-mushroom preparation, 105
on *Soma*, 90-92, 96-103, 170, 172
on *tlitiltzin*, 62
Wasson, Valentina Pavlovna, 82, 84-85
Wawatsári (Elder Brother), 121-132, 168
Weil, Andrew T., 7, 11n, 37
Weitlaner, Roberto, 65, 83
Where Our Mothers Dwell, 117-119, 120,
   124, 132
Where the Clouds Open, 118
Wilbert, Johannes, xii, 24-25, 31
wilka (huilca; Anadenanthera colubrina),
   27, 147
Wirikúta, 12, 113-119, 120-133
Witkop, Bernard, 161, 165

X, Malcolm, 36n
xi, 107
xibalbaj okox, 78
xochinanácatl, 73
Xochipala, 156
Xochipilli, God of Flowers, 73-74
Xochiquetzal, 72
xochitl, 73

yageine, 45
yajé, 44-56, 153
   dream, 56
   images, 46-51, 153
   preparation of, 149-150
   religion and, 47-48
   ritual, 46-48
   transcultural phenomena, 50-56
   also see ayahuasca; Banisteriopsis *entries*;
      vine of souls
Yajé Child, 46
Yajé Woman, 42-43, 46
Yanomamö (Waika), 29, 150-151
Yaqui, 8
Yaxchilán, 11, 12, 76
Yemen, nutmeg in, 37
yucca, 124
Yurimagua, 82, 87n

Zacatecas, 117
Zami ye Mebege, 41, 42
Zapotecs, 62, 65, 81
Zigmond, M. L., 25
Zinberg, Norman, xii,n, 14n
Zingg, Robert, 135
Zuñi, 122, 135, 139, 145, 168-169